SAP SD

for Beginners

Second Edition

SAP SD

for Beginners

Second Edition

THE X TEAM

K. A. Samad

Published in the USA by:

Arizona Business Alliance

SHROFF PUBLISHERS & DISTRIBUTORS PVT. LTD.
Mumbai *Bangalore* *Kolkata* *New Delhi*

SAP SD for Beginners, Second Edition

by K. A. Samad

 ISBN 13: 978-93-5023-389-4
Originally printed in India.

Published by Shroff Publishers & Distributors Pvt. Ltd., C-103, T.T.C. Industrial Area, M.I.D.C., Pawane, Navi Mumbai - 400 705, India. Tel: (91-22) 4158 4158
Fax: (91-22) 4158 4141, E-mail: spdorders@shroffpublishers.com.

Printing History:

First Edition: October 2009
Second Edition: July 2011

Reprinted in the USA by Arizona Business Alliance.
Under license from Shroff Publishers & Distributors Pvt. Ltd., India.

First USA Reprint: September 2011
ISBN 13: 978-1-61903-000-8

Published by **Arizona Business Alliance LLC** 7169 W. Ashby Drive, Peoria AZ 85383
Tel: 623 297 4448, Fax: 623 687 9524 e-mail: aba.us@hotmail.com

This book is dedicated to the following people:

My wife Beena Samad.

My elder son Alpha Samad.

My younger son Beeta Samad.

PREFACE

This book is a software book on SAP SD. It is a book for ERP professionals and explains only the fundamentals of SAP SD and hence it can be used by students who want to pursue SAP SD as their career. This book is full of SAP SD screen shots explaining all the important fields. With this book you can learn SAP SD fundamentals in about 30 days. You need to read other books for advanced features of SAP SD. This book covers the configuration setup to be done to start working on SAP after installing the SAP software.

This book is different from any other book in the market in such a way that each page of this book is sequenced in the proper order. Also care is taken not to explain irrelevant matters to avoid waste of your time in reading this book. The topics mentioned in the index of contents are not hooked up for a sales strategy.

Note that among various ERPs, SAP has the highest installation base in the world.

If you have access to SAP software, with this book you can learn SAP SD without anybody's help. If you have good software experience you will be able to learn SAP

SD with this book even without a SAP system because the screen shots are sequenced in such a way.

For a beginner, this book can be used to understand how an ERP works.

Also this book can be used as course material for SAP SD training.

It will help configure (Enterprise Definition, Enterprise Assignments, etc.) your system step by step after installing the SAP software.

First of all, it is a good decision that you have taken to learn SAP. You will realize it when you start practicing in SAP. The product is excellent and the support you get from SAP is amazing.

In some cases, SAP SD is known as SAP SCM Order Fulfillment.

As far as possible, explained here is only what is required to be understood about SAP SD fundamentals and much care is taken not to drag the matter.

Our aim is to make you learn SAP SD as quickly as possible. As SAP SD is a vast module, it is impossible to explain everything in a book of this size and hence, it is recommended to read other advanced books on SAP SD for more details. This book is intended for a beginner to begin as a SAP SD professional. Use this book as a reference study material. Also, it is useful for other module users such as MM, PP, FI/CO etc to have a general idea about how SD works.

Enormous time and cost have been spent in compiling this book and hence we do not like unauthorized copying and circulating of this book and depriving us of our small income through sale of each copy. I believe this book will make your process of learning SAP SD easier.

ASSUMPTIONS

The following assumptions are made while writing this book:

1. You know the basic terminologies (such as Database, Applications, transactions, Data etc.) used in the software industries.

2. You have basic domain knowledge about the sales and distribution activities.

3. You are attending or planning to attend a formal training on SAP SD. Hence, the navigation aspects (how to enter data, how to save data, how to close sessions etc.) are not mentioned in this book.

SCOPE OF THIS BOOK:

This book is not a complete book on SAP SD. It explains the complete fundamentals of SAP SD based on version 4.7 and later. These fundamentals are sufficient to answer technical questions for a job as a SAP SD beginner. After reading this book, you can easily learn advanced functions of SAP SD while working in SAP. Unless you know these fundamentals, you will never be able to understand any advanced functions of SAP SD which you will get only by working as a real time consultant in an ERP field. This book will help in certifying SAP SD in a faster way.

This book is most suited for SAP-University programs. Many universities have tied up with SAP to introduce teaching of SAP in their universities as their curriculum.

ACKNOWLEDGEMENT

Many working senior SAP consultants helped me in writing this book. They sent me many documents such as screen shots, guidelines, data, etc. to compile this book.

Many thanks to the following people:

1. My wife Beena Samad for co-operating with me to resign from my job to complete this book project.

2. Alpha Samad, my elder son, who continuously appreciated me to continue with this project.

3. My second son Beeta Samad, to co-operate with me for not spending much time with him.

4. H.R. Vishwa Karma, an IIT post graduate, professor and my ex-colleague, to give suggestions, guidance, etc. to complete this book.

5. Advance thanks to those who carefully read and gave me feedback for improving this book.

6. At last, to my God for giving me courage and time to complete this project.

GENERAL INTRODUCTION

Have you ever wondered why companies opt for standard ERPs(such as SAP, Baan, Peoplesoft, etc)?. Why do they not develop their own ERP? Why do people opt for more popular ERPs? The answer is ERP is a very vast product and by the time it is developed to the individuals' requirements, the developers would have left the company, business processes would have changed and finally you would be fed up with what is developed due to errors, documentations, etc. Hence, companies opt for standard and widely used products even if the standard products do not satisfy 100 percent of their requirements initially. Also, people experienced in the standard ERPs are available in the market to take over the position of employees, who have left the Organisation and to continue the business without any break.

SAP(Systems, Applications and Products in Data Processing) is an ERP. ERP stands for Enterprise Resource Planning. ERP is being implemented for Planning Resources of an Enterprise.

If you have decided to learn SAP ERP, you have taken a wise decision because, as per the present trend, SAP is going to be the world leader in ERP. Some of the reasons are as follows:

1. It is a very stable and well tested product.
2. The company is well managed and financially very sound.
3. The product is being improved continuously.
4. Well structured development centers and support centers are set up all over the world for customer satisfaction.
5. SAP takes feedback from all angles and the problems are addressed and the solutions are incorporated in later releases.

Man, machine, material, money (4 Ms) are resources. Banks, companies, offices etc are enterprises. You know that most of the banks use one or other ERPs. Generally, ERPs used by banks are known as Banking Software. Banks use ERP software for their accounting requirements such as money deposits, withdrawals, balance updates, etc. Similarly, a manufacturing company uses an ERP for accounting and updating material stocks, material purchases, goods sales, material transfers, material issues to production shop floor, updating credit balance of customers, receiving and updating invoices against sold goods, generating management reports, etc.

SAP ERP was first developed in 1972 by a few engineers who worked in IBM. The company name is SAP AG and is based in Waldorf, Germany. The first release of SAP was in R/2 (Realtime/ 2 tier). The 2 tiers(layers) were Application and database layers.

Later, R/3 (Realtime /3 tier) version was released in the 1990s. The 3 tiers are a)Presentation b) Application and c) Database layers.

The presentation layer is the front end that you use to insert data and also it displays data extracted from Database layer. SAP has developed and used it's own presentation layer called SAP GUI.

The Application layer contains the programs that work between the presentation layer and the database layer. It retrieves data from the database layer, manipulates the data, displays data in presentation layer and then puts back the data to the database layer. SAP has developed and used it's own programming language called

ABAP(Advanced Business Application programming) for writing the SAP codes. It is a 4 GL language.

The Database layer is the database where the data is stored and retrieved by the application layer. The main databases supported by SAP are Oracle, db2, infomix, etc.

The leading ERPs in the market are:

SAP, Baan, Oracle E- Business Suite, JD Edwards, Peoplesoft, etc.

SAP R/3 is a general ERP product of SAP company and other industry specific SAP products are IS-B(for banks),IS-OIL(for oil companies), IS- RETAIL(for retail business), IS-T(for Telecommunications) etc.

The main modules of SAP R/3 are SD(Sales and Distribution), PP(Production planning), MM(Material Management), FI/CO(Finance and Controlling), IM(Investment Management), TR(Treasury), QM(Quality Management),HR(Human Resources), PM(Plant Maintenance) WM(Warehouse Management), etc

Most frequently used sessions have Transaction Codes(T-Code) so that you can open the session directly by entering the T-Code. In this book, the T-code is entered in square brackets to identify them.

PROCESSES COVERED IN THIS BOOK

This book is meant for a beginner in SAP SD who has not even viewed SAP screens. Hence, in this book, only the details that are needed to understand the basic sales process are explained with the help of SAP screen shots.

The following basic processes are explained in this book:

- Defining the minimum mandatory Enterprise Units.
- Assigning these mandatory Enterprise Units.
- Creating the minimum mandatory master data.
- Setting up the minimum mandatory Pricing Condition Techniques.
- Setting up the minimum mandatory Determinations.
- Creating a simple sales order.
- Creating the delivery document for the sales order.

- Creating billing and accounting documents simultaneously for the above sales order.

The following chapters are also included in this book to understand the above processes in a simple way.

- Lean Warehouse Management
- BOM processes
- Period closing
- Tax calculations
- Number ranges

This book will guide you to set up all the needed information step by step to complete the above basic sales process after installing the SAP software.

If you can complete the above simple sales process, you will be able to understand, set up and experiment advanced features of SAP SD with the help of other advanced books and online help facilities of the SAP software.

1. Enterprise Definition:

In this area, all the relevant Enterprise Units such as Group Company, Company Codes, Plants, Distribution Channels, Shipping Points, etc are defined.

2. Enterprise Assignment:

In this area, all the above mentioned Enterprise Units are assigned properly. For example, assignments are made between branch companies to the Group Company, Plants to branch Companies, Distribution Channels to Sales Organisation, etc.

3. Miscellaneous setup:

Then some miscellaneous setups such as Currency conversion, Plant Parameter etc are done which are mandatory for working on SAP SD.

4. Master Data Set up:

After the above processes, all the relevant master data such as Sales Document Types, Item Categories, Account Groups, Customer Master Data, Material Master Data etc. are defined.

5. Pricing:

Pricing is the heart of SAP SD. The mandatory pricing set up needed is explained in this area.

6. Set up Determinations:

Then Determinations such as Item Category Determination, Pricing Procedure Determination, etc. are done. Determination set up is done in the system for the system to pick automatically certain data such as Item Categories, Material prices, etc while creating Sales Documents.

7. After the above set ups are made, a simple Sale Document is created and processed till the accounting document is created for the same.

It is recommended to use your own enterprise setup for your learning purpose rather than using the SAP standard setups. In many cases you will have to copy from the SAP standards and then make the modifications according to your needs.

Important: If you are a beginner in SAP SD, you must start with chapter 1 through 5 in sequence. For example, if you start reading from chapter 2 directly, you may not understand the process fully.

Table of Contents

Preface vii
Assumptions ix
Scope of this Book: ix
Acknowledgement xi
General Introduction xiii
Processes Covered in this book xvii

CHAPTER 1. ENTERPRISE SET UP IN SAP SD 1

Enterprise Definition. 4
Group Company[OX15] 4
Company Code[EC01] 6
Business Area[OX03] 8
Sales Organisation [OVX5] 9
Distribution Channel [OVXI] 10
Division [OVXB]. 11
Plant [OX10] 12
Storage location [OX09] 15
Shipping Point [OVXD] 16
Enterprise Assignment 19
Enterprise Assignment in a pictorial view 19
Assign Company Codes to Company [OX16] 21
Assign Plants to company code [OX18] 21
Assign Sales Organisations to company code [OVX3] 22
Assign Distribution channels to sales Organisation [OVXK] 22
Assign Divisions to sales Organisation [OVXA] 23
Set up Sales Area [OVXG] 23
Assign Plants to (sales Organisation +distribution channel) [OVX6] 24
Assign Sales Areas to Business Areas[OVF0 / OVF1] 24
Assign Shipping points to plant [OVXC] 27
Miscellaneous Setup 28

Currency conversion [OB08]. 28
Attributes of material [OMS2] 28
Plant Parameters [OLMB] 31
Value Area Setup [OMWD] 32
Specifying Posting Time Intervals [OB52] 33

CHAPTER 2. MASTER DATA. 35

Delivery Document Type [OVLK] 36
Billing Document Type [VOFA] 39
Sales Document Type [VOV8] 42
Accounting Document Type [OBA7] 49
Order Item Category [VOV7] 50
Delivery Item Category [0VLP] 56
Schedule Line Category [VOV6] 58
Account Group [OVT0] 62
Tax Set Up 66
Copy Control 70
Customer master data [XD01] 78
Material master data [MM01] 88

CHAPTER 3. PRICING 103

Introduction to pricing 103
1. Price Condition Table [V/03] 106
2. Price Access Sequence [V/07] 109
3. Price Condition Types [V/06] 112
4. Pricing Procedure [V/08] 120
5. Price Condition Record [VK11] 125

CHAPTER 4. DETERMINATIONS. 129

Introduction. 129
Order Item Category Determination [VOV4] 130
Delivery Item Category Determination [0184] 132
Schedule Line Category Determination [VOV5] 133
Pricing Procedure Determination [OVKK] 134

Partner Determinations. 134
Set Up Partner Determination for Customer. 137
Account Determination [VKOA] 140
Shipping Point Determination[OVL2] 144
Picking Location/ Storage Location Determination [OVL3] 146
Route Determination [0VRF] 146

CHAPTER 5. SALES TRANSACTIONS. 149

Introduction: 150
Sales Order Creation [VA01] 153
Pricing Analysis. 160
Delivery Document Creation [VL01N]. 161
Billing And Accounting Document Creation [VF01] 166
Sales Order Status 171

CHAPTER 6. APPENDIX 173

Period closing [MMPV]. 173
Stock creation [MB1C] 176
Stock viewing [MMBE] 178
Tax Calculation. 178
Defining Common Distribution Channels [VOR1] 192
Defining Common Divisions[VOR2] 193
BOM Process in SD 193
1. ABOM(Assembly Bill Of Material). 194
2. KBOM(Kit Bill Of Material) 194
Lean Warehouse Management (LWM). 206
Number Ranges for various SD processes. 216
Abbreviations Used in this book 219

Chapter

1

ENTERPRISE SET UP IN SAP SD

SAP is an ERP(Enterprise Resource Planning) system and hence we have to set up the Enterprise very carefully. Hence, a thorough study about the enterprise is to be done before defining various units of the enterprise and interlinking them together in the system. In fact the Organisation (the Organisation in which SAP is being implemented) should have selected the appropriate module(R/3 or industry specific solutions such as IS-OIL, IS-Retail, etc) based on their business nature.

Enterprise setup will be done differently for different SAP solutions and different industries. But, we are going to explain here a standard method of R/3 implementation. The purpose of this book is to understand the basics of SAP SD and it should not be considered as a real business mapping for an industry.

For making Sales Transactions, we have to create the Enterprise Set up, Master Data, Pricings and Determinations. Hence, first we will make the set up ready before we make the sales transactions. The set ups are done based on the SAP R/3 version 4.7. But there are no much differences for later versions as far as SD is concerned.

Note: When the SAP software is installed, many standard data such as Enterprise Units, Master data, Pricing, Determinations etc are created by default. This is just to guide you in case you need to use the default data and to copy from the standard to your own data.

SAP R/3 Login menu.

When you login to SAP R/3, version 4.7, as a super user, you will get the following menu.

Easy Access View (EA View)

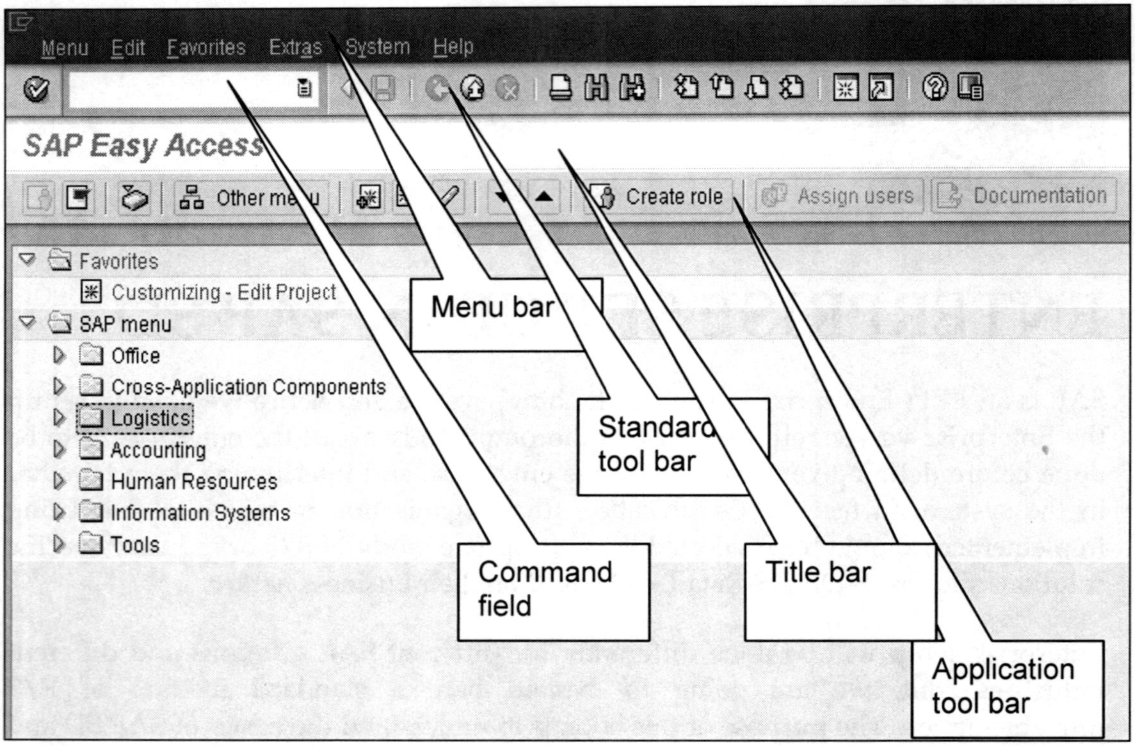

Fig 1-1

This view is called Easy Access view, shortly EA. You can come back to this view from any where in the system by entering /n or S000 in the command field. This S000 is the transaction code(T-code) for EA view. Like this, you can enter various T-codes in the command field to execute various transactions directly.

You can open up to 6 sessions at a time. If you know the T-code of a transaction, you can open another session and go to that transaction by entering /o and the T-code of that transaction directly. Eg: if you enter /OVA01, the system will open a new session and open the transaction Sales Order Creation[VA01].

Similarly, you can go to another mode of view called IMG(Implementation Guide) where most of the implementation settings for the enterprise are done. If you enter *SPRO* at the command field of EA view and then click on 'SAP reference IMG', you get the following IMG screen:

IMG view

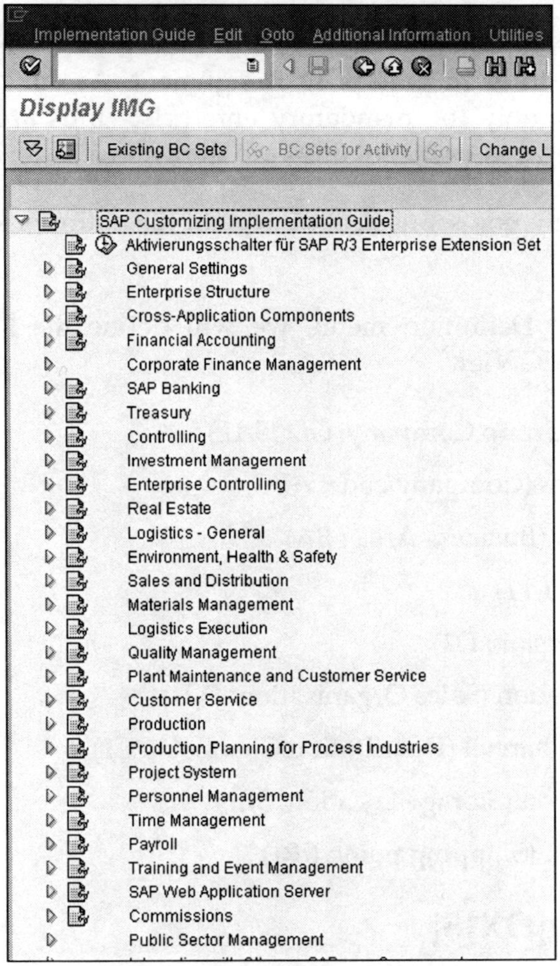

Fig 1-2

Path: [SPRO]- SAP Reference IMG

If you enter '/n' at the command field you will go back to EA view.

We will set up our own Enterprise Structure to understand the basic functions of the SAP SD. We will maintain the setup that is required only for our test scenarios. Later you can make additional setups depending upon your needs.

The Enterprise setup begins with IMG view.

Enterprise Definition

We have to define Organisational units first in Enterprise Definitions and then link these Organisational units in Enterprise Assignment. As our aim is to complete a simple sales process, only the mandatory enterprise units are defined here. The relationships of these Organisational units are shown in a pictorial view in fig 1-21

We are setting up only one set of data to explain the entire process. You can define more data later.

Hence, in Enterprise Definition menu, we will define the following mandatory Enterprise Units in IMG View:

1. Company (= Group Company: *GLOBAL*)
2. Company Code(Company code: *ABC*)
3. Business Area (Business Area : *BA*)
4. Plant (Plant: *PLT1*)
5. Division (Division: *D1*)
6. Sales Organisation (Sales Organisation: *SO1*)
7. Distribution Channel (Distribution Channel: *DC1*)
8. Storage Location (Storage Location: *SL1*)
9. Shipping point (Shipping point: *SP1*)

Group Company[OX15]

We must define at least one Group company to start work with SAP SD.

Group Company is sometimes called Parent Company, Holding Company etc. In SAP, Group Company is called just 'Company' and subsidiary companies are called 'Company Codes'. One group company can have many 'company codes'. But we are going to define one group company and one company code.

Let us define our group company 'GLOBAL'

Defining a new Group Company, *GLOBAL*[OX15]

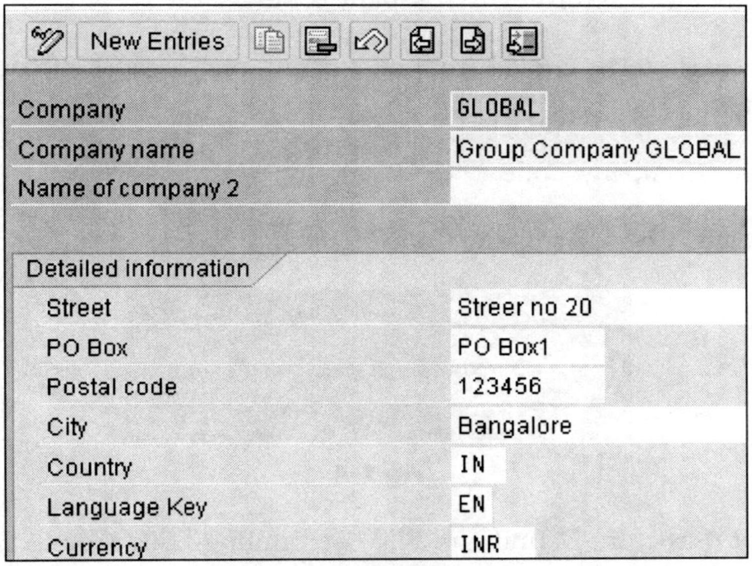

Fig 1-3

Path: IMG-Enterprise Structure-Definition- FIN Accounting-Define Company- New Entries.

Group company is just a code with it's description.

To a Company, we have to assign at least one Company Code for the Legal and Financial transactions. For our understanding, we are defining only one company code called 'ABC' and the same will be assigned to this company, GLOBAL.

The Country, Language and Currency are important in this session.

Company Code[EC01]

Company code, *ABC*

As said earlier, define at least one company code for the purpose of our study.

You can create and link many company codes to a group company. Each company code represents an independent accounting unit. Profit and loss statements (external legal reports) are taken according to company codes.

Company codes are to be copied from an existing one because of copying a lot of standard set ups.

Let us create our Company Code *ABC*.

Edit, Copy, Delete, Check Company Code

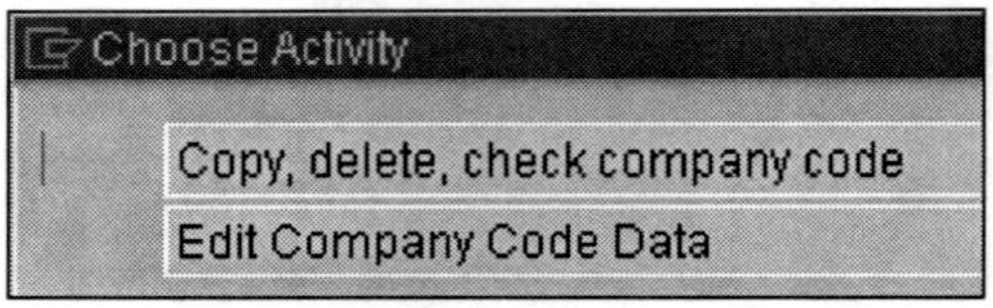

Fig 1-4

Path: IMG-Ent Structure-Definition- FIN Accounting-Edit, Copy, Delete, Check Company Code.

Choose first option: 'Copy, Delete, Check Company Code'.

When you select the first option, you will get the following blank screen.

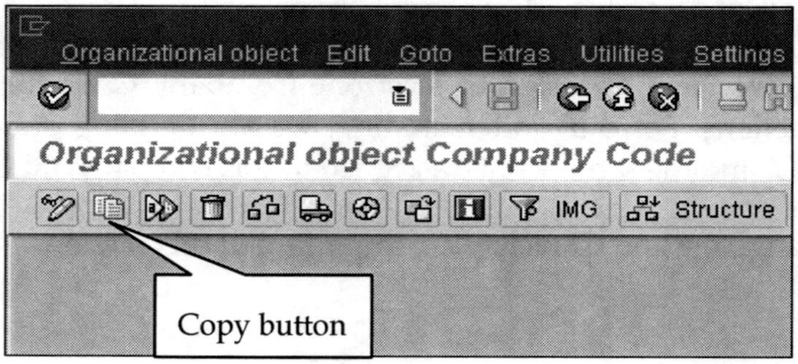

Fig:1-5

In this blank screen click on 'Copy' button (2nd button in the Application Toolbar).

Select the source company code as 1000, a standard existing company in the system and the target company code as ABC.

Important: Note down the source company code for future purposes. For example, it is needed to maintain currency conversion from the source currency to target currency.

Say Yes, when asked for copying General Ledger account.

Say Yes, for change of currency if the Target Company's currency is different from that of the Source Company and then enter the new currency. Currency of the source company 1000 is EUR and currency of the target company ABC is INR(Indian Rupees).

Similarly, say Yes for all other standard messages that appear.

Finally you will get the following screen:

Fig 1-6

Accept the above message and close the session.

Note: Number Ranges are explained in the Appendix.

Now select the 2nd option 'Edit Company Code Data' and edit the company code ABC for additional data as shown in the following screen.

Maintaining additional data for the Company Code ABC.

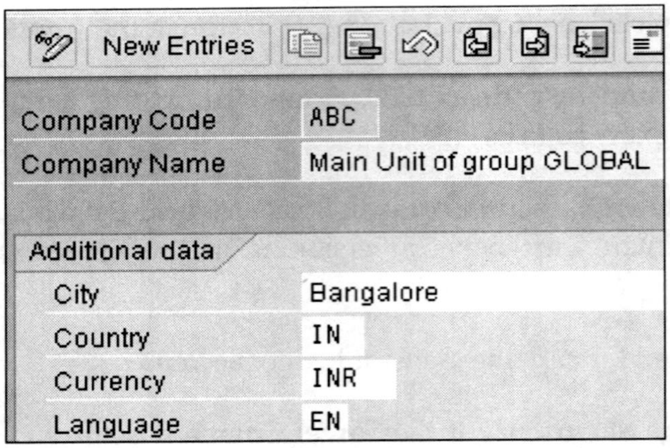

Fig 1-7

Here the field Country, Currency and Language are important.

Business Area[OX03]

Business Area is just a code with a description. Business Area is used for taking internal reports on business details by the finance department. Hence, you should discuss with FI/CO while defining Business Areas. Defining at least one business area for a company is mandatory. It is a company independent Organisational unit and can be used to take reports across companies, if needed. Hence, it is defined to take internal reports, for example based on plants and divisions. For each sales order item, a business area must be determined and hence a set of standard rules are defined in the system for determining sales areas.

Let us create our business area BA.

Defining Business Area, *BA*.

Defining Business Area[OX03]

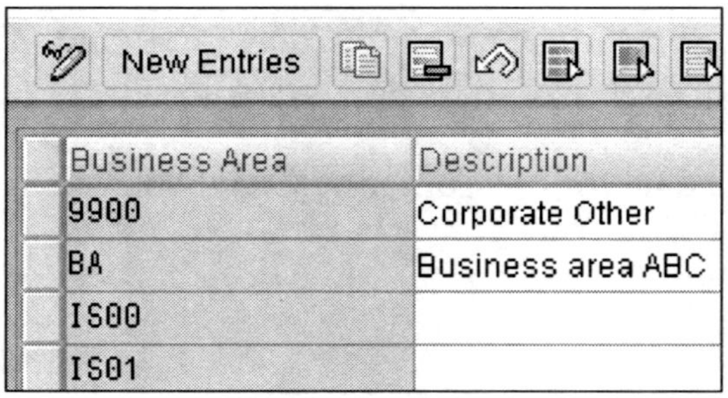

Fig:1-8

Path: IMG-Ent Structure-Definition- FIN Accounting- Define Business Area.

Refer assignment of 'Sales Areas to Business Areas' later in this chapter.

Sales Organisation [OVX5]

Sales Organisation is an Organisational unit controlling the marketing strategies, sales policies, extending the sales territory, etc. Generally only one sales Organisation will be defined for one company code, but in certain cases where the territory of sales is too large, there may be more than one sales Organisation for a company. Example: Sales- south, Sales north, Sales export, etc. At least one Sales Organisation must be defined in SD.

One sales Organisation is assigned to only one company code.

Each sales Organisation has it's own master data such as customer and material masters.

Let us define our sales Organisation, *SO1*.

Define, copy, delete, check sales Organisation[OVX5]

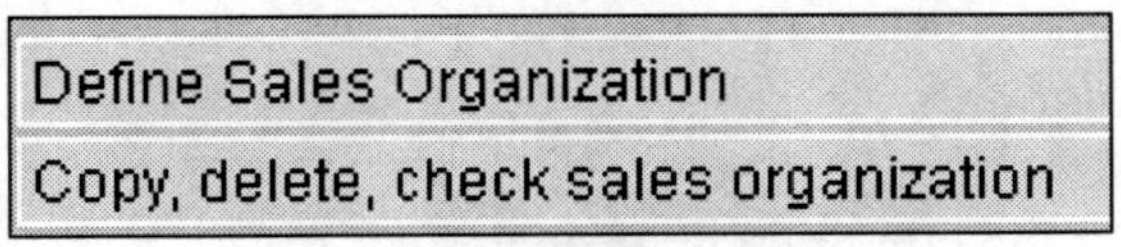

Fig:1-9

Path: IMG-Ent Structure-Definition- Sales and Distribution- Define, copy, delete, check sales Organisation.

Choose the first option.

Define Sales Organisation

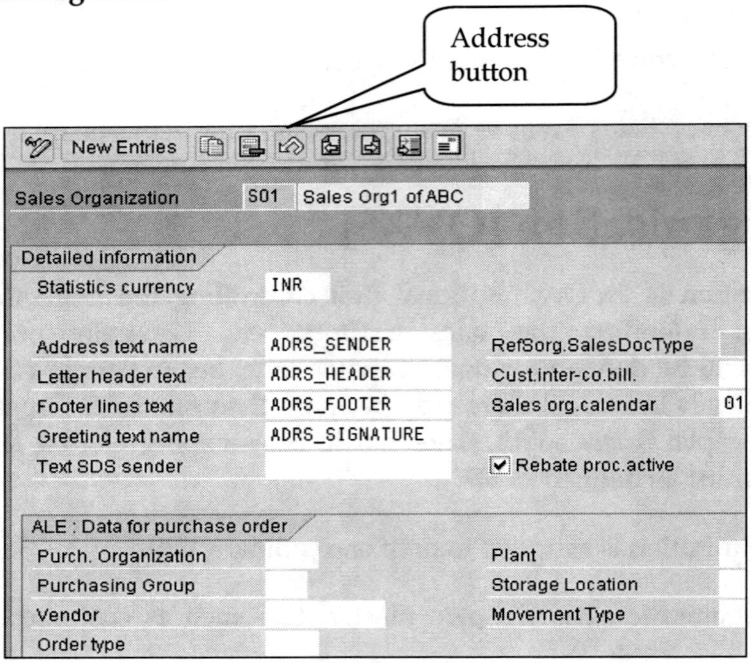

Fig:1-10

After saving, add the address by clicking on the address button

The following fields are important in this session:
Statistics currency.
Sales Organisation Calendar.
Rebate Process Active.
For our scenarios, only the currency is important.

Distribution Channel [OVXI]

Distribution Channel is the media through which the product or service reaches the customers. Example: Wholesale, Retail, Tele-booking, etc. Distribution Channel is a mandatory unit in SD.

Let us define our distribution channel *'DC'*.

Defining Distribution Channel [OVXI]

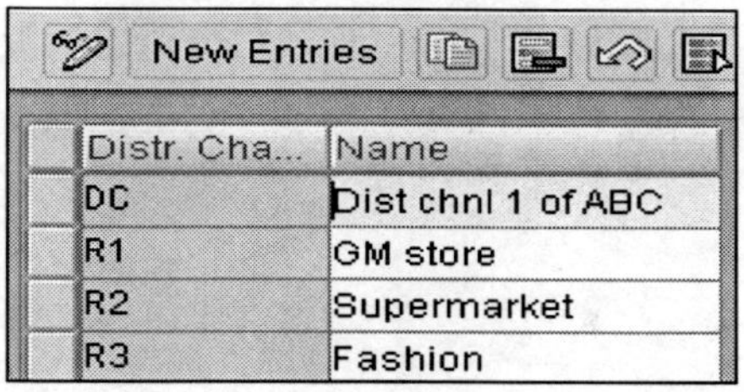

Fig:1-11

Path: IMG-Ent Structure-Definition- Sales and Distribution- Define, copy, delete, check distribution channel-Define distribution channel

Distribution channel is just a code with it's description.

Distribution channels are assigned to Sales Organisations in a many-to-many way. If sales orders are to be made from various distribution channels, link all those distribution channels to your sales Organisation.

Refer to the appendix if you want to set up common distribution channels for sharing master data of one distribution channel to other distribution channels.

Division [OVXB].

Division is a group of products earmarked for a specific purpose such as for identification, bifurcation, decentralized management, etc.

Example for a division is spare parts division, vehicle division, fabrication division, etc.

Division is a mandatory unit in SD. A material is always assigned to one division only.

Refer to the appendix if you want to set up a common division for sharing master data of one division to other divisions.

Let us define our division as D1.

Define, copy, delete, check division[OVXB]

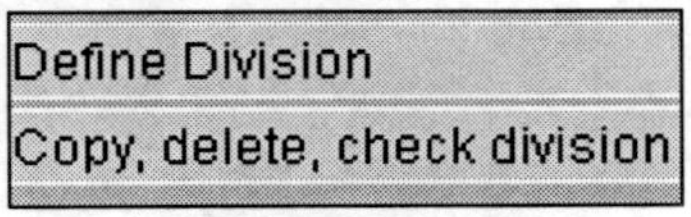

Fig:1-12

Path: IMG-Ent Structure-Definition- Logistics General- Define, copy, delete, check division. Choose option 1, Define Division:

Choose the first option .

Defining Division, *D1*.

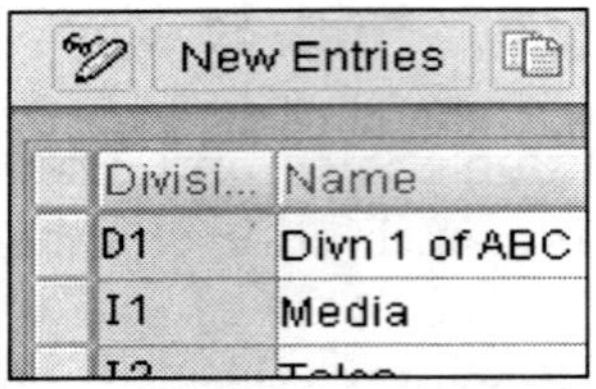

Fig:1-13

It is just a code and description

Plant [OX10]

Plant is an Organisational unit where the production is done and also it is considered as the material stocking place. Storage Locations are defined for each plant and assigned to plants. Material stocks are maintained at the storage location of plants. Many shipping points can be assigned to a plant. Also a plant can be used as Maintenance Planning Plant where all the plant maintenance activities are scheduled and carried out. Plant is a mandatory requirement in SD. In production, the plant is the production facility.

A company code can have many plants. A plant belongs to one country. Material creation, inventory management, material valuation, MRP planning, Production etc are done with reference to a plant. Hence, more than one company code cannot be linked to a plant. If you create a plant by copying from a plant that belongs to another country, you must change the country details of the new plant by going to the address area of the plant. Use plant 0001 or 1000 as a reference plant for copying.

Let us define our plant *PLT1*.

Define, copy, delete, check plant

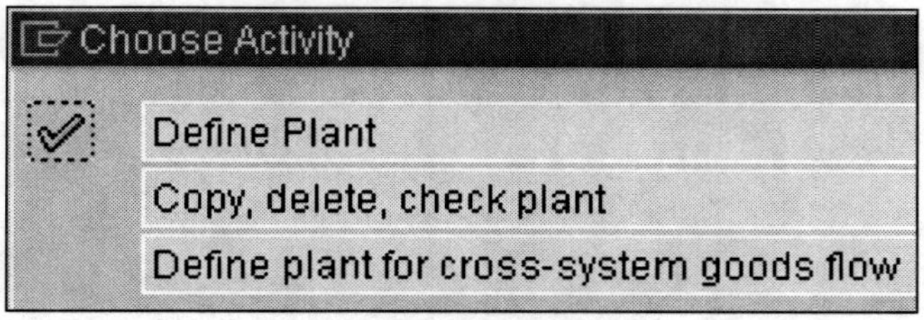

Fig:1-14

Path: IMG-Ent Structure-Definition- Logistics – General- Define, copy, delete, check plant. Choose option 1, Define Plant.

Choose the first option - Define Plant.

It is better to copy a plant from an existing one because many settings of the plant also get copied. But to understand better, you should create a new one instead of copying.

Define Plant [OX10]

Fig:1-15

After defining and saving the plant in this session, select the newly created plant and then choose the above button to enter the address data.

Entering the detailed information of the plant.

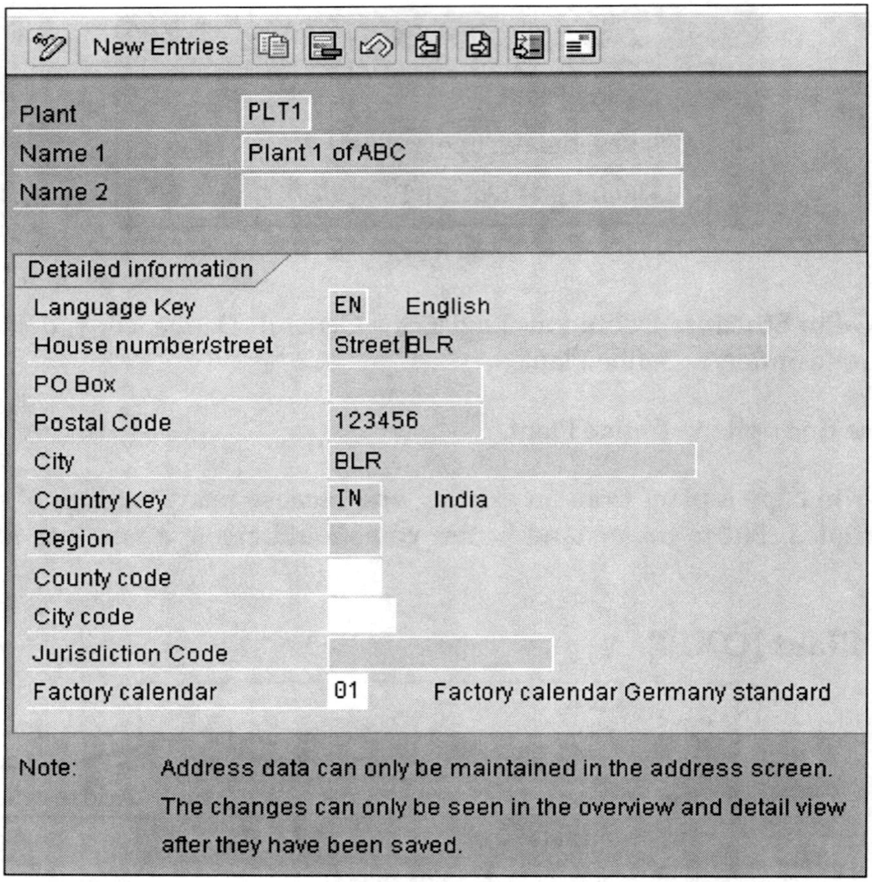

Fig: 1-16

Please Note: Plant is Language, City, County and Calendar based.

The country Key is very important because the tax details for materials that belong to this delivering plant are decided, based on this country. The tax classification code is entered in the material master.

If you copy a plant, the storage locations assigned to it also get copied.

After creating a new plant, what do you have to do? See the Enterprise Assignments and Miscellaneous Set up for your answer.

If warehouse management (full fledged WM or lean WM) is to be used in the sales process, a combination of plant and storage location must be linked to the warehouse. In such cases, materials are to be created with Warehouse Management view. If materials are already created without WM view, you can extend that material with WM view. If warehouse management is implemented, the material receipt and delivery process changes. If warehouse management is implemented, an interim location is used to receive the goods and a transfer order is to be created to move the materials to the final storage locations in the warehouse. For delivery also, a transfer order is required to transfer the material from the storage location to the interim location of the warehouse. But, in this book, the material handling process is explained assuming that the WM is not implemented. Refer to Lean Warehouse Management in the Appendix to know how to use simple warehouse management.

Storage location [OX09]

Storage locations are the locations where materials are kept in the plant. Storage locations are mandatory requirements for each plant. You can have many storage locations for a plant

Let us define one storage location SL1 for our plant PLT1.

Maintain storage location [OX09]

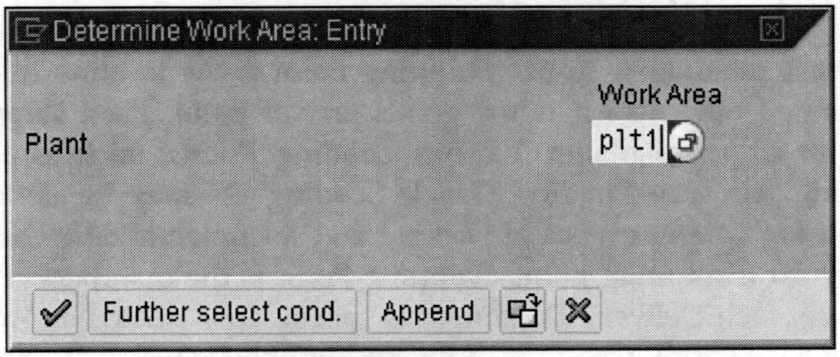

Fig:1-17

Path: IMG-Ent Structure-Definition- Materials Management- Maintain storage location.

Here you enter the plant to which you are going to create the storage locations.

Maintain storage location

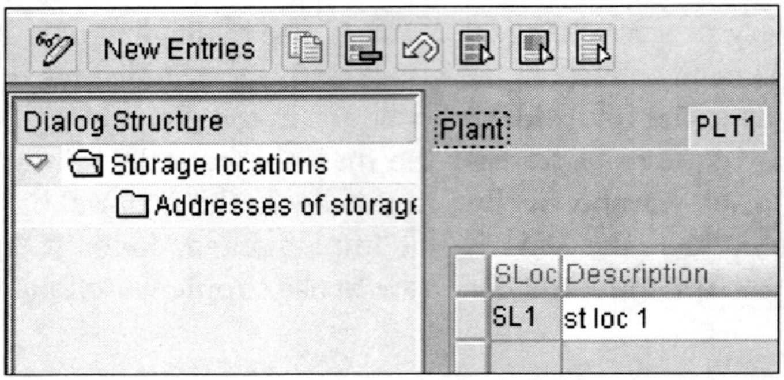

Fig:1-18

After saving the storage location, mark the same and then click on 'Address of Storage Location' and enter the address of the storage locations.

Defining a storage location and assigning the same to a plant is done in the same session. Hence, storage location can be defined only after defining the plant.

Shipping Point [OVXD]

Shipping point is mandatory in SD. Shipping Point is the location from where the goods are shipped out. Also it is the goods arrival point. Each shipping point is assigned to one or more plants. Various Loading Points; such as Rail Loading, Marine Loading Air way Loading, Truck Loading etc may be defined for each Shipping Point for different types of packing and documentations. Loading point is not mandatory for a shipping point. Shipping Point is the mandatory field for each Delivery. Hence, each Delivery Document is specific to a particular Shipping Point. If a customer needs entire lines to be delivered in one Delivery, all the lines should have the same shipping point. Shipping point can be determined by the system based on shipping point determination. Printer locations can be decided based on shipping points. One shipping point can be used by various plants.

Let us define our shipping point *SP1*.

Define, copy, delete, check shipping point[OVXD]

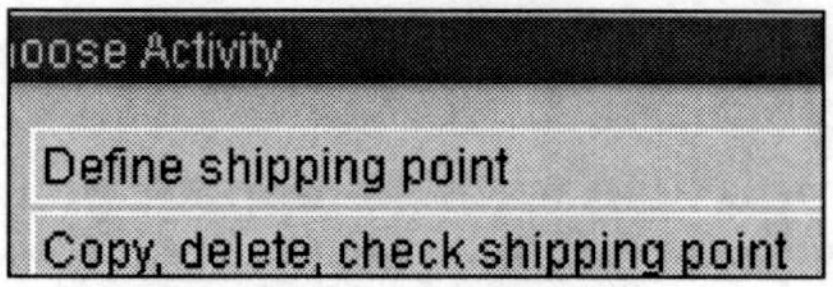

Fig:1-19

Path: IMG-Ent Structure-Definition- Logistics Execution- Define, copy, delete, check shipping point.

If you copy a shipping point, all the related tables are also copied and hence, it is recommended to create a shipping point by copying from an existing shipping point.

Choose the first option.

Define shipping point.

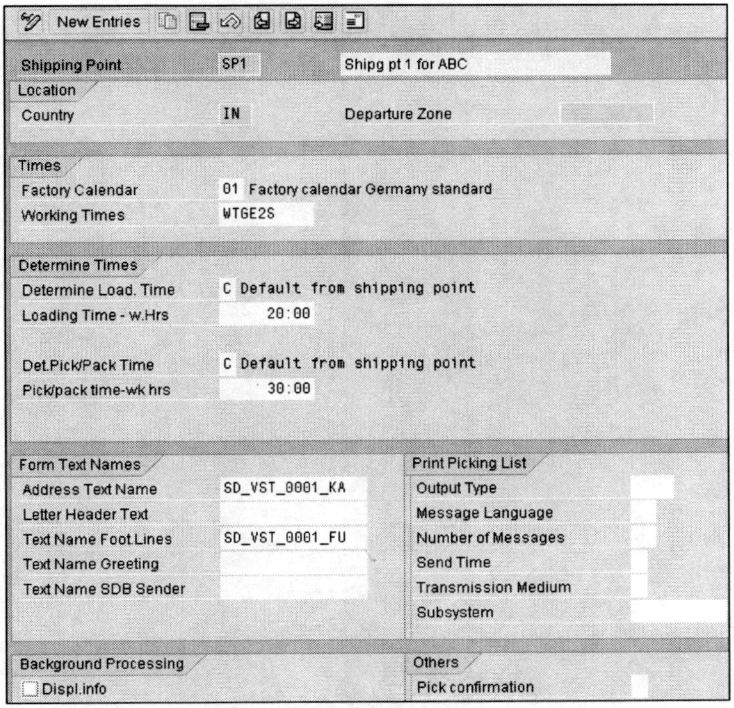

Fig:1-20

Some of the important fields from shipping point:

Country:

This country specifies the country from which the delivery originate.

Factory calendar:

Factory calendar that is applicable to this shipping point. Factory calendar is the calendar which specifies the working days and holidays for this shipping point.

Departure zone is used in Route Determination.

Loading Time and **Picking/Pack time** are used in Delivery Scheduling.

For our scenarios, only the country is important.

--- End of Definitions ---

Enterprise Assignment

Having defined all our mandatory Enterprise units, now we can interlink these units in this section.

Enterprise Assignment in a pictorial view.

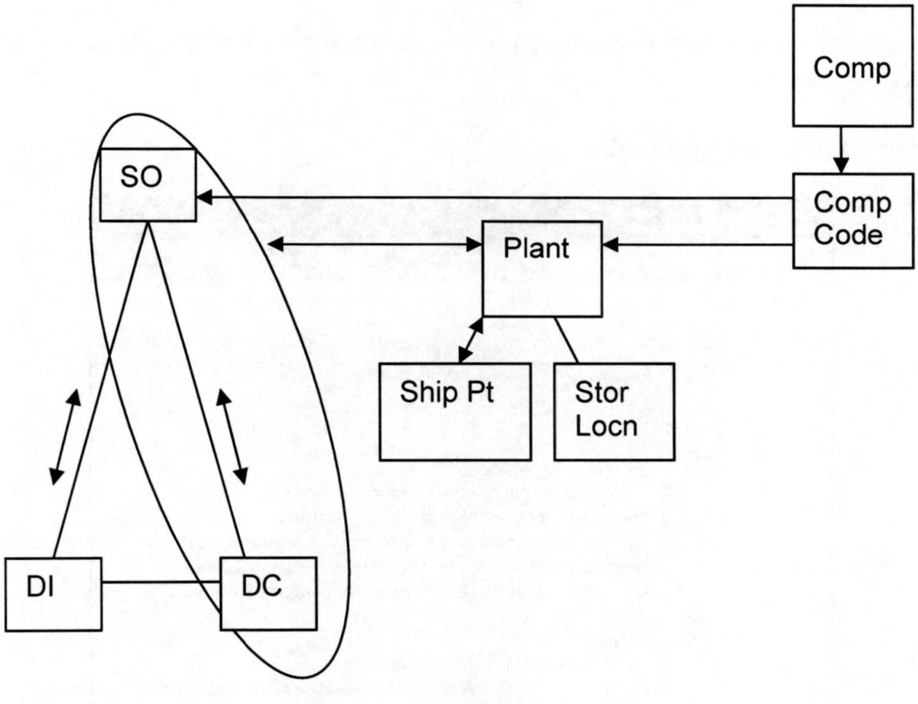

Fig:1-21

Assign:

- Company Codes to Company- Many to one assignment
- Plants to Company Code- Many to one assignment
- Sales Organisations to Company Code -Many to one assignment
- Plants to (Sales Org + Dist Channels)- Many to many assignment
- Distribution Channels to Sales Organisation- Many to many assignment
- Divisions to Sales Organisation- Many to many assignment
- Set up Sales Areas
- Shipping points to Plant- Many to many assignment
- Define Rules by Sales Areas and assign Business Areas according to the rules.

Rem: When you define a new plant, what are the enterprise assignments you have to make? Refer to fig 1-21 for your answer

Check up in the Miscellaneous Set Up also to know whether you have to do anything.

ENTERPRISE ASSIGNMENT

The Organisational units defined in the Enterprise structure must be assigned properly.

Menu paths for the assignment.

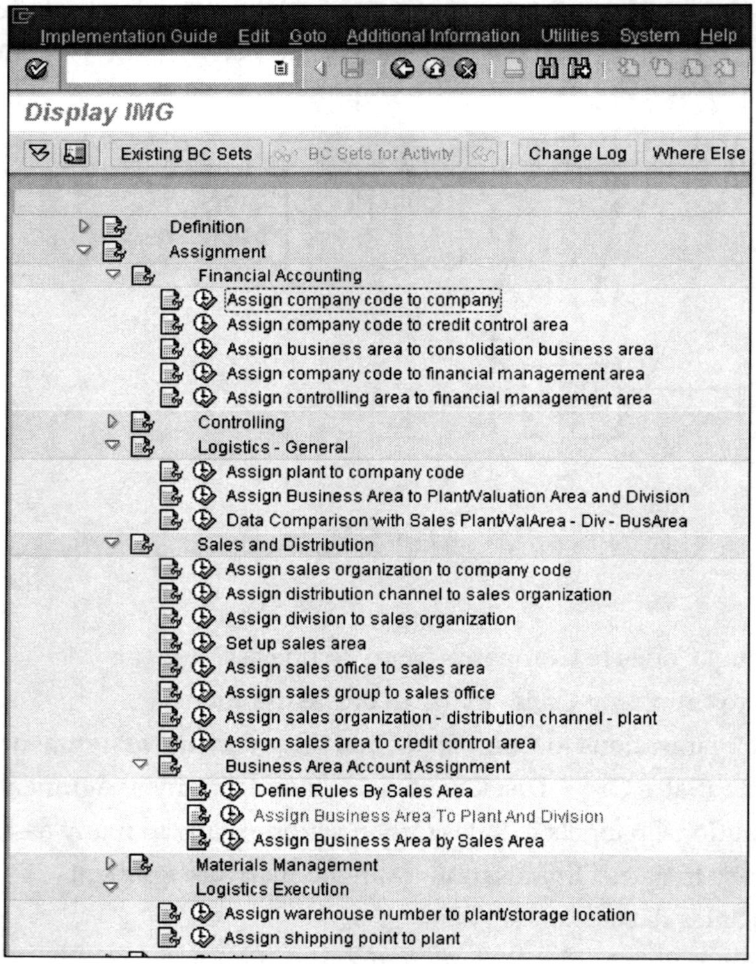

Fig:1-22

Path: IMG-Ent Structure- Assignment

Assign Company Codes to Company [OX16].

Let us assign Company code ABC to our Group Company GLOBAL

Assigning Company Codes to Company[OX16].

Fig:1-23

Path: IMG-Ent Structure- Assignment- Financial Accounting- Assign company code to company.

Here company code ABC is linked to the group company GLOBAL. Similarly all company codes are to be assigned to the group company.

Assign Plants to company code [OX18]

Assign plants to company code[OX18]

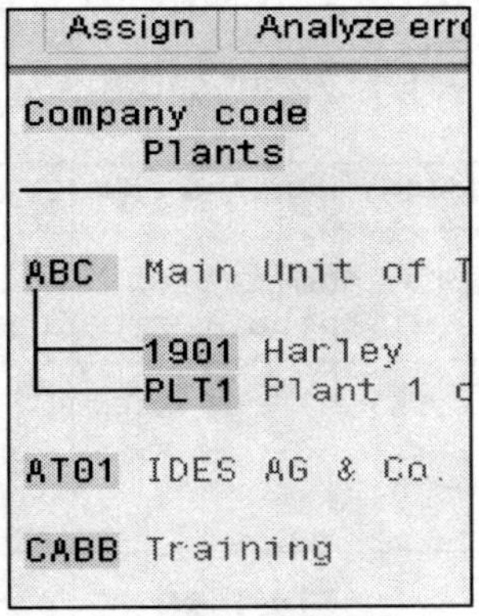

Fig: 1-24

Path: IMG-Ent Structure- Assignment- Logistics General- Assign plant to company code.

Plants belong to a particular company. One plant cannot be assigned to many companies.

Assign Sales Organisations to company code [OVX3]

Assign sales Organisations to company code[OVX3]

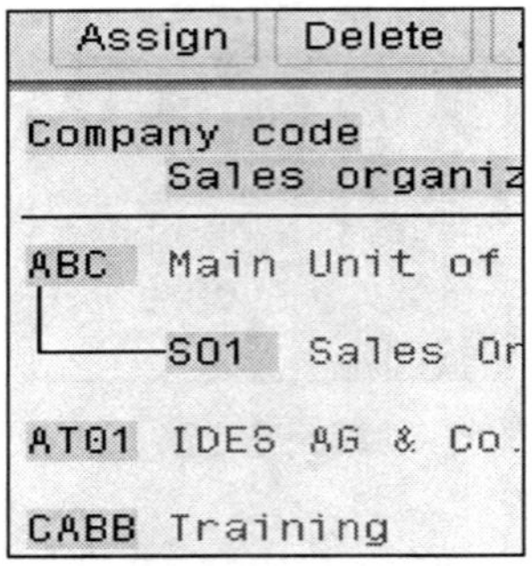

Fig:1-25

Path: IMG-Ent Structure- Assignment- Sales and Distribution- Assign sales Organisation to company code.

You can assign many sales Organisations to a company code. But one sales Organisation belongs to one company code only.

Assign Distribution channels to sales Organisation [OVXK]

Assign distribution channels to sales Organisation[OVXK]

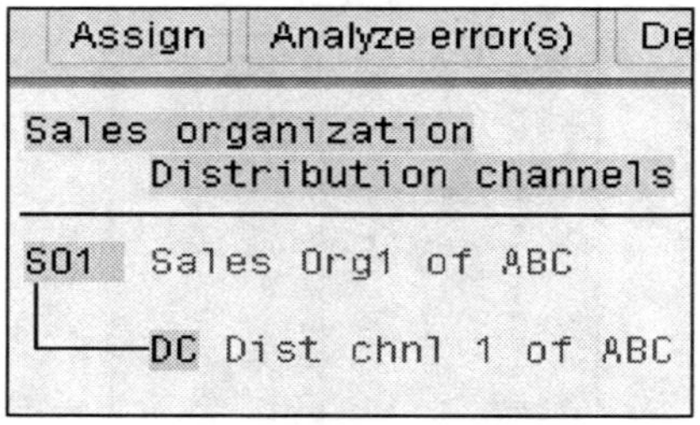

Fig:1-26

Path: IMG-Ent Structure- Assignment- Sales and Distribution- Assign distribution channel to sales Organisation

Assign Divisions to sales Organisation [OVXA]

Assign divisions to sales Organisation[OVXA]

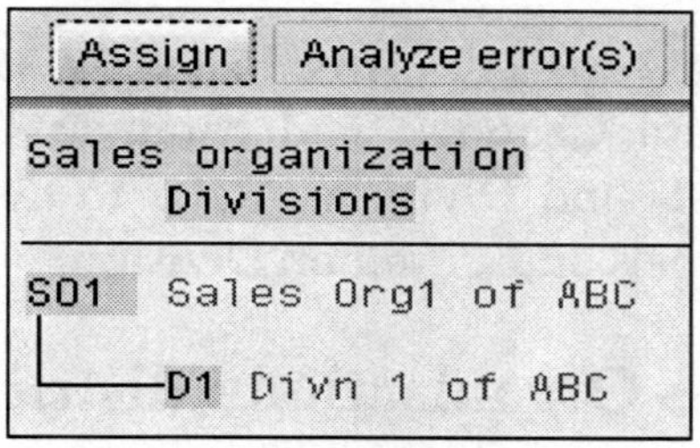

Fig:1-27

Path: IMG-Ent Structure- Assignment- Sales and Distribution- Assign division to sales Organisation.

Set up Sales Area [OVXG]

Set up Sales Area[OVXG]

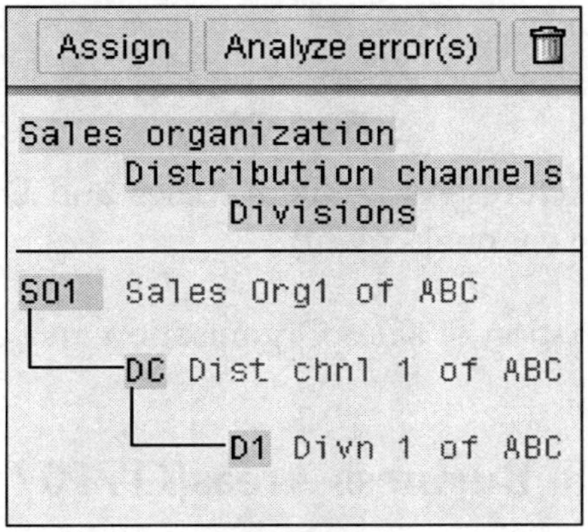

Fig:1-28

Path: IMG-Ent Structure- Assignment- Sales and Distribution- Set up sales area.

Sales Area is a combination of Sales Organisation, Distribution channel and Division.

You cannot say any combination of sales Organisation, distribution channel and division as a Sales Area. You must set up these 3 units here to call them as a Sales Area.

Sales documents(Sales orders, sales inquiries, sales quotations etc), customer masters etc are created against Sales Areas and hence, you must set up the relevant Sales Areas in this session before such actions.

Hence, you must have at least one Sales Area to test the sales order creation. You can set up common Distribution Channels and common Divisions for sharing data among Distribution channels and Divisions. Refer to the appendix to know about common Distribution Channels and Common Division.

Assign Plants to (sales Organisation +distribution channel) [OVX6]

Assign plants to (sales Organisation +distribution channel)[OVX6]

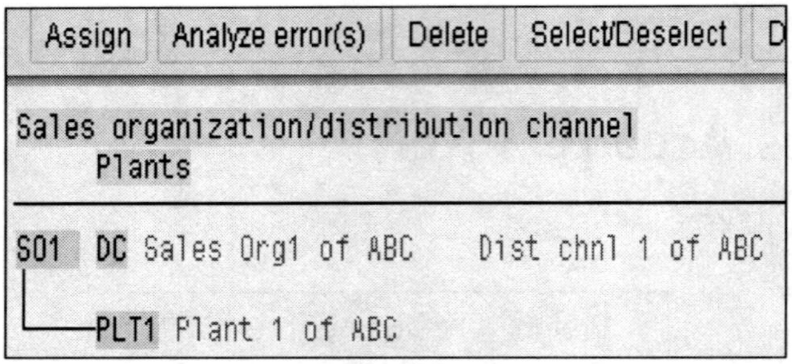

Fig:1-29

Path: IMG-Enterprise Structure- Assignment- Sales and Distribution- Assign (sales Organisation - distribution channel - plant)

Here you assign a combination of sales Organisation and distribution channels to a plant.

Assign Sales Areas to Business Areas[OVF0 / OVF1]

Assign Sales Areas to Business Areas.

Business Areas are defined and used for taking internal reports and they can be mapped to separate accounts in finance for evaluation of sales based on each Business area.

Note: For taking external reports (for example, balance sheets for legal purposes), Company Code is used.

Business Area usage is not a mandatory requirement by law, but it is a mandatory requirement for SAP SD to work. You cannot maintain sales orders if Business Areas are not set up properly.

Business Area is determined by the system in sales orders for each line item. This determination is based on assigning a rule to a combination of Sales Organisation, distribution channel and division in which we make sales orders. The determined business area can be seen in the accounting document.

For all the combinations of Sales Organisation, Distribution Channel and Division, you must assign a rule for how the business area is to be determined by the system when the sales order is created. Three rules are available to select from.

They are:

Business area determination by (Plant + Division)- Rule 1.

Business area determination by Sales Area- Rule 2

Business area determination by (sales Organisation+ distribution channel + item division)- Rule 3.

Hence, first assign rules for Business Areas as follows[OVF2]:

Let us assign rule 1 for our sales area SO1 + DC + D1.

Define Rules for Business Area[OVF2]:

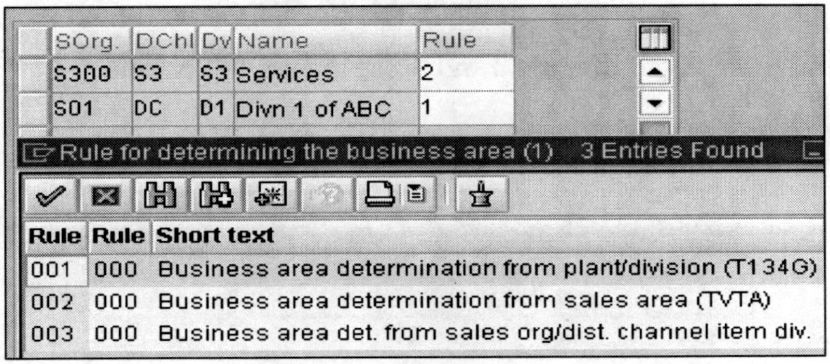

Fig:1-30

Path : IMG-Ent Struct-Assgnt-SD-Bus Area Account Assignment- Define rules by sales area.

When you set up a Sales Area, the same appears in this session (Fig 1-30) to assign a rule.

Fig 1-30 shows that rule 1, 'Business Area determination based on Plant and Division' is set for the combination of SO1+DC+D1.

Hence, any sales made in SO1 + DC +D1 will use the business area assigned for the relevant plant and division.

Now assign our (plants + divisions) to our Business Area:

As we have set rule 1 for SO1+ DC+D1, we must assign a Business Area to our plant and division (PLT1 + D1) for creating sales order in (SO1 + DC + D1).

Assigning our Business Area to our plant and division[OVF0]

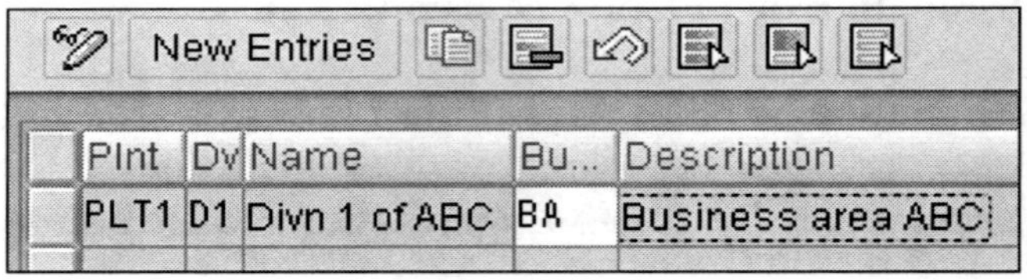

Fig:1-31

Path :IMG-Ent Struct-Assgnt-SD-Bus Area Account Assignment-Assign Business Area To Plant And Division

Now, if any sales order is made from plant PLT1 and division D1 in (SO1 + DC + D1), Business Area 'BA' will be determined by the system.

To understand more about the rule 2 and 3, see the session below.

Assigning Business Area to Sales Area [OVF1]

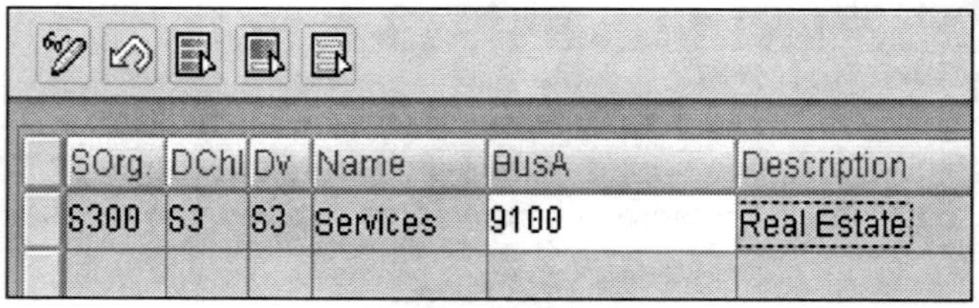

Fig:1-32

Path :IMG-Ent Struct-Assgnt-SD-Bus Area Account Assignment- Assign Business Area by Sales Area.

Note: In this session you do not have a New Entry option. You will see here only those Sales Areas which are linked with rule 2 or 3. Hence, you will be able to link a Business Area to those Sales Areas for which rules 2 or 3 are set.

In this session you cannot see our sales area(SO1+DC+D1) to link to a Business Area because we have linked rule 1 to our sales area.

The determined Business Area can be viewed in the accounting document([VF02]-Goto-Item-Item Details).

Assign Shipping points to plant [OVXC]

Assigning shipping points to plant[OVXC]

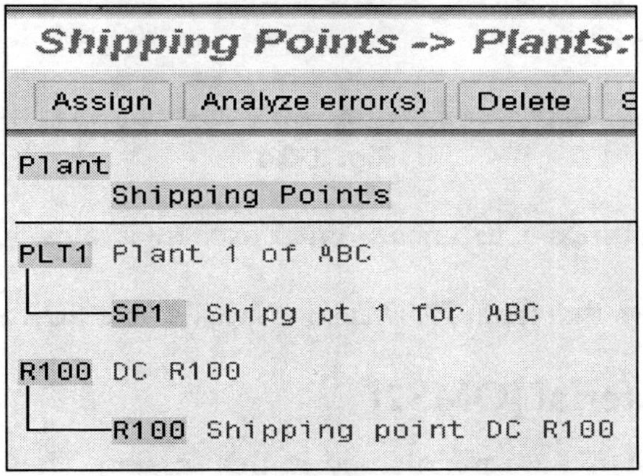

Fig:1-33

Path :IMG-Ent Struct-Assgnt- Logistics Execution- Assign shipping point to plant.

-- End of Assignments--

Miscellaneous Setup

As part of the setting up of Enterprise for SD point of view, some miscellaneous settings also need to be done for proper function of all functions in SD. The following are the settings to be done.

Currency conversion [OB08].

When you copy a company code of one currency to another company code of a different currency, you may have to set up currency conversion factors as follows.

Enter Exchange Rates.

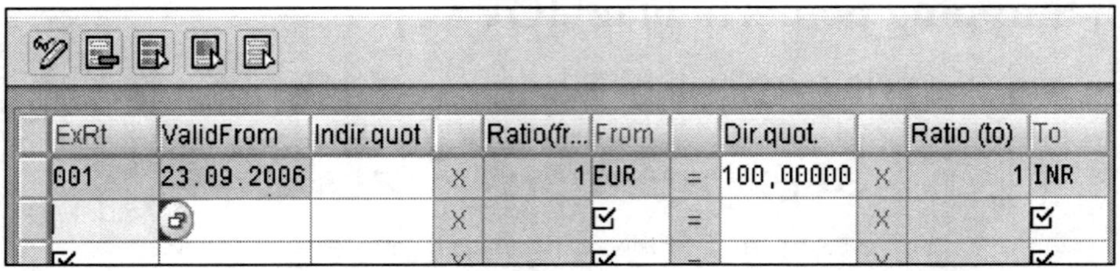

Fig: 1-34

Path: IMG-General Settings- Currencies- Enter exchange rates- New Entries.

The above entry shows that from 23.09.2006 onwards, one EUR is equal to 100.0 INR.

Attributes of material [OMS2]

Two attributes of material are maintained in this session. These attributes are to be maintained before creating material masters. They are:

1. Attribute of Material Type

2. Attribute of Quantity/Value Update of materials.

1. Attribute of Material Type.

In addition to other data, Material Type is used while creating material master. Almost all Material Types are already defined in SAP system. A few examples are FERT(Finished Product), FRIP(Perishable), ERSA(Spare Parts), HAWA(Trading Goods), etc.

Attributes of material Type controls many features while creating material master. Refer to Material Master Data[MM01] in the chapter Master Data.

Let us go to the session Define Attributes of Material Types.

Define Attributes of Material Types[OMS2]

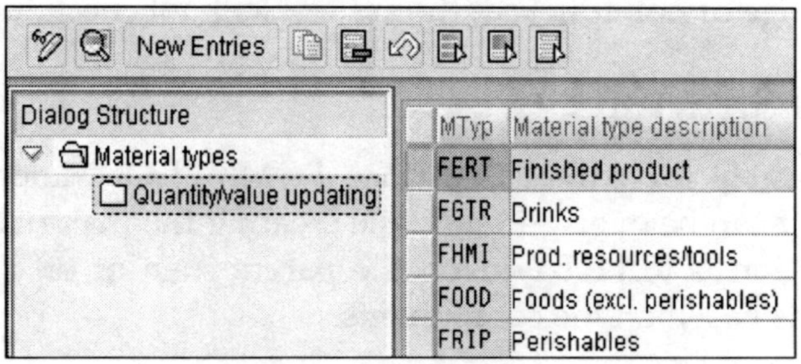

Fig:1-35

Path: IMG-Logistics General-Material Master-Basic Settings-Material Types-Define Attributes of Material Types.

Let us view the attributes of material type FERT(Finished Product.)

Attributes on Material Type FERT(Finished Product.)

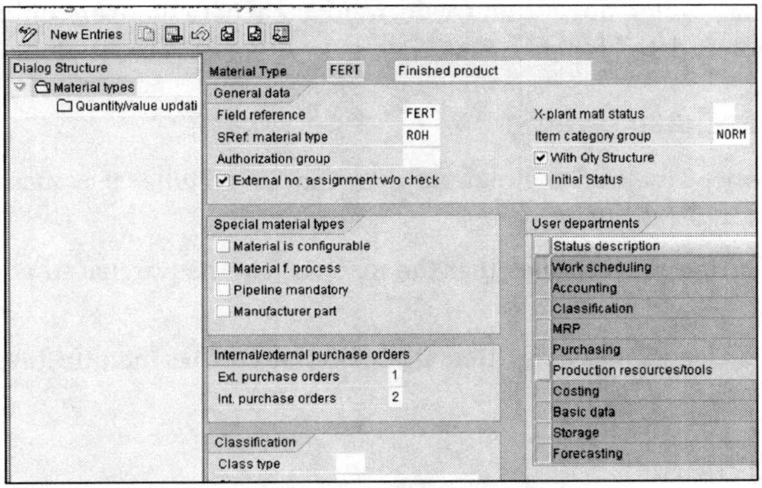

Fig:1-36

The following features are controlled by material type attributes while creating materials[MM01]:

Screen Reference material type:

Which screens appear and in what sequence, is controlled by this field.

External Number of assignment w/o check:

In case we enter the material number externally, the system should ask the user to tick the number range or not. If ticked, the system will not check the number range.

With Quantity Structure:

This field is applicable for parent item in a BOM(Bill Of Material). This is for a default value, but it can be overwritten while creating the material master. It shows whether the valuation is to be based on the parent item or on the components. If ticked, the costing is based on the components.

Material is configurable:

Whether this material is intended for a specific purpose such as configurable material or process material?

Pipeline mandatory:

Whether pipeline material features are mandatory or not? An example for pipe line materials are water, air, cotton waste, mud, etc where there are unlimited supply and stock is not updated for such materials.

External purchase orders:

What procurement method the material has; that is, whether it is manufactured in-house, or procured externally.

Ext purchase orders =1 indicates that the material can be purchased with a warning message.

Int Purchase order =2 indicates that the material can be manufactured without a warning message.

User departments:

Which user departments (Data entry screens) are allowed to use while creating the material master.

2. Attribute of Quantity/Value Update of materials.

This is also a very important set up. If it is not set, you cannot even create stock for the material in the particular plant.

Attributes on 'Quantity and Value Updates' is used for material transactions.

Let us view the following screen to know how it can be set up.

Attributes on Quantity and Value Updates[OMS2].

Fig: 1-37

Here you select, as marked, for all the plants and Material Types that you deal with.

It shows that materials created in the plant PLT1 with Material Type FERT are updated on quantity as well as value in the appropriate ledger accounts.

Plant Parameters [OLMB]

Let us view the Plant parameter session.

Plant Parameters [OLMB]

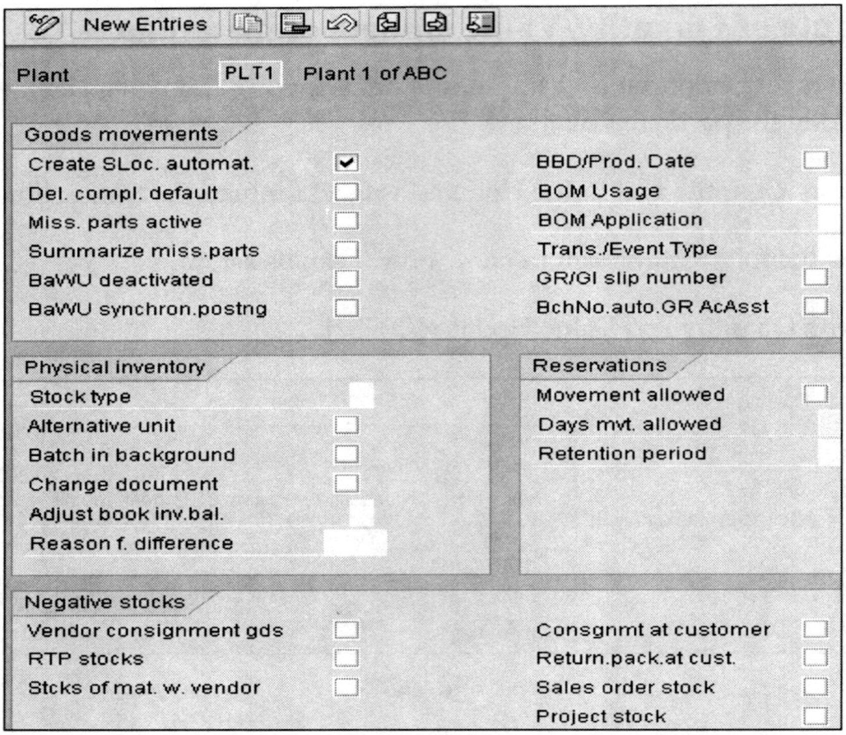

Fig:1-38

Path: IMG- Materials Management- Inventory Management and Physical Inventory- Plant Parameters.

The minimum setting in plant parameter to be done in SD point of view is 'Create Storage Location automatically'. Further settings are done by PP and MM consultants.

If you create a plant by copying from another plant, the parameters are also copied.

It indicates that automatic creation of storage location in the material master at the time of first goods receipt is allowed. If it is not set, you must maintain the storage location data of a material before you post the first goods receipt in the relevant storage location.

Value Area Setup [OMWD]

Account Determination for Value Areas(Plants)- [OMWD]

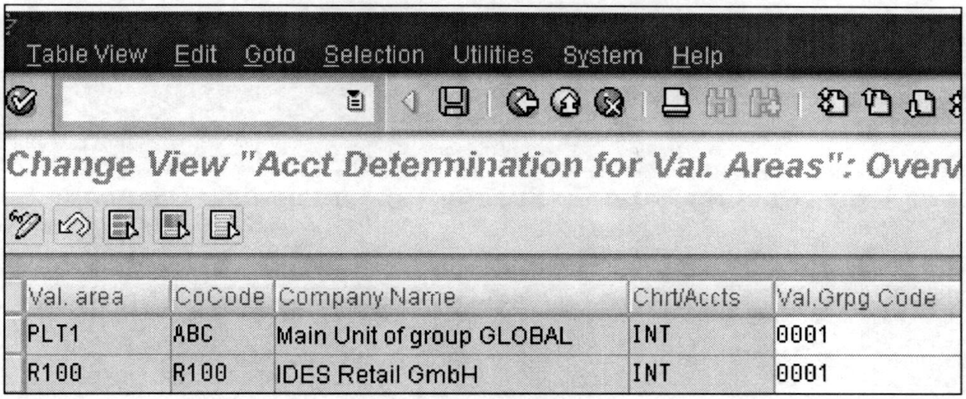

Fig:1-39

For each plant you must set up the above data.

Use the Valuation Grouping Code 0001.

Valuation Grouping Code determines the ledger accounts to which goods movement is to be posted. It is set by FIN consultant and is used in MM for inventory Valuation.

Specifying Posting Time Intervals [OB52]

SPECIFY POSTING TIME INTERVALS [OB52]

If the company code is created by copying from an original company(In our case company code ABC is created by copying from company code 1000 and hence Variant 1000 of company code 1000 is copied to the new company code), you have to modify the posting periods of the relevant variant to future periods as mentioned below.

Actually, this will be set up by FIN consultant. But for your learning purpose, set up the data as shown in fig 1-40:

Changed Data

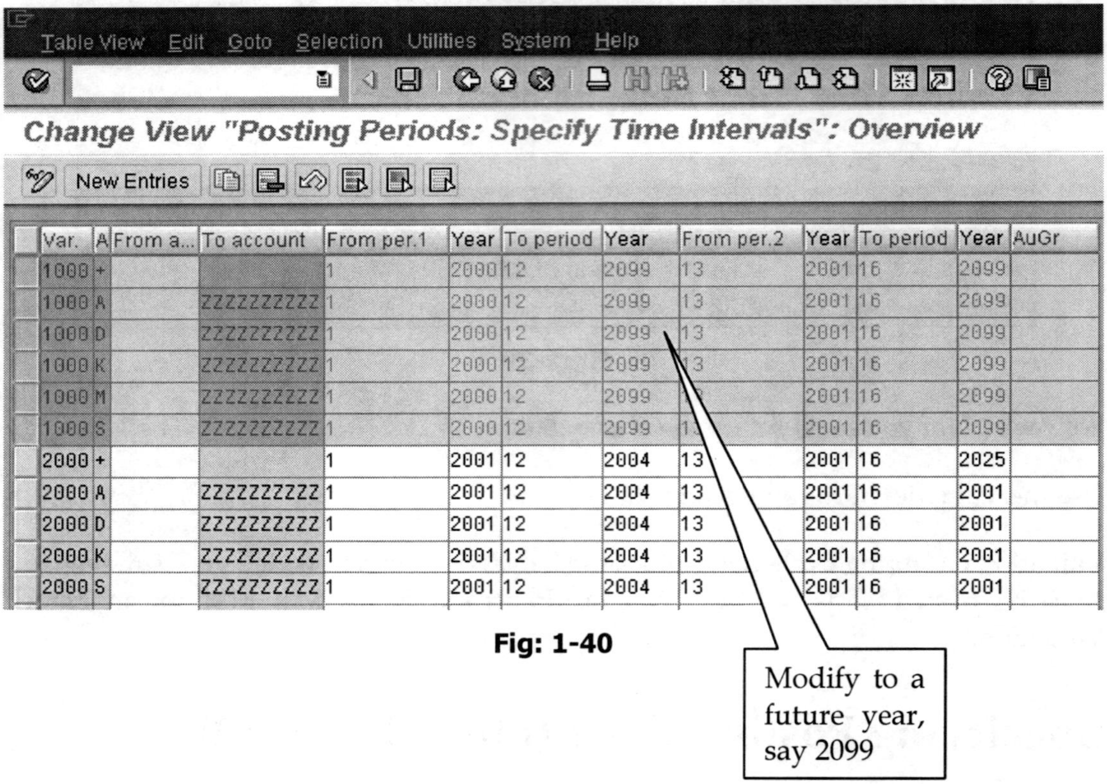

Var.	A	From a...	To account	From per.1	Year	To period	Year	From per.2	Year	To period	Year	AuGr
1000	+			1	2000	12	2099	13	2001	16	2099	
1000	A		ZZZZZZZZZZ	1	2000	12	2099	13	2001	16	2099	
1000	D		ZZZZZZZZZZ	1	2000	12	2099	13	2001	16	2099	
1000	K		ZZZZZZZZZZ	1	2000	12	2099	13	2001	16	2099	
1000	M		ZZZZZZZZZZ	1	2000	12	2099	13	2001	16	2099	
1000	S		ZZZZZZZZZZ	1	2000	12	2099	13	2001	16	2099	
2000	+			1	2001	12	2004	13	2001	16	2025	
2000	A		ZZZZZZZZZZ	1	2001	12	2004	13	2001	16	2001	
2000	D		ZZZZZZZZZZ	1	2001	12	2004	13	2001	16	2001	
2000	K		ZZZZZZZZZZ	1	2001	12	2004	13	2001	16	2001	
2000	S		ZZZZZZZZZZ	1	2001	12	2004	13	2001	16	2001	

Fig: 1-40

The above figure 1-40 shows that the posting period year of 'To period 1' is modified to 2099 for the original company code 1000 and hence for our company code ABC also.

--- End of Miscellaneous setup--

Chapter 2

MASTER DATA

After finishing the enterprise setup, we should set up the master data. For most of the business needs, the master data is already available in the system. Hence, it is recommended to use the same master data if possible. If you want any modification to the existing master data, you copy them to new codes and then modify the new ones. Never make any changes to the existing master data. Only the essential master data such as customer masters and material masters required for our sales scenario will be created.

We will use the following abbreviations for the master data throughout the book for easy reference. Let us study about the following master data:

Delivery Document Types (DDT)

Billing Document Types(BDT)

Sales Document Types (SDT)

Accounting Document Types(ADT)

Order Item Categories(OIC)

Delivery Item Categories(DIC)

Schedule Line Categories(SLC)

Account Groups

Tax Set Up

Copy Control

CUSTOMER MASTER DATA

MATERIAL MASTER DATA

Except for Customer Master and Material Master, all this master data is available in the system for global purposes. Global means this master data is independent of company code, sales Organisation, etc.

We will explain and create all the above master data in the above given sequence. Then we will use them in our sales transaction exercise.

Delivery Document Type [OVLK]

DELIVERY DOCUMENT TYPE(DDT)

'Delivery Doc Type', sometimes referred to as 'Delivery Type' is a document which controls the delivery of materials.

It is used in Delivery Item Category(DIC) determination[0184]. DDT is assigned in SDT.

Delivery Document Type LF is used for Std Delivery, LO is used for delivery without reference, LR is used for return sales delivery with reference to a sales order and NL is used for Replenishment delivery.

We will use the existing DDTs for our exercise.

Delivery Document Type, LF [OVLK]

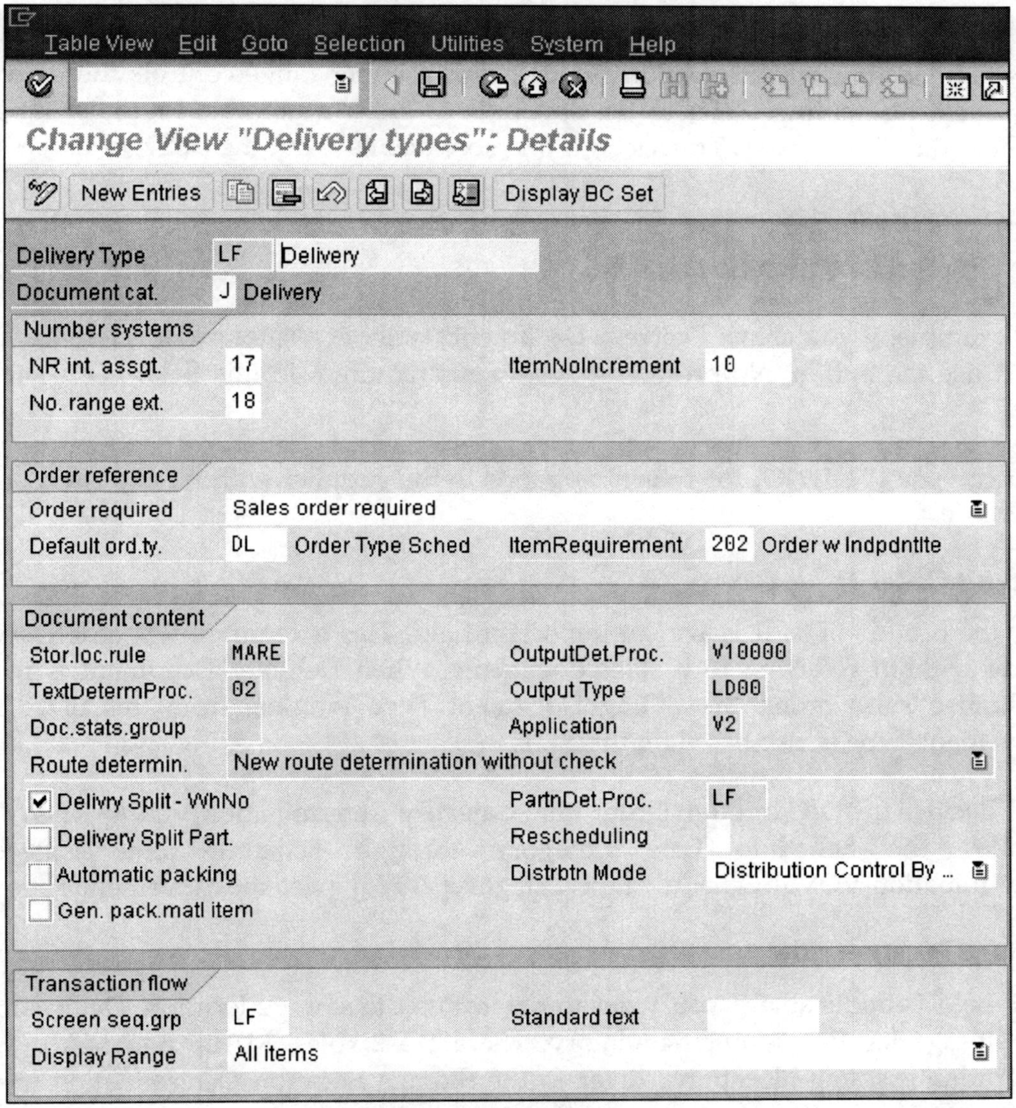

Fig: 2-1

Path: IMG-Log exec-Shipping –Deliveries-Define Delivery Types.

Important fields' descriptions in DDT:

Document Category:

This is an important field. This field is accessed from a common table for SDT, DDT, BDT etc. For DDT, you must use only J(Delivery).

Number Range:

It is defined through the session [VN01]. This number range controls the delivery document numbering. Refer to the appendix to know more about number ranges. Refer to the chapter Sales Transactions for more details about the Delivery Process.

Order required:

Use appropriate options in this field.

For example, if you create Delivery Documents without a sales order reference, you must use the option 'No preceding documents required' in this field. *LO* is such a DDT.

You can use [VL01NO] for returning goods to the supplier without any sales order reference.

Default Order Type, DL:

It is the pseudo SDT. It is also an important field. This is required when delivery is made without referring to a sales document. When Delivery Document is made without a sales order, the Billing Document Type is taken from this SDT. The Movement Type is also based on this SDT.

SDT decides the OIC through Order Item Category Determination[VOV4]. Then OIC decides the Schedule Line Category through Schedule Line Category Determination[VOV5]. Schedule Line Category[VOV6] gives the Movement Type.

Storage Location rule:

This field is applicable if you want to determine the storage location. Determining the storage location is not mandatory. There are 2 rules, MALE and MALA, for determining storage locations. Refer to the Storage Location Determination in the chapter Determinations for more details.

Refer to the screen below to know about DDT for returning the sold materials.

DDT for Return Sales Delivery[OVLK]

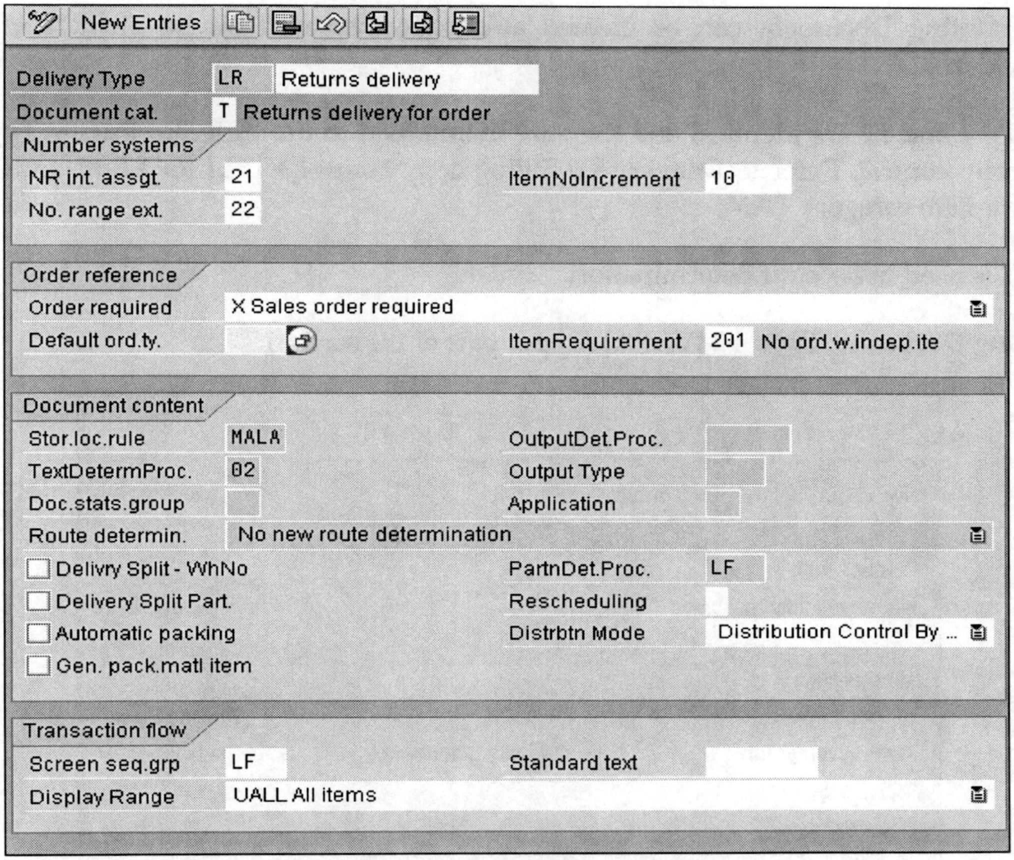

Fig:2-2

Path: IMG-Log exec-Shipping –Deliveries-Define Delivery Types.

Billing Document Type [VOFA]

Billing Document Type(BDT).

BDT controls billing document as well as accounting document created through the session VF01. Billing document generates the legal invoice and the accounting document is a document for internal use. BDT is assigned in SDT. Accounting Document Type(ADT) is assigned in BDT at the field 'Document type'. If no ADT is assigned at this field, by default, the system takes ADT *'RV'*. ADT decides the number range for Accounting Documents. Use [OBA7] to view ADT. The number range for ADT is created through the session [FBN1] and the number range for BDT is created through the session [VN01].

Accounting Document can be created automatically based on the field 'Posting Block' in BDT.

BDT *F1* and *F2* are identical and they are maintained to use different Pricing Types in copy control. Refer to Delivery-To-Billing copy control[VTFL] for LF-F1 and LF-F2 for item category TAN.

BDT is used in account determination.

Billing Document Type, F2 [VOFA] (upper part of the screen)

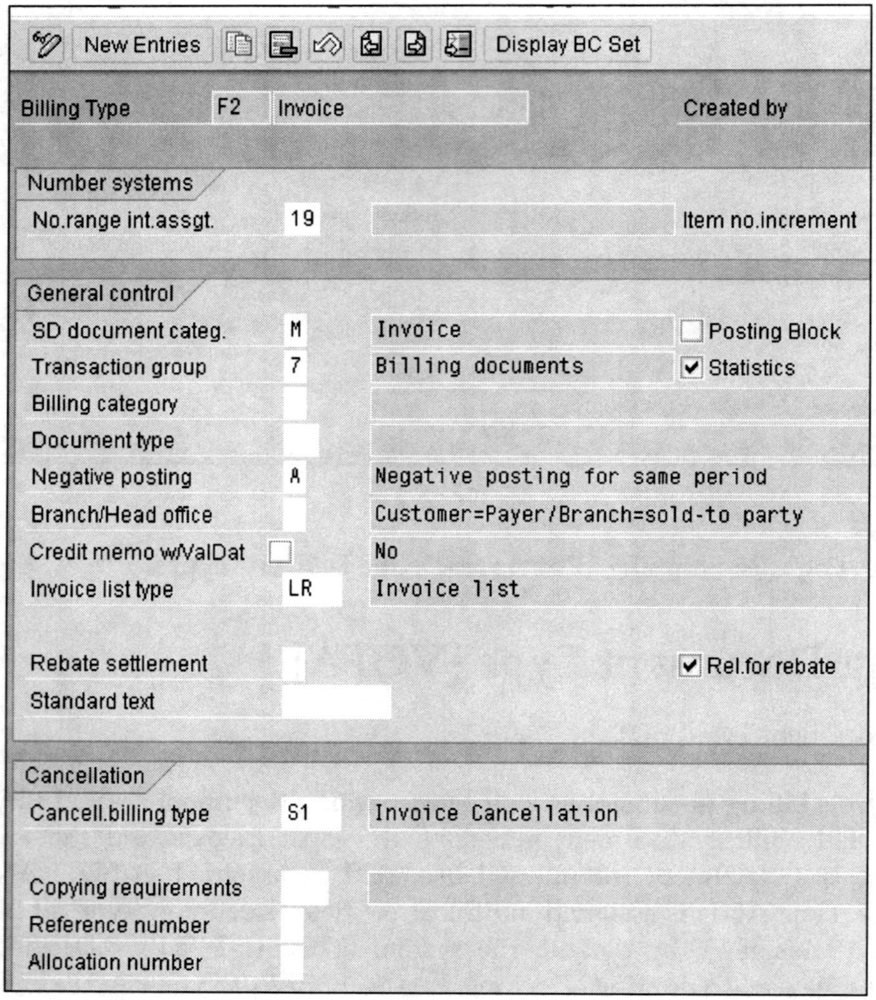

Fig:2-3

Path: IMG-SD-Billing- Billing Docs- Define Billing Types

Please note that the Billing Document can be generated only by internal numbering.

Some of the important fields in BDT are explained here:

Number Range:

The billing Document uses only internal numbering. It is maintained through the session [VN01].

Posting Block:

It is an important field. If marked, while saving the Billing Document, the Accounting Document will not be generated. In such case, you can manually generate accounting document from the billing document by going to Toolbar-Billing Document- Release To Accounting.

Document type (= Accounting Document type) :

This is also an important field.

Here you assign the Accounting Document Type [OBA7]. If no Accounting Document Type (ADT) is assigned here, the system takes Accounting Document Type *'RV'* by default. Accounting Document Type is mandatory to create Accounting Documents. Accounting Documents are created while or after creating the Billing Documents. The number range for ADT is maintained through [FBN1]. You can see the ADT in Accounting Overview of the Billing Document.

Bottom part of BDT F2 [VOFA]

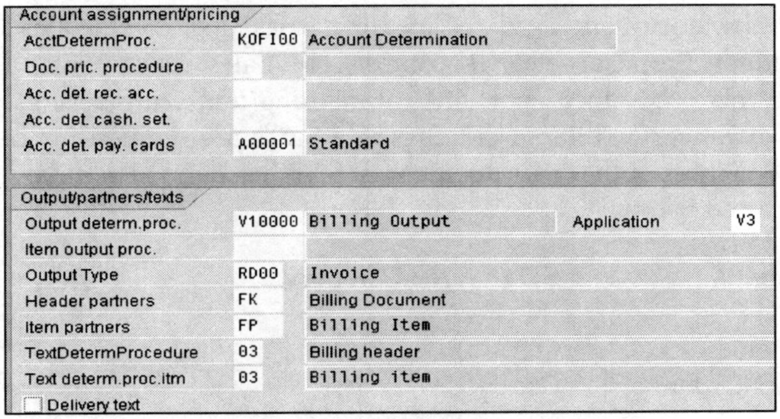

Fig: 2-4

Path: IMG-SD-Billing- Billing Docs- Define Billing Types

Fields:

Account Determination Procedure:

It is an important field and is used for account determination.

This Account Determination Procedure links the Account Determination Type, Chart of account, Sales Organisation, Account Key and G/L Account. Hence, for Account Determination Procedure linked here, there must be valid G/L account numbers defined and assigned for creating accounting documents.

Refer to Account Determination later in this book for more details.

The following fields in BDT integrate SD with Finance:

1. Posting Block
2. Document Type (= Accounting Document Type)
3. Account Determination Procedure

Now for our exercise, create two exact copies of Billing Document Types ZF1 and ZF2 by copying from F2. The reason for this will be clear when you read SDT.

Sales Document Type [VOV8]

Sales Document Type(SDT)

In SAP, SDT is referred to as 'Order Type' in many areas.

For our needs, we will create our own SDT *ZOR* by copying the existing SDT *OR*

SDT is a header document used for creating sales documents(Sales Order, Sales Inquiry, Product Proposal etc). It controls, in Sales Documents, features like document numbering, document line numbering(Item numbering), subsequent processes like Delivery , Billing, etc. Separate SDTs are defined for separate Sales Documents. For most of the sales documents, SAP has defined standard SDTs, a few of which are listed below:

Sales Documents	**SDT**	**Doc Category**
Sales Inquiry	IN	A
Sales Quotation	QT	B
Standard Sales Order	OR	C
Product Proposal	MS	D

T- code for creating some of the sales documents are as follows:

Sales Order	VA01
Credit Memo Request	VA01
Sales Inquiry	VA11
Sales Quotation	VA21
Scheduling Agreement	VA31
Sales Contracts	VA41

In this book we describe only the sales order process because if you understand the sales order process, you can easily understand all other processes of SD.

For the Sales Order itself, there are various SDTs defined in the system. For example, OR is used for Standard Sales Orders, RO is used for Rush Sales Orders, CS is used for Cash Sales Orders, etc. In SAP, normal sales order is referred to as Standard Order or Standard Sales Order.

It is recommended not to modify any of the SAP standard SDTs. If you want to make any modification to the existing SDT, it is recommended to copy them to a new SDT and do the modifications in the new one. Prefix the letter Z for the new SDT. Z is recommended by SAP for some technical reasons. Hence, if you want to make a copy of OR, create ZOR or ZR, etc.

So, it is recommended to create your own SDT, even if it is the exact copy of an existing SDT.

Also, while copying, certain linked set ups such as Copy Control Rules, Item category determination,etc. are copied to the new SDT.

SDT is used in Sales Document Creation, Order Item Category Determination, Pricing procedure determination, Copy Control, Delivery Document Type(DDT), etc.

Note: Delivery Document Type and Billing Document Type are linked in Sales Document Type whereas Accounting Document Type and Account Determination Procedure are linked in the Billing Document Type.

Let us copy the SAP standard SDT *OR* to *ZOR* and modify the fields 'Item Number increments', fig 2-5 and 'Billing Document Types, fig 2-6' for our exercise:

As SDT is a big screen, we will split it into 2 parts to accommodate in the page.

Sales Document Type, *ZOR* [VOV8] (Upper part of the screen)

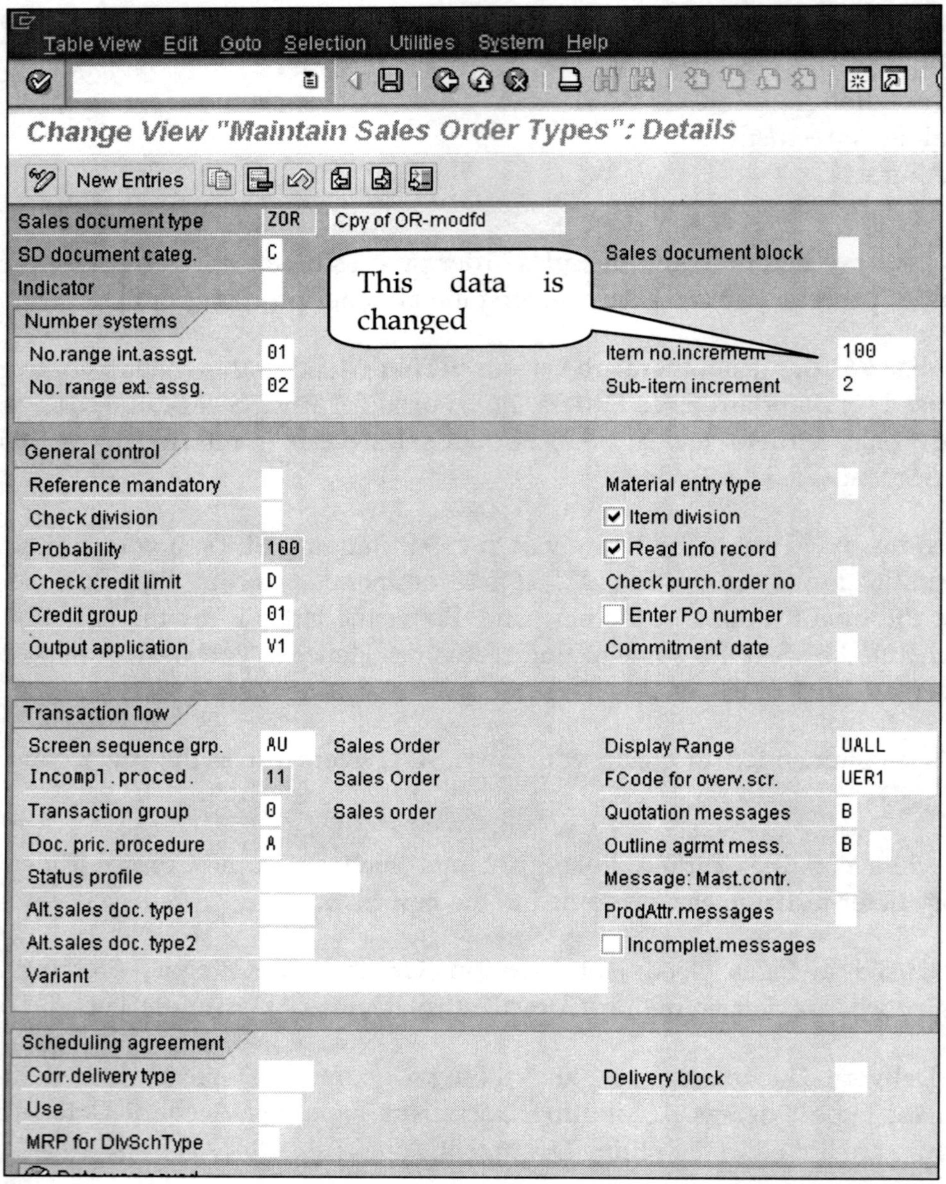

Fig:2-5

Path: IMG-SD-SLS-SLS DOC-SLS DOC HEADER-Define Sales Document Types.

Some of the important fields are explained here. If you want details on other fields, it is recommended to take field help from SAP system.

Document Category:

It indicates categories of sales documents such as 'A' for Sales Inquiry, 'B' for Quotation, 'C' for Sales Order, 'D' for Product Proposal, etc. There is some program built under this code. For example, if you create sale order[VA01] with SDT *'IN'*, the system will give a message indicating that this Order Type is not for sales order. Hence, you must use SDTs with document category 'C' while creating sales orders[VA01].

Sales Doc Block:

If selected, a new SO(Sales Order) cannot be created but an already created SO can be processed.

Number Range(Number Series):

Internal number range is used for the system to use it's own consecutive numbers as per the definition of number ranges. External number range is used for creating sales documents with your own number systems. If you want to create SO with your own number code, enter the number code while creating SO. Use [VN01] to view various number ranges for sales documents. Please observe in [VN01] that if the external indicator is not marked, it is assumed that it is an internal series. If you do not want to create sales documents with external numbering, remove the external number range in SDT.

Item Number increment:

It is used for incrementing line numbers(item numbers) in the Sales Document.

Sub Item Increment is used for numbering components in BOMs(Bill Of Material). Refer Bill Of Material in the appendix for more information.

Reference mandatory:

If selected , a reference document is mandatory while creating sales document with this SDT. Some of the options are as follows:

' ' means no reference is needed.
'A' means with reference to a Sales Inquiry
'B' means with reference to a quotation
'C' means with reference to a Sales Order
'M' means with reference to a Billing document.

Item Division:

If selected, the division in the sales order line will be that from item(Material master). Otherwise it is taken from the header data(Division entered as per fig 5-2). This field is used for cross division sale(Items of different divisions in one sales order). If a sales order is to be created with items from various divisions, this field should be selected.

Enter PO number:

If this field is selected and if you save the sales document without entering anything at the field 'PO Number', the system puts, by default, the Sales Document number at the field 'PO Number'.

Note: When incompletion procedure '11' is linked and also if this field is selected, the Sales Document will be saved without any incompletion log.

Incompletion Procedure:

'Incompletion Procedure' will work in conjunction with the field 'Incomplete Message'.

Incompletion Procedure is a list of fields for which if data is not maintained, the incompletion will be logged in an incompletion log for information and will allow continuation with the subsequent processes.

But, if an incompletion procedure is linked and also if the field ' Incomplete Message' is selected, the system will not allow to save the document and proceed further.

Here the incompletion procedure '11' is linked to this SDT through the path IMG-SD-BF-Log of incomplete Items. Procedure '11' is list of the following fields with a warning indicator for the field 'PO number'

Document date
Document currency
PO number
Incoterms
Pricing date
Payment terms

Each of the above fields is assigned with an 'incompleteness status group'. The status group decides which processes(Sales, Delivery, Billing, etc) should be logged in the incompletion log if the data is not maintained.

Status Group '01' is assigned to the field 'PO number'. Status Group '01' is marked for logging only the Sales Document. Hence, if the field ' Incomplete Message' is selected and then you try to save the sales order without filling the field 'PO Number', the system will not allow you to save the sales order. You must edit the sales document(VA02- Edit- Incompletion log) and enter the PO number for processing the sales document further.

Document Pricing Procedure:

It is a very important field and is Used for Pricing Procedure Determination.

Sales Document Type, *ZOR* [VOV8] (Bottom part of the screen)

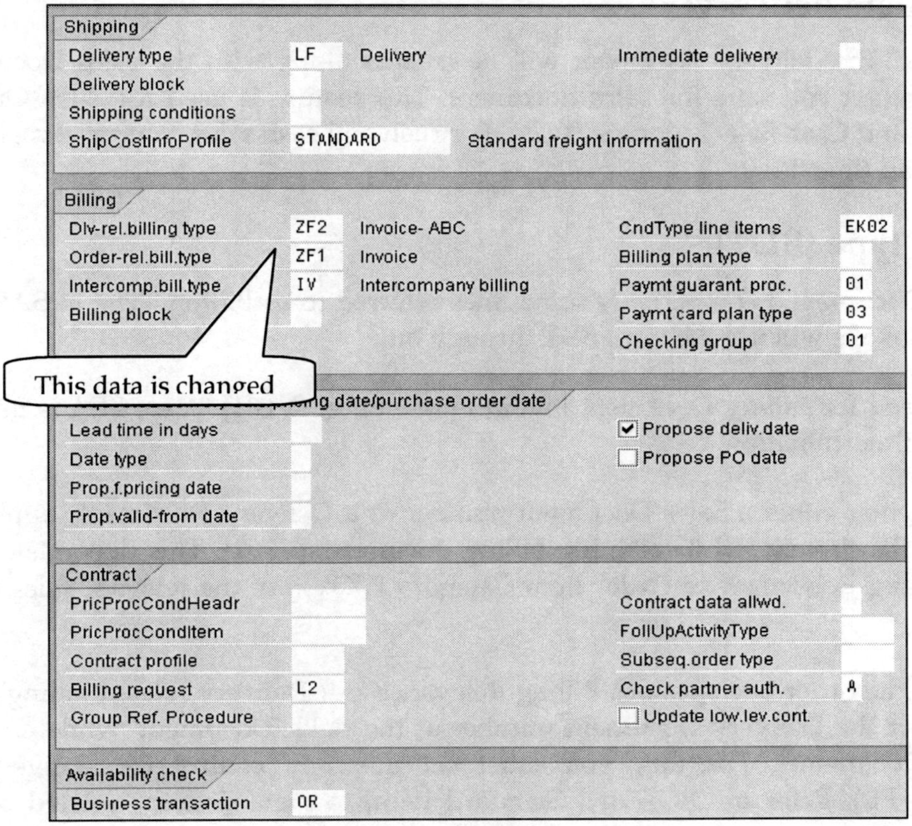

Fig:2-6

Path: IMG-SD-SLS-SLS DOC-SLS DOC HEADER-Define Sales Document Types.

Delivery type:

'Delivery Document Type(DDT)' is sometimes referred to as Delivery Type in SAP. But in this book we will use the term DDT through out.

DDT will be used while creating Delivery Document of the Sales Order [VL01N]. Also, DDT is used in Delivery Item Category(DIC) determination. DDT controls the number ranges of the delivery document.

For generating Delivery Document, Copy Control is to be set up through [VTLA] for this SDT and DDT.

If blank, no delivery document will be created.

Immediate delivery:

If selected, the delivery document will be created along with the Sales Document number when you save the sales document. This feature is used for Rush Orders(SDT *RO*) and Cash Sale Orders(SDT *CS*). For rush and cash sales, you must make the Order Lead time 0.

Billing type (BDT):

'Billing Document Type(BDT)' is sometimes referred to as Billing Type in SAP. But in this book we will use the term BDT through out.

BDT is used for Billing Document(invoice) generation [VF01]. Also, BDT is used in Account Determination.

You can enter either a Sales Document number or a Delivery Document number at the field 'Document' while creating billing documents[VF01]. This depends on the field 'Billing Relevance' in Order Item Category [VOV7] of the relevant sales order lines.

If OIC of the order line specifies Billing Relevance 'A'(Delivery related billing), you must enter the Delivery Document number at the field 'Document' while creating Billing Documents. For this, you must set up copy control for Delivery To Billing[VTFL]. Refer to OIC *TAN*(Standard Item) to view delivery related billing item.

If OIC of the order line specifies Billing Relevance 'B'(Order related billing), you must enter the Sales Order number while creating the Billing Document. For this, you must set up copy control for Order To Billing[VTFA]. Refer to OIC *BVN*(cash sale) to view order related billing item.

If you want to ensure that the invoice should be generated only after delivery of the materials, you can use delivery related billing.

For our exercise, use ZF2 for Delivery related billing and ZF1 for order related billing. Actually these are for default values while creating billing documents. You can enter manually other BDTs while creating Billing Documents.

If these fields are blank, the billing documents cannot be generated.

Refer to SDT *CF*(consignment fill up) for which Billings are not applicable.

Lead time in days:

Lead Time is used in Delivery Scheduling/ Shipment Scheduling. It is the time required for picking , packing, loading, transportation, etc.

Make this field blank(= 0 days). When it is blank, the delivery date in the sales order will be the current date. If the current date is not a working day, the system may give the next working day as the First Delivery Date.

For example, if you enter 7 in this field, by default the 'First Date' in our Sales Document will be 7 working days in advance from the date of order creation.

Hence, create a new SDT *ZOR* by copying from OR and make the above changes in *ZOR*.

Accounting Document Type [OBA7]

ADT is controlled by FIN consultant and it is displayed here only for your reference.

Accounting Document Type [OBA7]

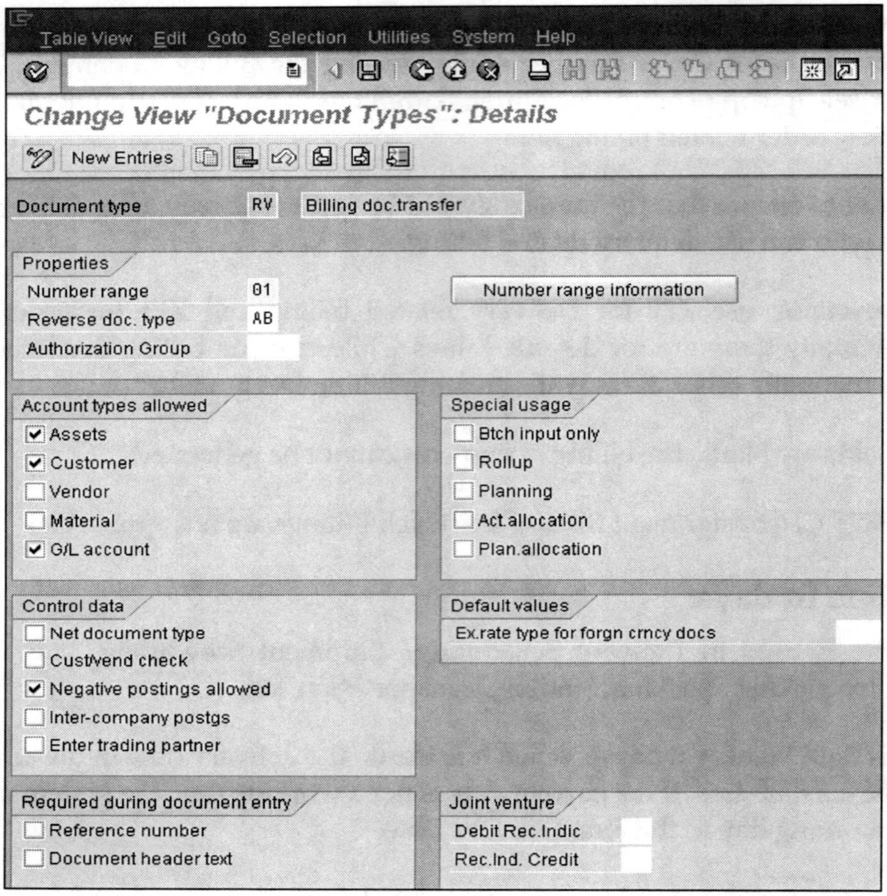

Fig: 2-7

Path: Financial Accounting- Financial Accounting Global Settings- Document- Document Header- Define Document Types.

ADT is assigned in BDT. The number range for ADT is maintained through [FBN1]. You can see the ADT in the Accounting Overview of the Billing Document.

Order Item Category [VOV7]

There are two types of item categories and hence to differentiate them we will use OIC for Order Item Category and DIC for Delivery Item Category. For simplicity, SAP uses the term 'Item Category' for OIC. But in this book, we will use OIC instead of just mentioning as Item Category.

OIC is used in Sales Documents and DIC is used in Delivery Documents.

OIC is a controlling document which controls certain features of the sales document lines(Items). It specifies for the line material whether Pricing is applicable, Delivery is applicable, Costing is to be done, Break down to be done in the case of BOM etc. In the case of service contract, it specifies the reference material for service contract.

Order Item Categories are automatically determined by the system while creating sales documents. This selection is based on the Order Item Category Determination. Refer to the Item Category Determination in the chapter Determination. Order Item category in SO decides the Schedule Line Category of the same SO line. Refer to the Determination Of Schedule Line Category.

For our scenarios, we will use SAP standard OIC *TAN*

Order Item Category, TAN-[VOV7]

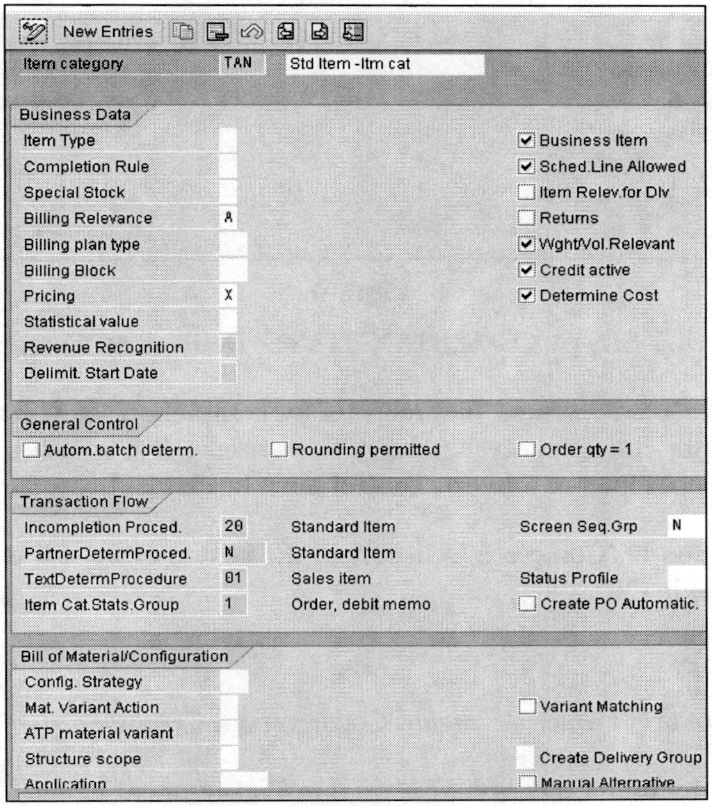

Fig:2-8

Path: IMG- SD- SLS- SLS DOCS- SLS DOC ITEMS- Define Item Categories.

Field descriptions:

Item Type:

Blank means Std physical Item (Means pricing, delivery, scheduling etc can be applicable for this line). Other Item Types are Text item, packing item etc.

Completion Rule:

This field is applicable mainly for quotations and contract lines.

Example for OIC *AGN* used in sales quotation lines [VOV7] .

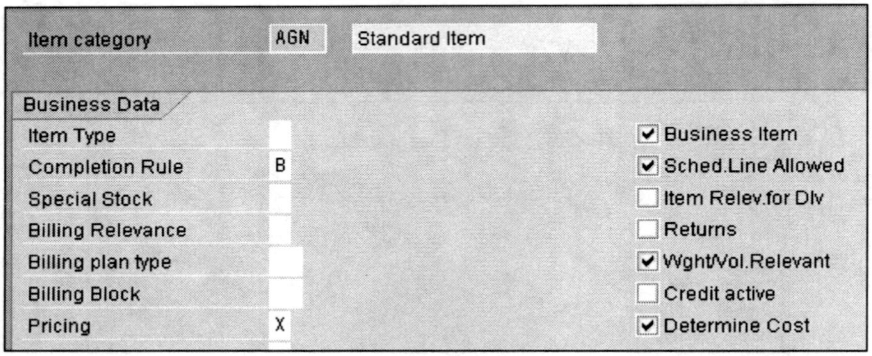

Fig:2-9

Path: IMG- SD- SLS- SLS DOCS- SLS DOC ITEMS- Define Item Categories.

Completion Rule 'Blank' means 'Not relevant for completion'. Rule B means the Item is completed after full quantity has been referenced . If B is used, the check box 'Update Document Flow' in the copy control must be checked.

Note: The function of 'Complete Delivery' in the customer master is different from Completion Rule in OIC.

Special Stock:

Blank means Not applicable, 'W' means Consignment-Customer.

Example for Order Item Category, *KEN* used in Consignment Issues[VOV7]

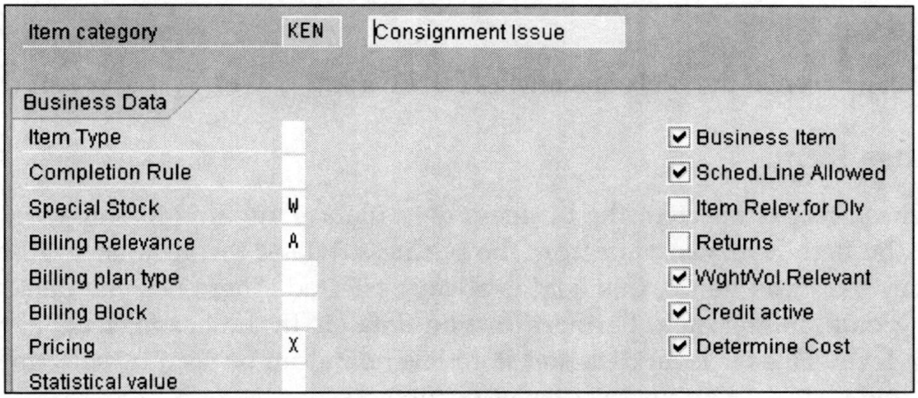

Fig:2-10

Path: IMG- SD- SLS- SLS DOCS- SLS DOC ITEMS- Define Item Categories.

Billing Relevance:

It is an important field. Refer to the explanation on the field 'Billing Document Types' in Sales Document Type.

Blank means No billing.
'A' means Billing is done based on the Delivery Document
'B' means Billing is done based on the Sales Document(Sales order).

Billing plan type:

Blank means no billing plan. '01'milestone Billing(based on the project progress), '02'periodic Billing(Based on a fixed frequency).

Billing block:

Billing can be blocked due to various reasons eg: 01, Calculation missing, 03 prices incomplete etc. If blocked, no billing document can be generated till the block is removed.

Pricing:

X means std pricing is applicable.

Stat value:

Blank means normal methods of statistics can be used.

Business Item:

If this check box is selected, the business data (data pertaining to shipping, billing etc.) at the Item level can vary from the business data at the Header level. In most cases they vary and hence, this field is always selected. There is some data such as Shipping data, Billing data, Partner function data etc in the header level as well as the item level. Header level data and Item level data can be seen by selecting Goto-Header and Goto-Item in the sales order documents.

Schedule Line Allowed:

If this check box is not marked, you cannot enter quantity in the sales document.

Schedule Lines are created for sales orders and not for delivery documents.

This is the field which decides whether physical delivery is applicable for the sales order lines or not. If marked, the schedule lines are created for sales orders lines(Items) and the items can be delivered. But even if the schedule line is created for a sales order line, the SLC linked in the schedule line finally decides whether the delivery is applicable or not. You can see the schedule lines and SLC after creating the sales order and selecting Goto- Item- Schedule lines.

The fields 'Item relevant for delivery', 'Movement Type', etc. of the SLC control the creation of delivery lines in the delivery document.

Items that are not relevant for delivery, such as items in contracts (eg: OIC *KMN*) and credit memo requests, do not have schedule lines. Except the Text Items, items that are not marked in this field cannot be copied into a delivery.

Item Relevant for delivery:

This field is applicable for text and value items only(Item type A and B) for which schedule lines will not be applicable. This field can not be marked for standard items. Catalogues of a product, warning instruction printouts, stickers, labels, etc can be considered as text items because normally stocks for such items are not controlled. Material masters are not created for them. In the sales order line, details are entered in the description field of the sales order line without order quantity.

You can use the field 'Usage' in the item category determination in this case. For text item types, schedule lines will not be created.

Hence, if this field is marked, the system copies item directly from the Sales Document to the Delivery Document without a schedule line created for sales order line. Refer to OIC *TATX* for Sales order and *AFTX* for Sales Inquiries.

Determine cost:

It Indicates whether, during pricing, the system determines the cost (stock value) of a sales document item. The system checks the cost determination indicator mentioned here as a requirement before applying the Pricing Condition Type in the pricing procedure that calculates the cost. Pricing Condition Type *VPRS* is used in pricing procedure to pickup standard cost to pricing.

Incompletion Procedure:

During the Sales Document process, you can make entry of certain fields mandatory and if they are skipped without entry, the same will be logged in the incompletion log. This is done through incompletion procedure. The incompletion procedure defines the fields in which the user must enter information. Example: Validity periods and customer purchase order numbers are required entries for both contracts and scheduling agreements. Refer to the explanation on incompletion procedure in SDT for more details.

Structure Scope:

Structure of certain materials can be detailed through BOM and material configuration. In such case this field is used.

To understand this feature as well as Higher Lever Item Category, BOM process is explained in the appendix of this book.

Here blank means no structure change, A means BOM explosion to single level, B means BOM explosion to multi level, C means Configuration without BOM explosion, etc.

Application:

This field is applicable where Structure Scope is applicable. SD01 is for Sales and Distribution, PP01 is for production, etc.

Bottom part of OIC *TAN* [VOV7].

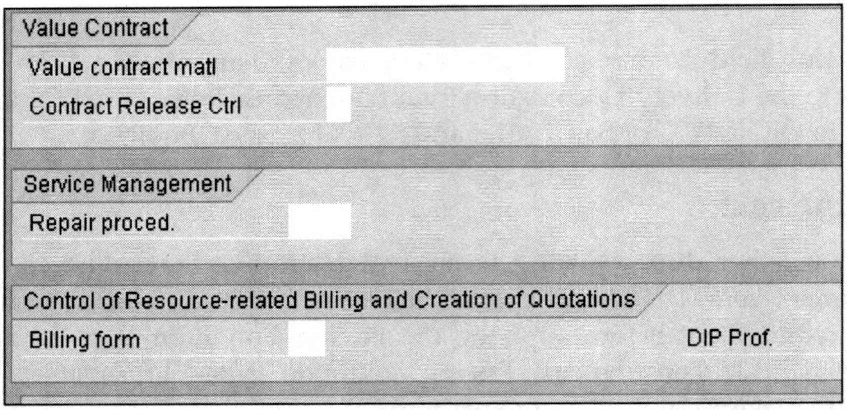

Fig: 2-11

Path: IMG- SD- SLS- SLS DOCS- SLS DOC ITEMS

Value Contract Material:

This field is applicable for value contract with assortment module only. When you create Value Contract with assortment module, the system needs a reference material. You enter that material code here. The Assortment module is created with [WSV2] and value contract with the assortment module is created with [VA41] using SDT *WK1*.

Delivery Item Category [0VLP]

Delivery Item Category(DIC)

Please note that DIC (Delivery Item Category) is different from OIC (Order Item Category). T-code for DIC is 0VLP and T-code for OIC is VOV7.

The code of OIC and DIC should be the same. When you create a new OIC, a DIC is also created automatically with the same code. Normally OIC is created by copying and hence even Order Item Category Determination and Delivery Item Category Determinations are copied.

You cannot create a DIC directly in [0VLP] if the same code is not available in OIC. But you can delete a DIC, which creates a lot of fuss in the system.

An item category is mandatory for all Sales Document lines and Delivery Document lines.

If the Delivery Document is created with reference to a sales order, the code of the DIC in the delivery document will be the code of OIC of the sales order. For example, if OIC of a sales order line is *TAN* and when you create a delivery document for the same sales order line, the DIC of this delivery document line also will be *TAN*. But if you want to add one more line manually to this delivery document, a new DIC will be picked up as per the Delivery Item Category determination[0184].

For example, if you want to add packing materials in a delivery document manually, you should have set up DICs for the same packing materials. Similarly if a delivery Document is to be created manually without any order reference, you need to set up DIC.

Delivery can be created directly(without any order reference) with the T-Code [VL01NO] with delivery document type LO.

Delivery Item Category, DLN-[0VLP]

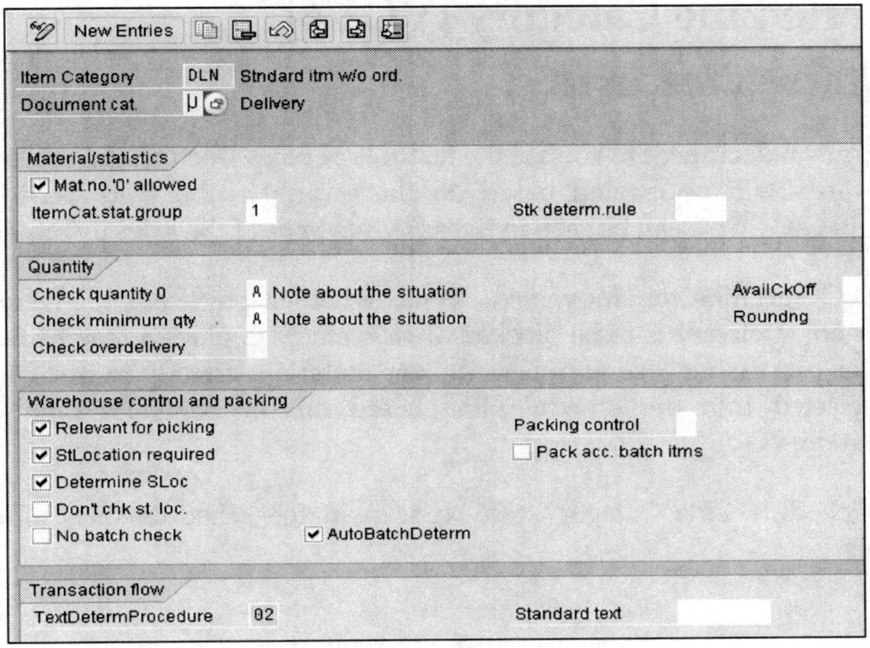

Fig: 2-12

Path: IMG-Logistics Execution-Shipping-Deliveries-Define Item Categories for Deliveries.

Document Category:

This is an important field. This field is accessed from a common table for SDT, DDT, BDT, DIC etc. Refer to the field help of SDT in this book for more information. For DIC, you must use only J(Delivery).

Relevant for picking:

If marked only, you can enter pick quantity in the delivery. If the warehouse management is implemented, you can create the transfer order[LT03] if this field is marked. For the non stock text items, it need not be marked.

Note: Both Picking and Packing relevance for an item is set in DIC.

Storage Location Required:

If ticked, entry of storage location in the Delivery Document becomes mandatory.

Schedule Line Category [VOV6]

SCHEDULE LINE CATEGORY(SLC)

SLC is a control document to control the features of Sales Documents' schedule lines. Schedule lines will be created based on the setting in the field 'Schedule Line Allowed' in OIC. SLC can be seen in the schedule lines of the sales documents.

Mainly SLC specifies the Movement Type, whether physically delivery can be created or not, Delivery is to be blocked always etc. SLC plays a major role in third party order processing (our suppliers deliver materials directly to our customers). SLC is selected into the schedule line based on the Schedule Line Category Determination[VOV5].

[VOV6], Schedule Line Category can be seen in the schedule lines of the sales documents.

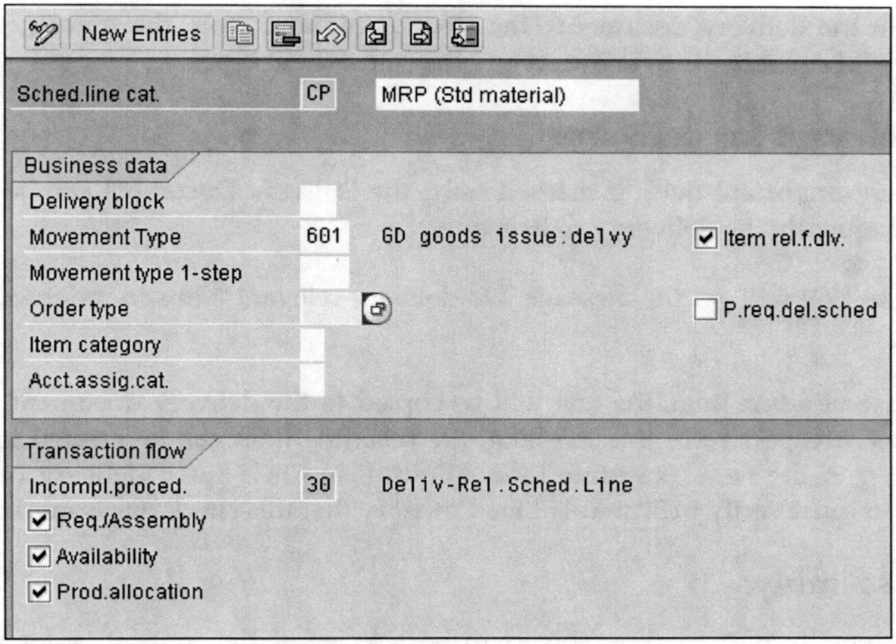

Fig:2-13

Path: IMG-Sales and Distribution- Sales- Sales Documents- Schedule Lines- Define Schedule Line Categories.

Imp: Schedule line category is very important because, if the schedule line category is not proper, the system will not allow delivery of the goods.

Delivery block:

There are some sort of deliveries that when delivery documents are created and saved, the deliveries are to be blocked immediately. For example, when a free-of-goods sales delivery is saved, it must be automatically blocked. The reason is that all free goods delivery is to be approved by somebody and then the block must be removed, if required, manually, before proceeding further.

Delivery block can be set at SDT, DDT and SLC levels.

Movement types:

It is defined by MM consultants. There are different movement types configured separately for SD purpose. 601 is one among them and this is generally used for normal delivery processes. 601 specifies that when Goods-Issue is posted (PGI is clicked in the delivery document), the stock is reduced from the unrestricted use. Consult MM consultants to know about other movement types.

Item relevant for delivery:

It is a very important field. If marked only, the Delivery Document can be created and subsequently the delivery can be made.

Otherwise, you will get the message 'No delivery-relevant items in order xxx, order type yyy'.

In the case of a text item, the text will be copied to the delivery document. But for text items, irrespective of this marking, the schedule lines can be created based on the setting in the field 'Schedule Line Allowed' in OIC. But if delivery has to be made, you must verify in Schedule Line Category that this check box is marked.

Req/Assembly:

Requirement transfer to Assembly is to be selected if the transfer order is to be created for picking or procurement process. Transfer Order is applicable if the WM is implemented.

An example for schedule line category without Movement Type [VOV6]

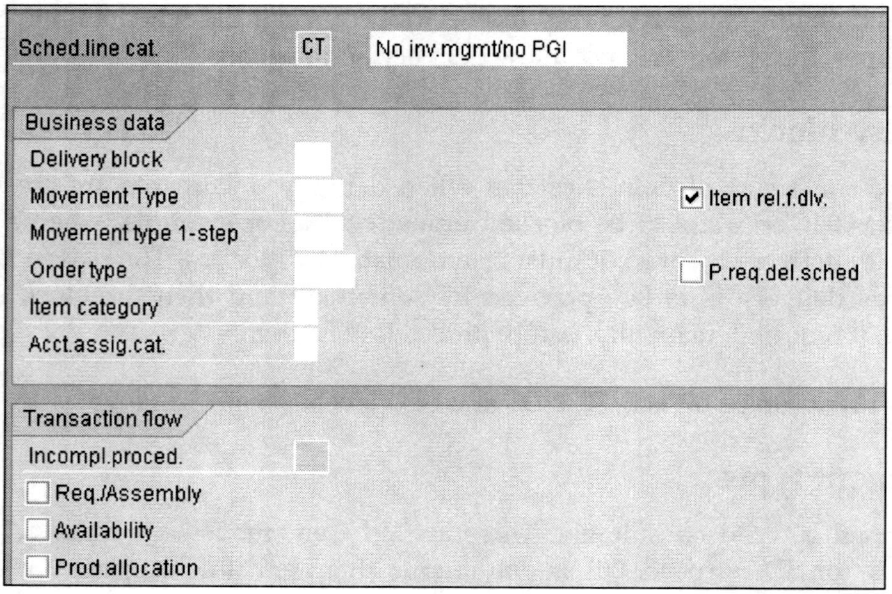

Fig:2-14

Path: IMG-Sales and Distribution- Sales- Sales Documents- Schedule Lines- Define Schedule Line Categories.

This can be used for text items, for example catalogues, stickers, etc.

For trading goods(for which stock will not be maintained), the following Schedule Line Category can be used. In this case when a sale order is created for this item or for its parent, a Purchase order will be created by the system. This process is called third party order process.

An example of schedule line category for third party process [VOV6]

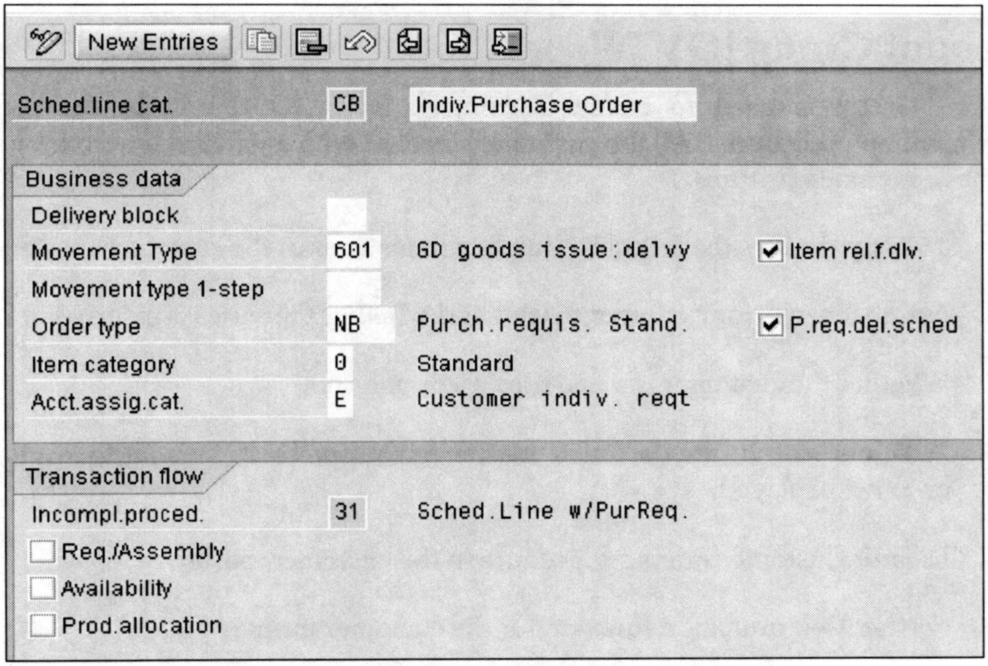

Fig:2-15

Path: IMG-Sales and Distribution- Sales- Sales Documents- Schedule Lines- Define Schedule Line Categories.

Order Type 'NB':

Here Order Type means 'Purchase Order Type' for standard items.

Item Cat '0':

Here Item Category is Purchase Item Category(PIC) which controls aspects like whether material receipt is allowed, Invoice allowed, etc.

Other fields:

Fields 'Acct Assignment Category', 'Purchase Requisition Delivery Schedule', etc. are applicable for purchase order creation through sales order.

Here the Requirement Transfer, Availability Check and Production Allocation are not applicable.

Account Group [OVT0].

Account Group is used to create Customer Master[XD01] and in the partner determination procedures. All the customers created with a particular account group will have the same features.

Account Group decides the following important features in the customer master:

1. Number series for customer master and whether the series is external or not.
2. Whether the customer is a one time account or not
3. Which entries in the customer master are suppressed, mandatory, optional, or to be displayed.
4. Default Customer Pricing procedure in the customer master.
5. Partner Determination function for the customer master.

Many Account Groups are already defined in the system such as 0001 for General purpose(to act as SP,SH,BP and PY), 0002 exclusively for SH(Ship To party), 0003 exclusively for Payer(PY) and 0004 exclusively for Bill To Party(BP), etc.

If you want to use a different Account Group, it is recommended to copy an existing one to your own and modify to your requirement. SAP has defined various account groups with various options and in case you want your own, it is recommended to copy an existing one to a new code with a Z- prefix.

Defining Account groups

Let us study the existing account groups 0001 and 0002.

Account Group 0001.

Define Account Groups and Field Selection for Customers [OVT0]

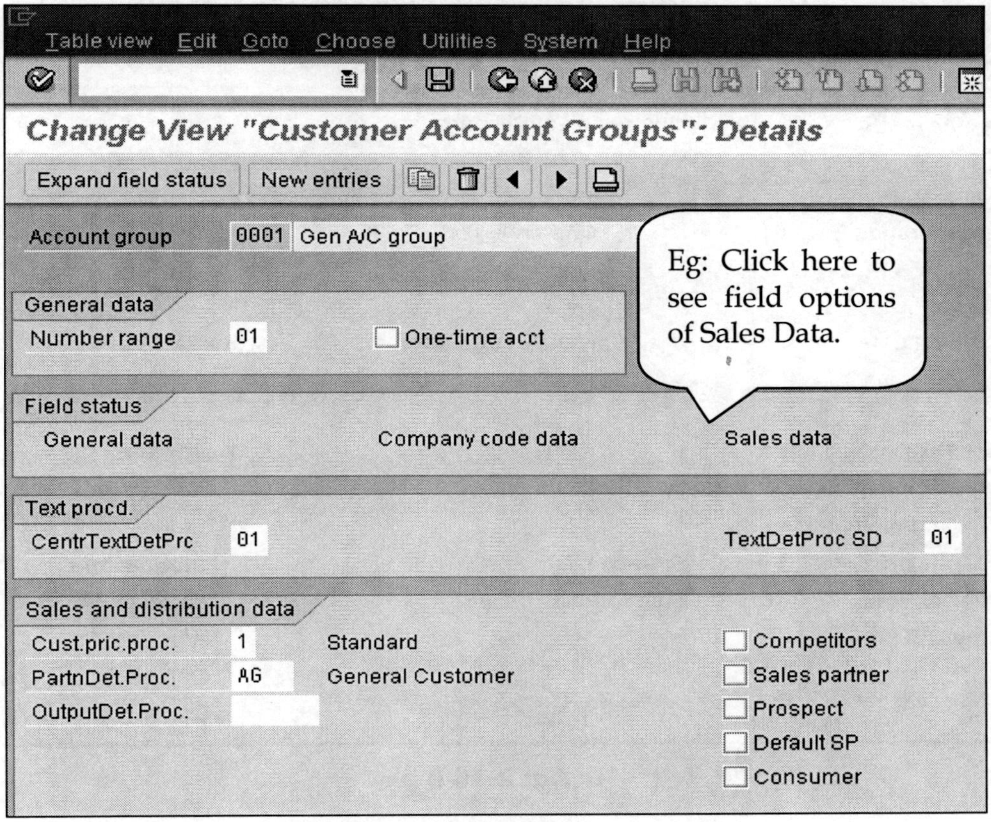

Fig: 2-16 A

Path: IMG-Logistics – General- Business Partner- Customers- Control- Define Account Groups and Field Selection for Customers.

Account Group 0002.

The following is the existing account group 0002.

Define Account Groups and Field Selection for Customers [OVT0]

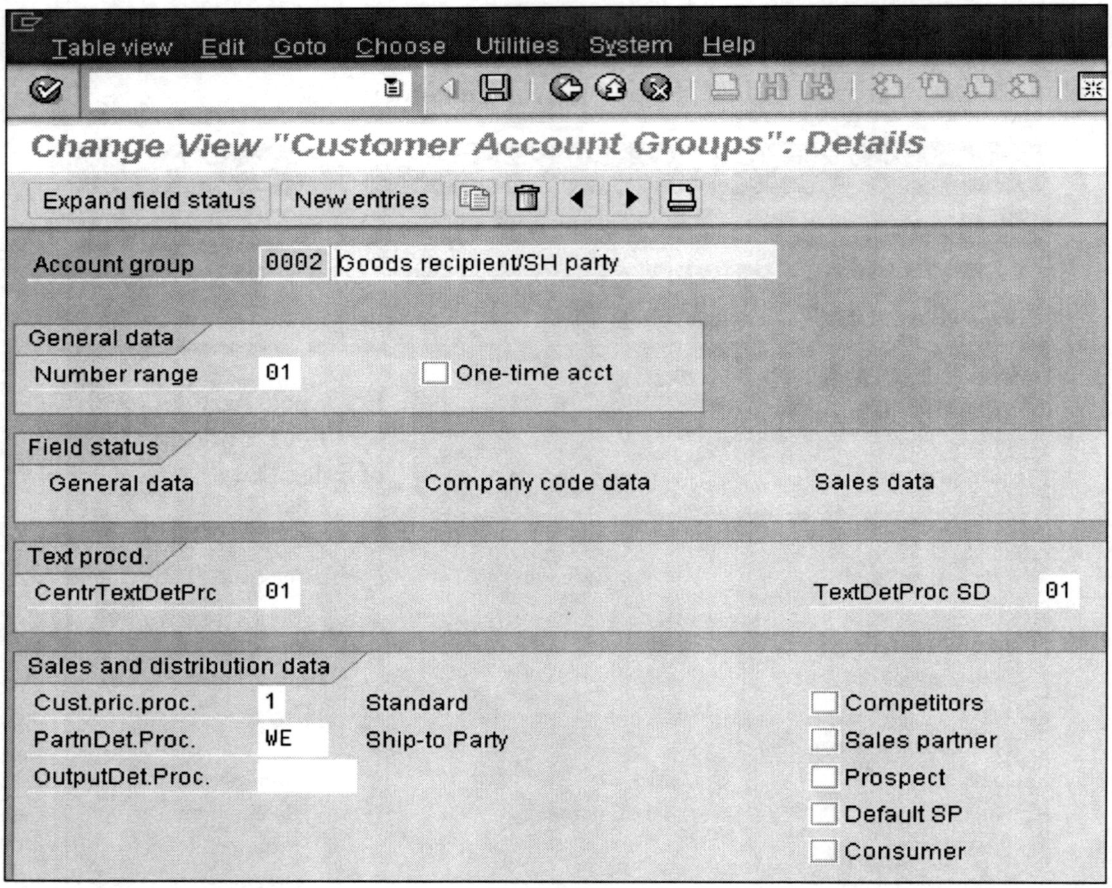

Fig: 2-16 B

Path: IMG- Logistics – General- Business Partner- Customers- Control- Define Account Groups and Field Selection for Customers.

Note the difference in the Partner Determination Procedures(PDP) in both the account groups.

PDP *AG* will be linked to 4 partner functions (SP,SH,BP &PY) and PDP *WE* will be linked to only SH. Refer to partner determinations in the chapter Determinations for more details.

Number Range:

It is defined through the session [OVZC]. Refer to the Number Range for Customers in the Appendix.

General Data/ Company code data/ Sales data:

These tabs control field selections in the customer master.

Click on these tabs to know which fields are mandatory, which fields are optional, etc.

For example, account group 0002(for Ship To Party) requires information relevant for shipping only. Billing information is suppressed.

If you suppress all fields in a screen, the same screen will not be displayed during customer master creation.

Customer pricing Procedure:

It is entered here only for a default value while creating the customer master.

Partner Determination Procedure(PDP):

It is an important field. When you create a customer master with Account Group(0001), the Partner Determination Procedure AG is used. Four partner functions (SP,SH,PY,BP) are assigned to AG in Partner Determination Setup and hence, when you create customer master with account group(0001), these four partner functions will be automatically added to the customer master.

Refer to the chapter Partner Determination Procedure for more details.

The account group will not work without a Partner Determination Procedure.

Example for field options in shipping screen under General Data tab for account group 0001.

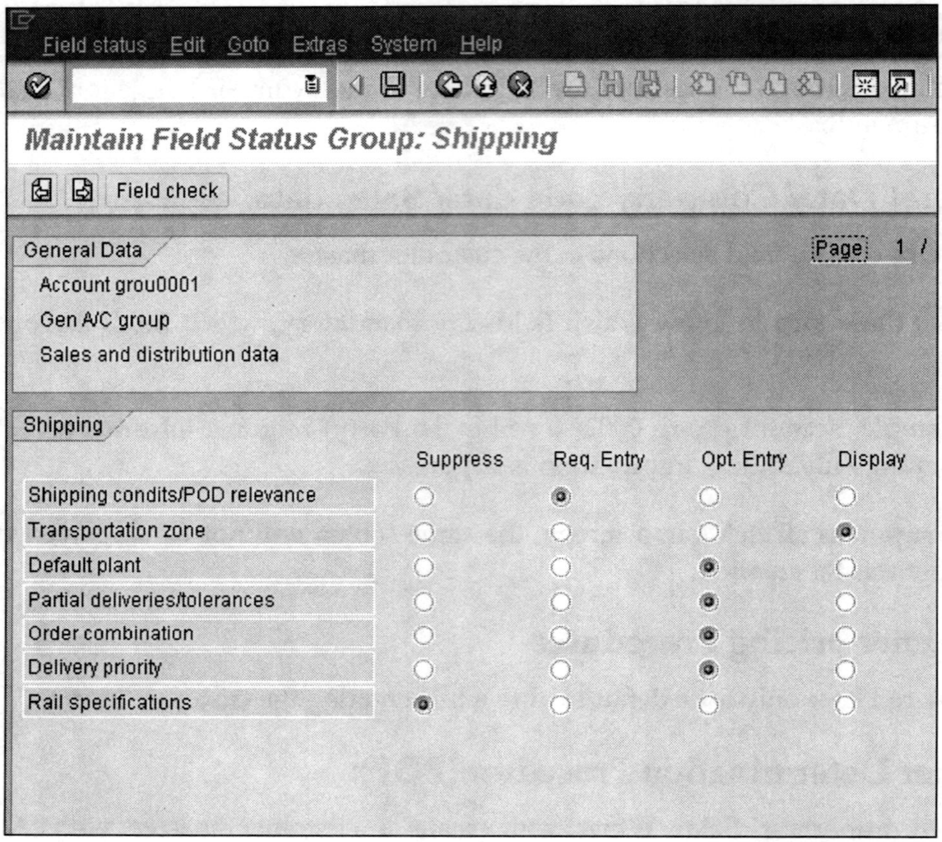

Fig:2-17

Tax Set Up

Various countries have various types of taxes and in many cases they are complicated and taxing rules vary very often. There are a few third party softwares which can be linked to SAP. In many cases the responsibility of updating the tax rules as and when there is a change, lies with the third party vendor for which there will be an agreement for the same. But some basic set up is to be done in SAP for the same and they are explained here. These basic setups are to be done whether you have a tax system or not. If you do not have any tax system, maintain tax as zero tax.

During sales order processing, the system applies the tax category according to:

1. The country of your delivering plant.
2. The country of the customer receiving the goods.
3. Tax classifications in the customer master and the material master records.

To have tax indicators in the Customer Master(in the Billing Document tab) and the Material master(in the Sales Org-1 tab), the country codes to which these master data belong(in our case IN) should be listed in the following session(Maintain Tax Categories by Country).

Define Tax Determination Rule (Maintain Tax Categories by Country) [OVK1].

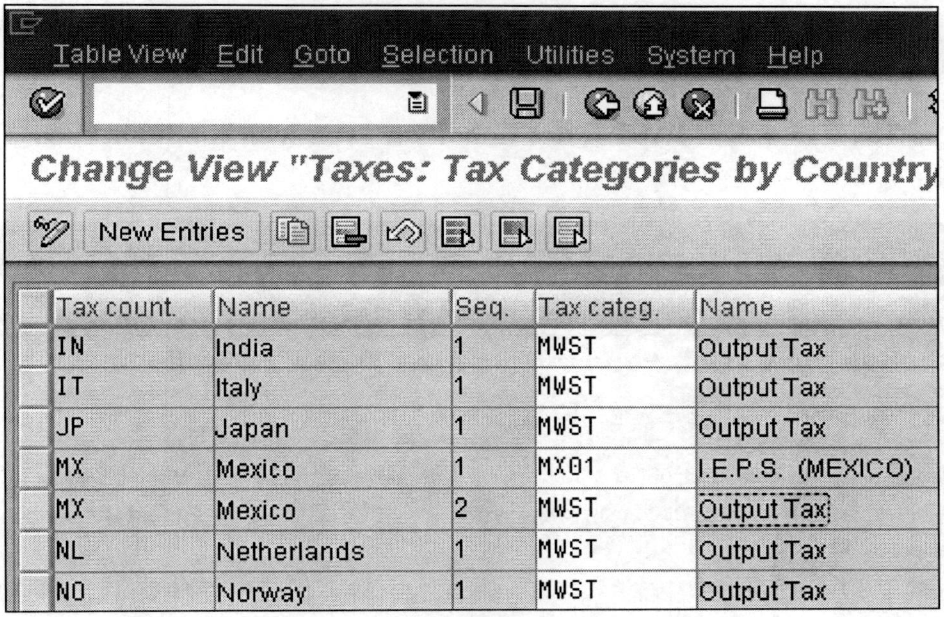

Tax count.	Name	Seq.	Tax categ.	Name
IN	India	1	MWST	Output Tax
IT	Italy	1	MWST	Output Tax
JP	Japan	1	MWST	Output Tax
MX	Mexico	1	MX01	I.E.P.S. (MEXICO)
MX	Mexico	2	MWST	Output Tax
NL	Netherlands	1	MWST	Output Tax
NO	Norway	1	MWST	Output Tax

Fig:2-18

Path: IMG-Sales and Distribution- Basic Functions- Taxes- Define Tax Determination Rules.

Here you list out all tax countries and Tax Categories(Price Condition Types with

Condition class 'Tax'- [V/06]).

For example, here India(IN) has only one tax category and Mexico has 2 tax categories.

If you do not list the country codes here, you cannot maintain tax indicators in the customer master and Material master records.

If you have not set up taxes, the following error messages may appear at various levels:

- 'Material xxx not defined for sale from country yyy'.
- 'Error occurred in Derivation Rule'.
- 'No calculation procedure assigned to country xxx'.

First, define the Tax Categories(Price Condition Types with condition class D, Taxes).

Defining Tax Category; MWST (Price Condition Type with condition class 'Taxes') [V/06]

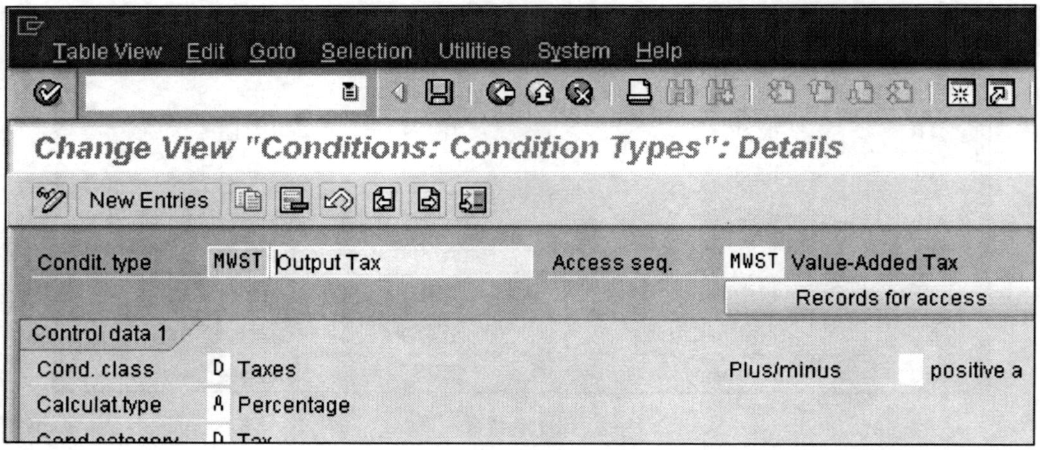

Fig:2-19

Path: IMG-Sales and Distribution-Basic Functions-Pricing-Pricing Control - Define Condition Types-Maintain Condition Types.

Price Condition Types are explained under the chapter Pricing.

Now maintain Customer Tax Classes(that must be entered in Customer masters) and Material Tax Classes (that must be entered in Material masters), as follows:

Maintain Customer Tax Classes[OVK3]

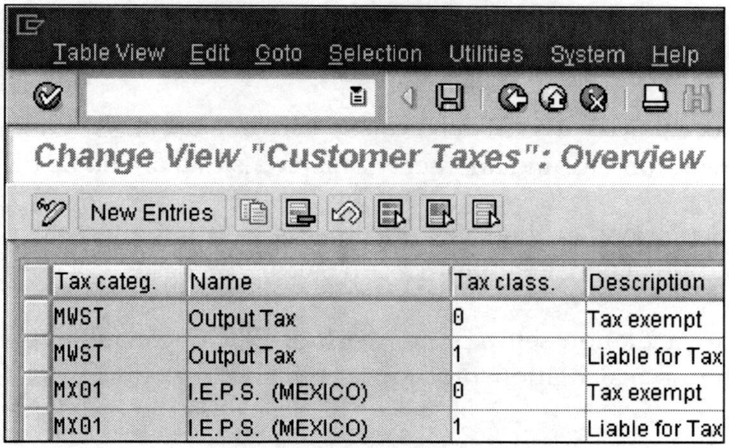

Fig:2-20

Path: IMG-Sales and Distribution- Basic Functions- Taxes- Define Tax Relevancy Of Master Records- Customer Taxes.

Define tax classes(a single character) against the Tax Category in this session.

If you do not maintain data in this session[OVK3], you cannot maintain tax data for customers.

Maintain Material Tax Classes[OVK4]

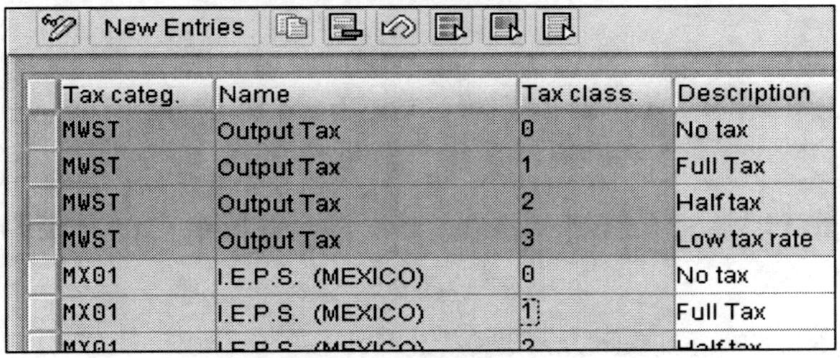

Fig: 2-21

Path: IMG-Sales and Distribution- Basic Functions- Taxes- Define Tax Relevancy Of Master Records- Material Tax.

Define the tax classes(a single character) against Tax Category in this session.

If you do not maintain data in this session[OVK4], you cannot maintain tax data for materials.

Example: For tax category MWST, you can specify one tax classification for materials that are exempted from tax and another for materials that are liable for full taxes.

To have tax calculations in the sales documents, you have to set up tax details in IMG- FIN accounting Global Setting- Tax on Sales/Purchase.

Though the tax calculation setup is the work of FI/CO consultants, if you want to know about the tax calculation procedure, refer to the topic 'Tax Calculation' in theAppendix.

Copy Control

COPY CONTROL RULES

You have to set up Copy Control Rules for copying and referencing data from one sales document to the other.

Example:

For copying Sales Inquiry(with SDT 'IN') to Sales Order (with SDT 'OR'), you have to set up copy control rules for Sales Document to Sales Document because both are sales documents.

For copying data from Sales to Delivery, you have to setup copy control for Sales Document to Delivery Document.

The set up is to be done for Sales Document Types, Item Categories and Schedule Line Categories.

The following 6 types of set ups are to be done:

1. Sales to Sales.
2. Billing to Sales.
3. Sales to Billing.
4. Billing to Billing.
5. Delivery to Billing.
6. Sales to Delivery.

Schedule Line Level copy control are needed for the first two types because schedule lines are created for sales orders only.

1. [VTAA] Sales Document to Sales Document(eg: Copy an existing Sales Order to a new Sales Order, Quotation to Sales Order, Product Proposal to Sales Order etc).

   Path: IMG- Sales and Distribution- Sales- Maintain Copy Control for Sales Documents- Sales Document to Sales Document.

2. [VTAF] Billing Documents to Sales Documents(eg. Invoice to Return Sales Order).

   Path: IMG- Sales and Distribution- Sales- Maintain Copy Control for Sales Documents- Billing Document to Sales Document.

3. [VTFA]Sales Document to Billing Document(eg: Cash sales to Invoicing, Credit Memo Request to Credit Memo)

   Path: IMG- Sales and Distribution - Billing - Maintain Copying Control For Billing Documents -Sales document to billing document.

4. [VTFF] Billing Document to Billing Document (eg: Invoice Correction)

   Path: IMG- Sales and Distribution - Billing - Maintain Copying Control For Billing Documents - Billing document to billing document.

5. [VTFL]Delivery Document to Billing Document (eg: Sales Delivery to Sales Invoicing)

   Path: IMG- Sales and Distribution - Billing - Maintain Copying Control For Billing Documents - Delivery document to billing document.

6. [VTLA]Sales Document to Delivery Document (eg: Sales order to Delivery, Return sales order to Ret delivery etc).

   Path: IMG- Log Exec- Shipping- Specify Copy Control for Deliveries.

We will explain Sales to Sales type and Sales to Delivery types in this book. You can explore other rules at your own pace.

Copy Control rule for Sales Inquiry to Sales Order

For sales to sales, you must set up copy control at three levels, they are:
Header level
Item(Line) level
Schedule Line level.

[VTAA],Copy control set up at header level for SDT *IN(Sales Inquiry)* to SDT *OR(sales order)*

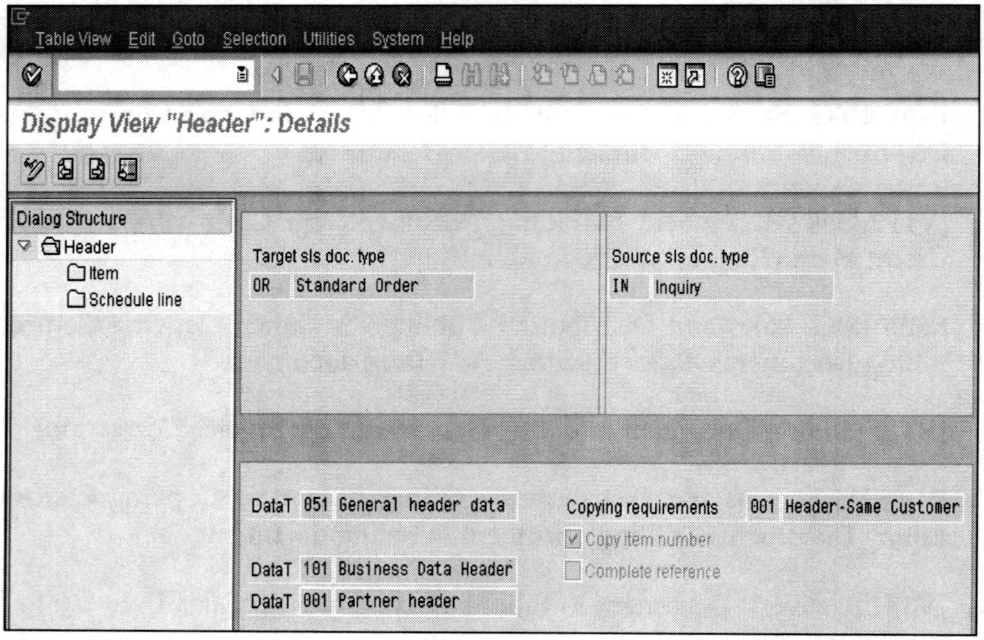

Fig:2-22

Path: IMG-Sales and Distribution-Sales-Maintain Copy Control for Sales Documents-Copying Control: Sales Document to Sales Document.

Data Transfer routines and Requirements are created in ABAP for copying data from one document to the other.

Example for Data Transfer routines:

1. You can specify that Terms of payment should be copied from the Customer master instead of copying from the previous document.
2. Reference document in the Billing Document must be the PO number.
3. Invoicing quantity should be the delivered quantity, Etc.

[VTAA], Example to show list of OICs used for copy control from SDT *IN* to *OR*.

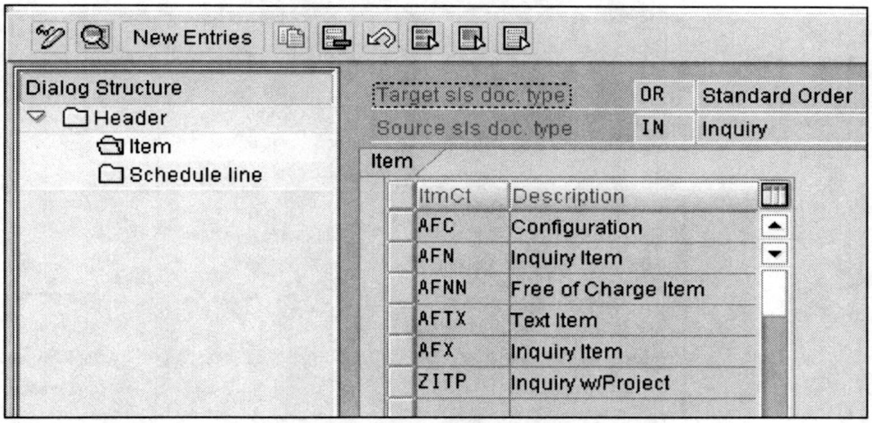

Fig:2-23

Path: IMG-Sales and Distribution-Sales-Maintain Copy Control for Sales Documents-Copying Control: Sales Document to Sales Document.

The fig: 2-23 shows the header data of copy control for creating Sales Order with SDT *OR* with reference to Sales Inquiry with SDT *IN*.

The Item Categories seen in this session are the probable OICs in the source sales documents.

You must set up copy control for all probable OICs and SLCs for each combination of *OR* and *IN*. For example, If you do not maintain copy control for OIC *AFN*, you will not be able to create the Sales Order from Sales Inquiry with OIC *AFN*. If copy control is not maintained for SLCs, schedule lines cannot be created for Sales Orders.

If you do not setup proper copy controls, you may get a message like 'Copying is not possible because ---

For standard document types, the set up is already done in the system. If you copy one Document Type to the other, the copy control also gets copied.

[VTAA] Example for setting copy control at **Item level** for OIC, '*AFN*'.

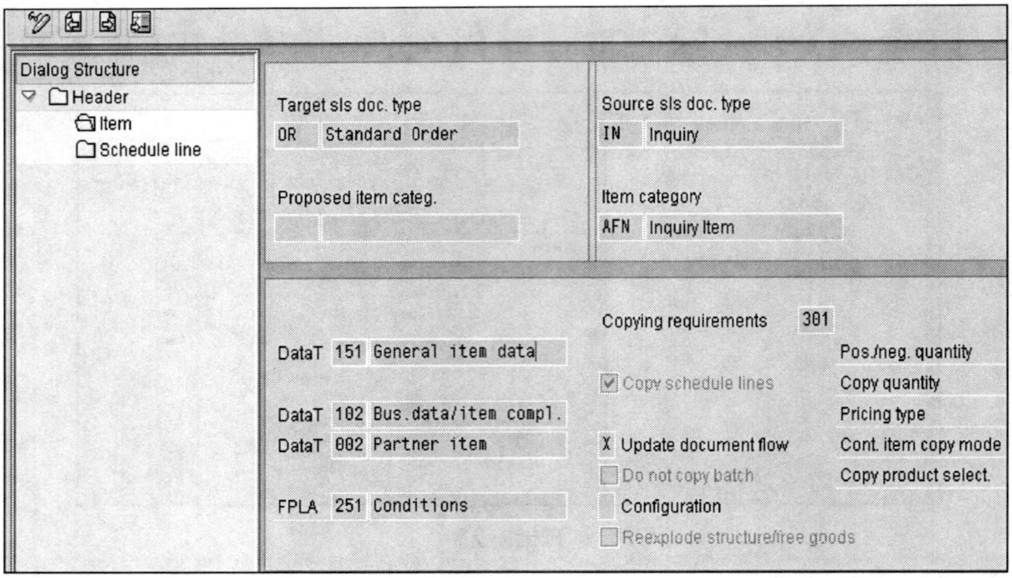

Fig:2-24

Path: IMG-Sales and Distribution-Sales-Maintain Copy Control for Sales Documents-Copying Control: Sales Document to Sales Document.

If the field 'Proposed Item Category' is left blank, the item category in the target document is decided by the Item Category Determination procedure defined for the target SDT.

If you want a specific item category in the target document, you must specify the same in copy control.

Example: Suppose you copy a free-goods item from Sales Inquiry with item category AFNN to Sales Order and you want the item category in the Sales Order as TANN by default. In this case the system should not carry out item category determination in the sales order and hence you enter the source item category as AFNN and the target item category as TANN.

Field 'Update document flow':

A document flow record contains information about the quantities and values that have been copied from the source document to the target document. The system uses the document flow to determine the status of the source document. You must select this check box for the same.

For example,
Source document: customer quotation.
Target document: sales order.
The sales order creates a document flow record for the quotation.

[VTAA] Example for setting copy control at **Schedule Line level** for *IN* to *OR*.

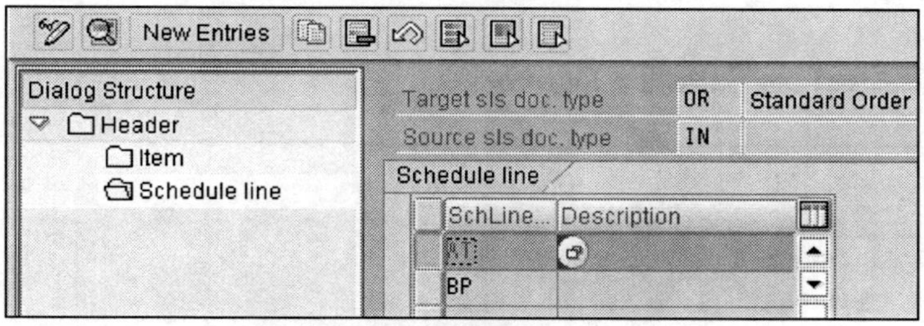

Fig:2-25

Path: IMG-Sales and Distribution-Sales-Maintain Copy Control for Sales Documents-Copying Control: Sales Document to Sales Document.

Note: Schedule Line Level copy controls are applicable for copying a document to a sales order because schedule lines are created for sales orders only.

Details:

[VTAA] Details of copy control at **Schedule Line level** for SLC, '*AT*'.

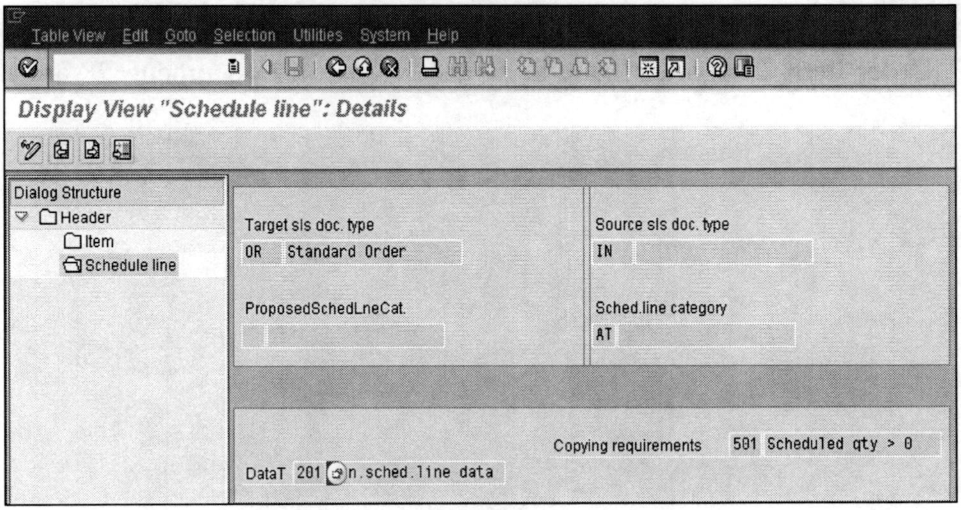

Fig:2-26

Path: IMG-Sales and Distribution-Sales-Maintain Copy Control for Sales Documents-Copying Control: Sales Document to Sales Document.

Copy Control for Sales Order to Delivery Document:

[VTLA]Copy Control for Sales To Deliveries.

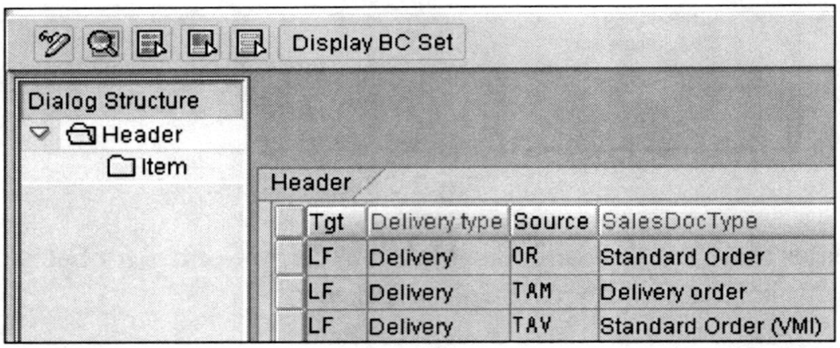

Fig:2-27

Path: IMG-Logistics Execution- Shipping- Copying Control- Specify Copy Control for Deliveries.

Fig 2-27 shows the header level copy control.The header details for OR to LF are shown in fig 2-28

[VTLA]Order Item Categories likely to be used for source document *OR* are shown here

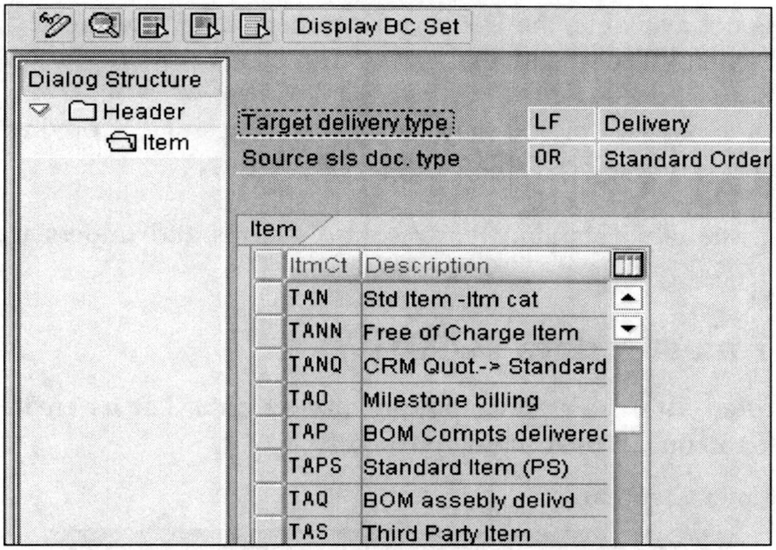

Fig:2-28

Path: IMG-Logistics Execution- Shipping- Copying Control- Specify Copy Control for Deliveries.

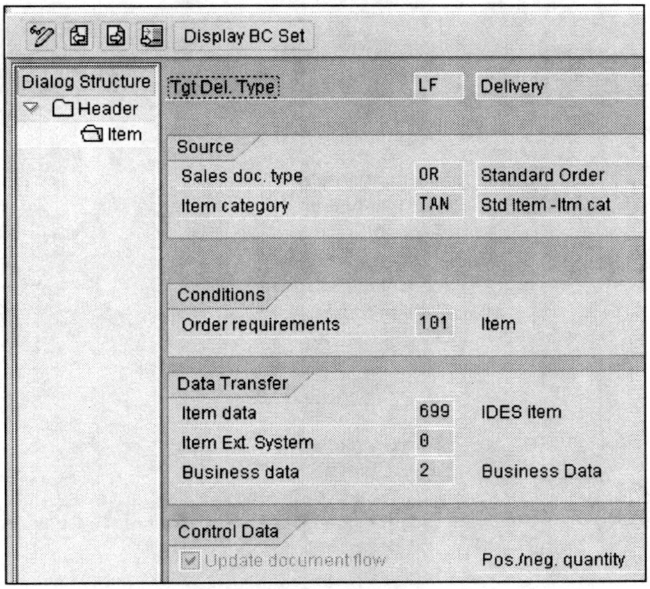

Fig:2-29

Path: IMG-Logistics Execution- Shipping- Copying Control- Specify Copy Control for Deliveries.

If this setup is not available, the Delivery Document cannot be created for the sales order created with SDT *'OR'* with OIC *'TAN'* and DDT *LF.*

If copy control is not set up, you may get the error message: 'Copying not possible because an entry is missing in Table TVCPL : LF TA TAN'.

Now you can see other standard copy control setups and understand them in a better way.

Customer master data [XD01]

Customer master data is a very important master data. Let us create a customer master '123' for all our future training purposes.

Path for Customer Creation.

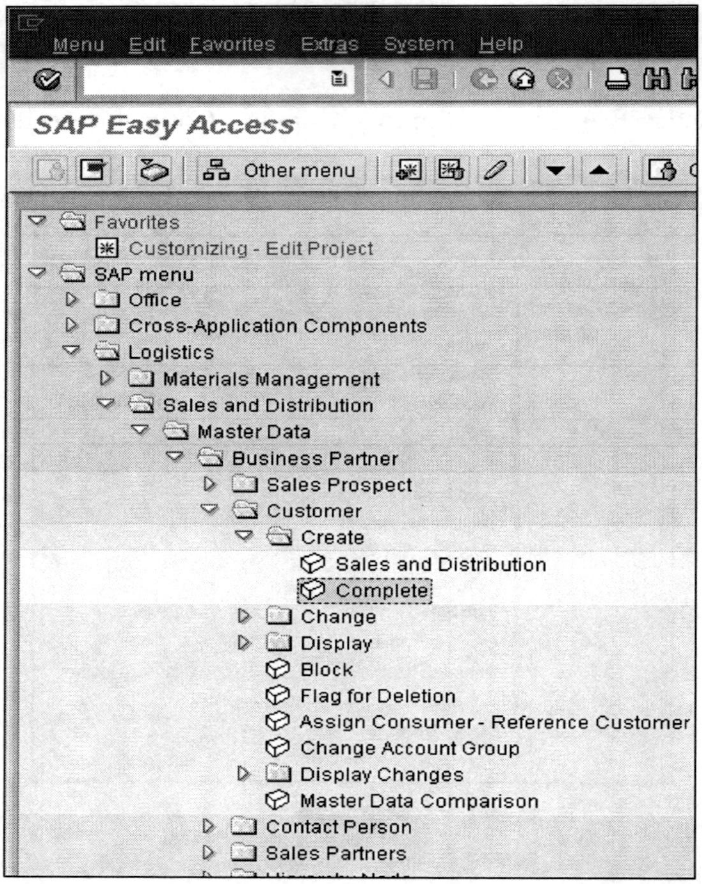

Fig:2-30

Path: EA-Logistics- Sales and Distribution- Master Data- Business Partner- Customer- create- complete.

For processing sales orders, the following partner functions are mandatory:

1. Sold To Party (SP) (= One who places the order)
2. Ship To Party(SH) (= One who receives the goods/ services)
3. Bill To Party (BP) (= One who receives our invoice/Bills)
4. Payer (PY) (= One who actually pays us)

Let us create a customer master who has to act as SH(Ship To Party), BP(Bill To Party), PY(Payer) in addition to SP(Sold To Party). Hence, we have to select a suitable Account Group for the same so that all these partner functions are added automatically in the customer master.
Let us create our customer master 123.

[XD01], Create Customer-Complete

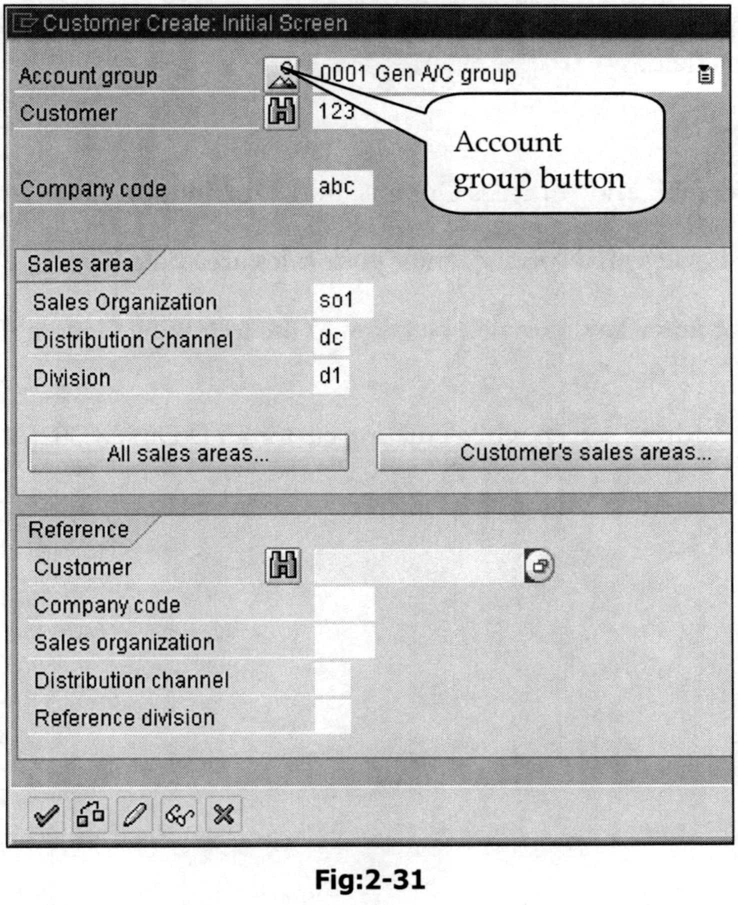

Fig:2-31

Path: Logistics-SD-Master Data-BP-Customer-Create-Complete.

Account group:

Account Group decides the customer number coding pattern, partner functions, field options etc. Click on 'Account group' button(ball button) and select the account group 0001. Refer to the topic 'Account group' in the Master Data for more details.

Customer:

As the account group 0001 specifies using external numbering with numerals, you must enter numerals to create the customer code. Also, the Customer Number entered here (123) should lie in the number range interval mentioned in the account group. Refer to the number ranges in the appendix for more information.

Company code:

Enter the company code here. If created through VD01(Customer-SD), there will be no access to this field.

Sales area:

Sales area is a combination of Sales Organisation, Distribution Channel and Division.

As a customer is sales area specific, enter your sales area data here.

On pressing the Enter key, you will be taken to the following General Data- Address screen automatically.

General Data- Address screen while creating customer [XD01/XD02].

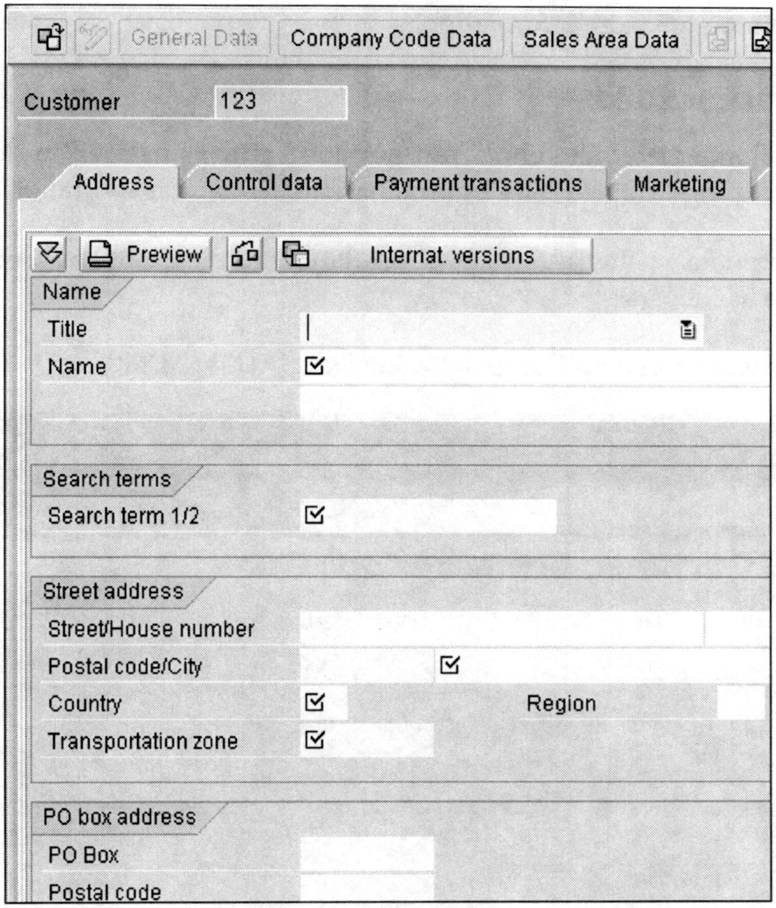

Fig:2-32

Fill up the address data (ticked fields are mandatory fields).

Search term ½:

It is an important field. This field is used to Search/Find customers. Hence, during your learning period, put your name in this field to search customers created by you. You can use wild character(*) to search the customers.

Country:

If the country you enter in this screen is not listed in the session Maintain Tax Categories by Country[OVK1], you will get an error message ' No calculation procedure assigned to country xxx'

Refer to Tax Setup for more information.

Transportation zone:

It is used in Route Determination. Transportation zone is defined in IMG-Logistics Execution-Shipping-Routes-Route Determination-Define Transportation Zones.

After entering data in this screen, click on the main tab Company Code Data and enter the data as follows:

Account management tab in Company Code Data [XD01/XD02].

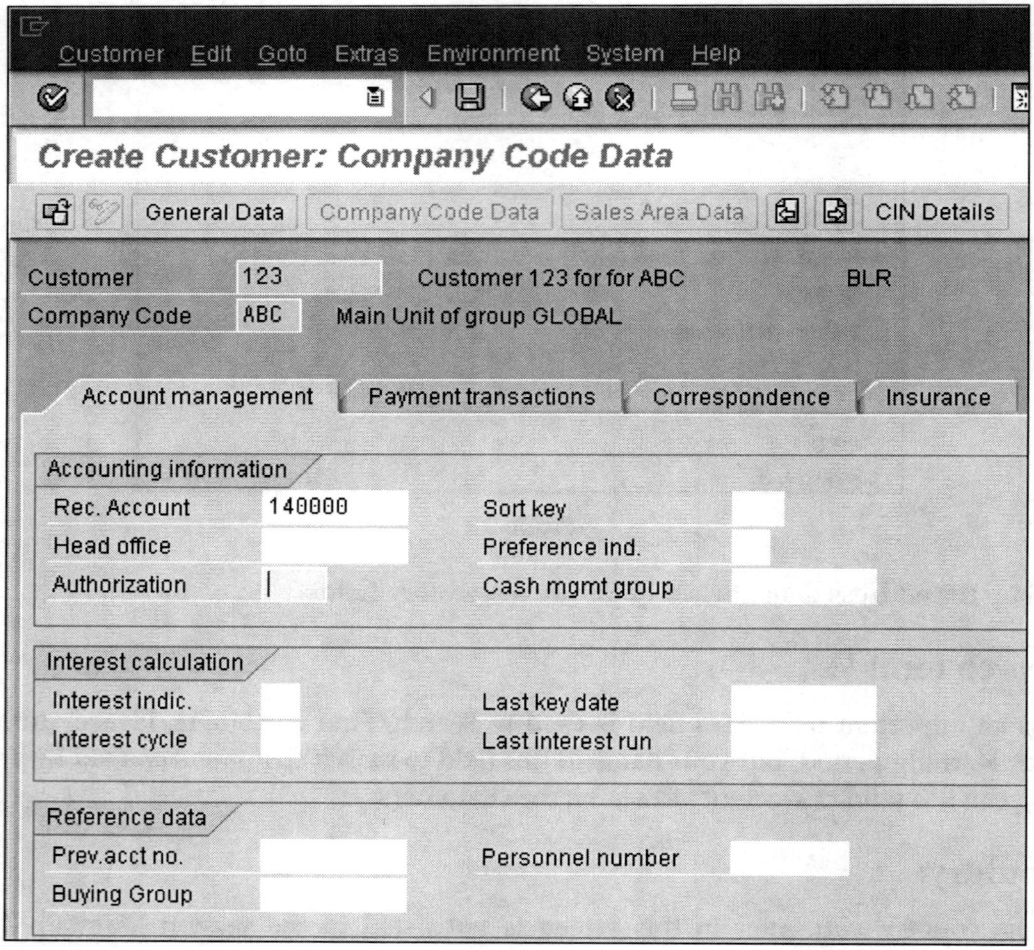

Fig:2-33

In this screen, the mandatory field is Reconciliation A/C. Enter 140000, Trade Receivables - domestic. Then click on the main tab 'Sales Area Data':

Sales tab in Sales Area Data of customer master [XD01/XD02].

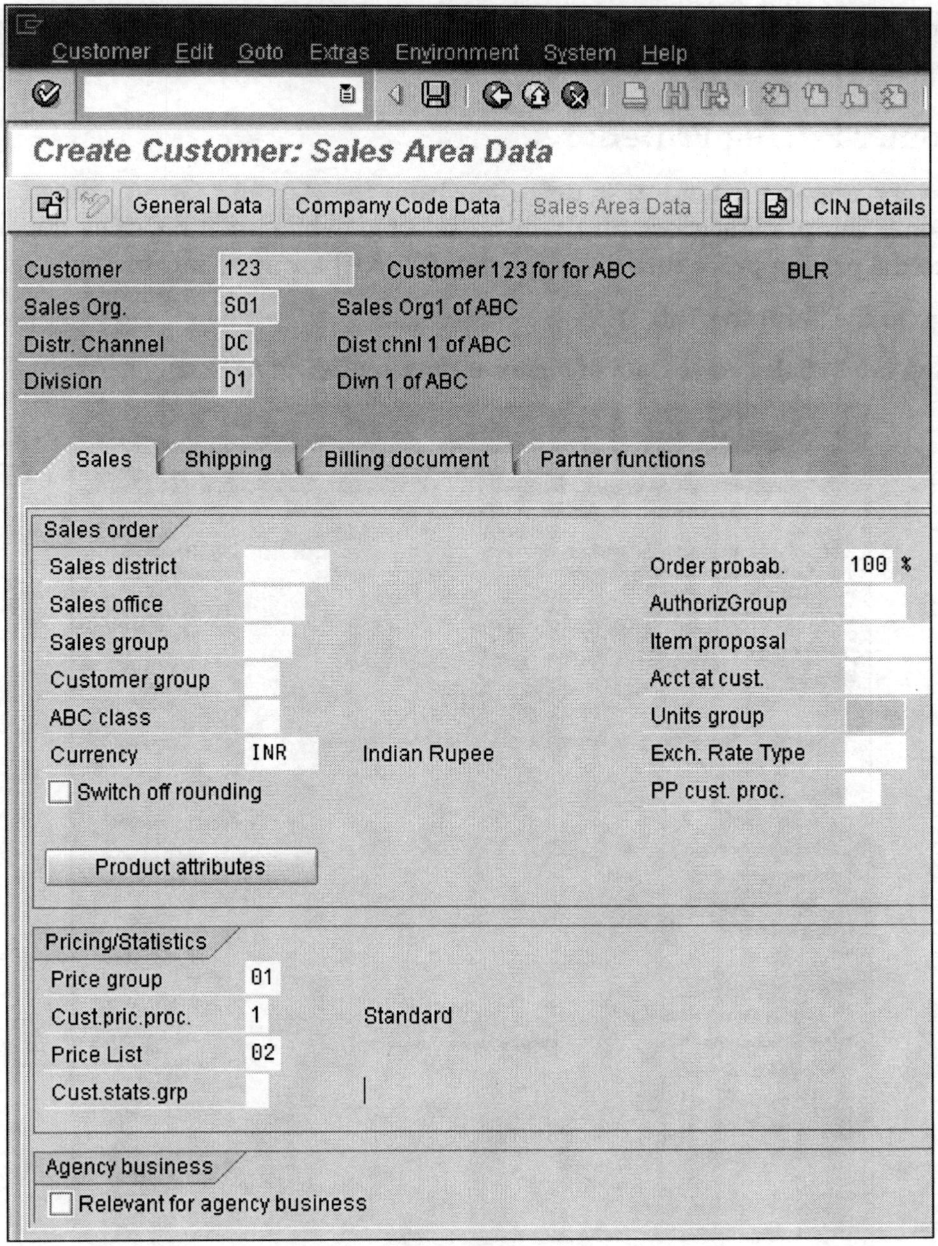

Fig:2-34

Price group, Customer Pricing Procedure and **Price List** are to be given. Customer Pricing Procedure is defaulted from the Account Group.

Price Group(01) and Price List(02):

Path for defining them is: IMG- Sales and Distribution- Basic Functions- Pricing-Maintain Price-Relevant Master Data Fields.

Customer Pricing Procedure:

It is a very important field. It is defaulted from the Account Group. Based on this value only the pricing procedure will be selected while creating sales documents. Refer to the pricing procedure determination[OVKK] for more information.

Then go to the Shipping Tab.

Shipping tab in Sales Area Data of customer master [XD01/XD02].

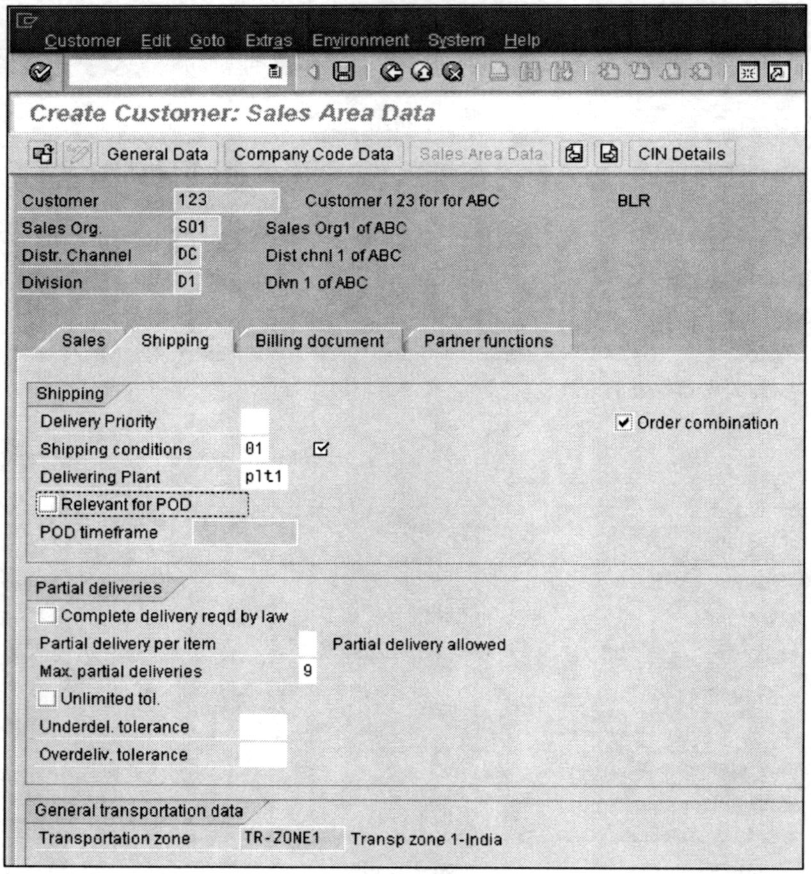

Fig:2-35

Shipping condition and Delivery Plant to be entered.

Shipping condition:

Path to define Shipping Condition: IMG-Logistics Execution- Shipping- Shipping Point and Goods Receiving Point Determination- Define Shipping Conditions.

Shipping Condition is a mandatory field in the customer master and is used in Shipping Point Determination.

Shipping Condition can be assigned in SDT also.

Delivering Plant:

The default plant from which material will be delivered to the customer.

Partial Delivery Per Item:

This field controls partial delivery of the material. Please do not confuse this with the field 'Completion Rule' in OIC.

Then go to the Billing Document tab.

Billing document tab in Sales Area Data of customer master [XD01/XD02].

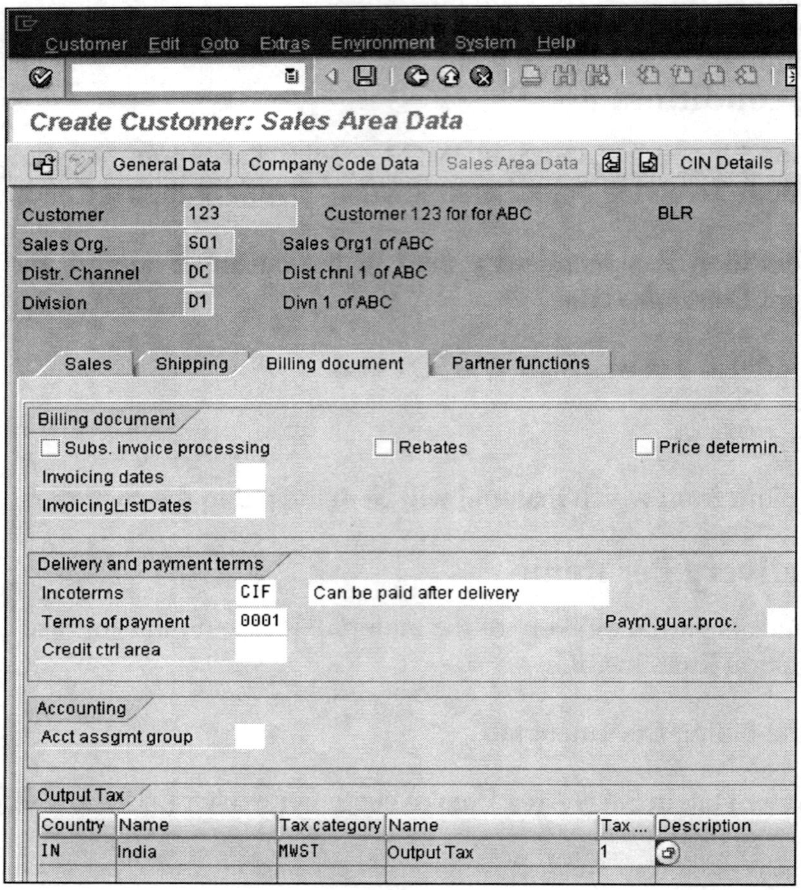

Fig:2-36

Incoterms(International Commercial Term for Shipping rules):

If you enter incoterm here, the same will be defaulted while creating the sales document. The standard terms are available in the system.

Terms of payment:

This is defined by FI consultant and will be defaulted while creating sales documents.

Account Assignment Group:

This field is used for Account Determination.

Output Tax.:

A mandatory entry. Tax info area(Output Tax) does not appear if created through VD01(without company code). One company belongs to only one country and tax is based on the country of ship to party.

Tax Data can be maintained only if the Tax Category By Country[OVK1] is maintained and also the Tax Classifications are defined in the session Maintain Customer Taxes[OVK3]. Refer to the chapters Tax Set Up and Pricing for more details. The country (here IN) is the country from which the materials are sent.

Then go to the 'Partner functions' tab and see that all the needed partner functions are available as follows:

Partner function tab in Sales Area Data of customer master [XD01/XD02].

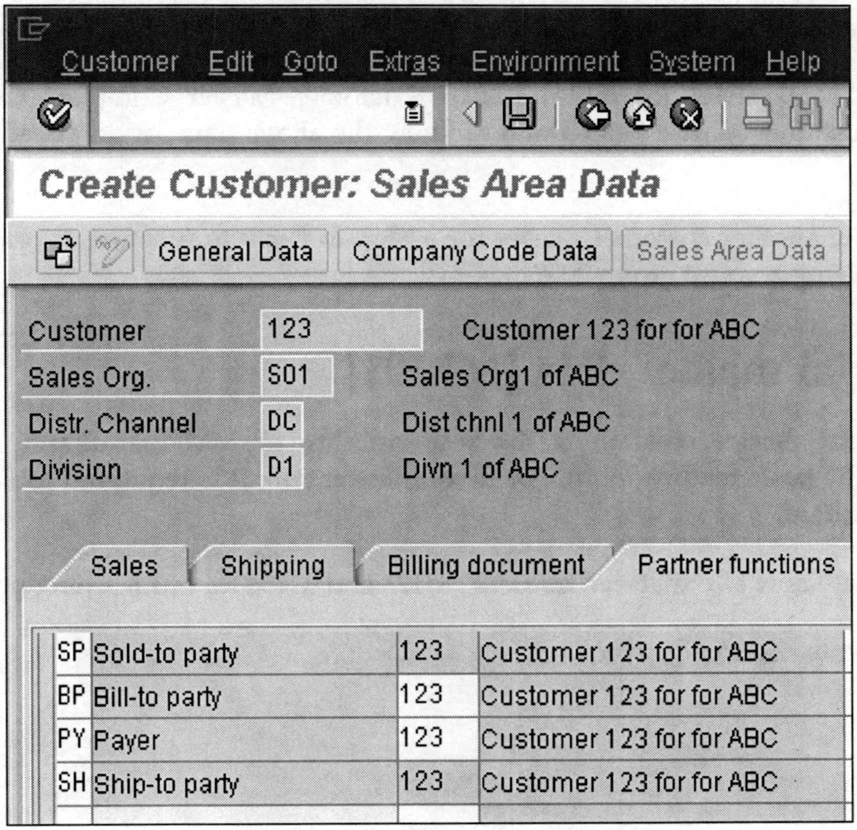

Fig:2-37

Here it shows that the customer 123 is acting as SP, BP, PY and SH.

These partner functions are defaulted based on the Partner Determination Procedure linked to the account group. Refer to the Partner Determination Procedure.

Then save the data.

Why do you see here the partner functions BP and PY as editable ? Refer to the account group and partner determination procedure for the answer.

If you want to use the same customer code across various sales areas, you can extend this master data to those sales areas.

Use XD02 for modification and XD03 for display of already created customers.

See Extras- Admin Data to know against which account group this customer master was created.

Use [SE17] or [SE16] for tables KNB1(Customer Master Company Code) and KNVV(Customer Master Sales Data) to know the above data for an already created customer.

Now create another customer master for a Ship-to Party to function as only Ship-to Party by using account group 0002.

Material master data [MM01]

As Material master creation is the responsibility of MM consultants, here we describe the basic features only. For more information, it is requested to consult an MM consultant.

Let us create now two material masters, M123 and M456 for our learning purposes.

Path to create material master.

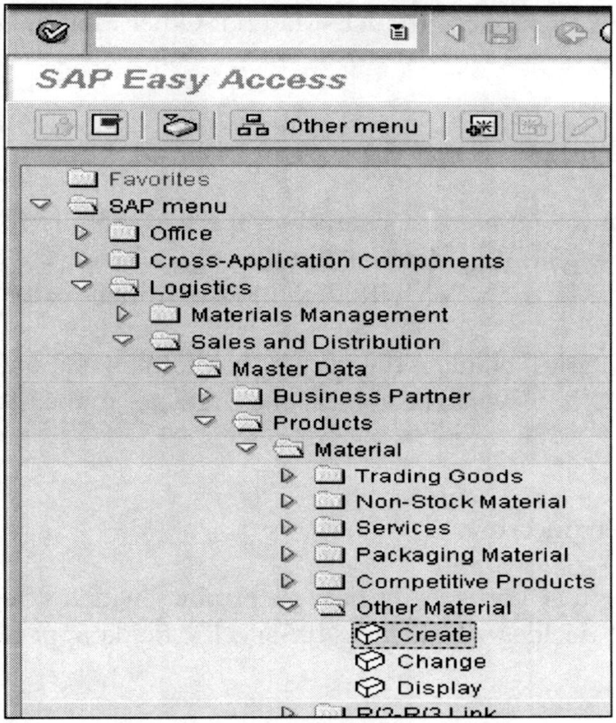

Fig:2-38

Path: EA-Logistics-Sales and Distribution- Master Data- Products- Material- Other material.

Create material [MM01] - Initial screen

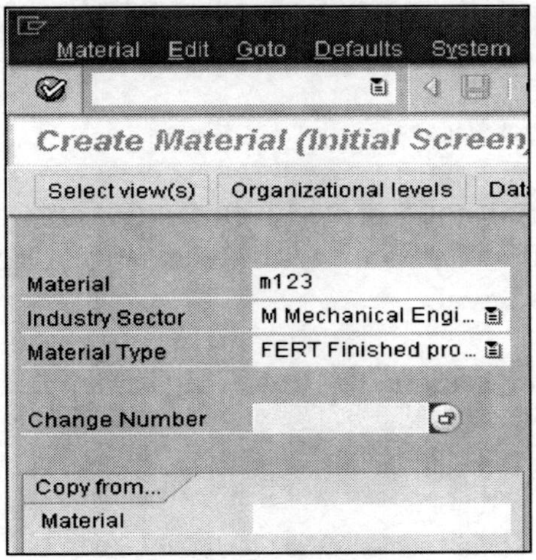

Fig:2-39

Path: Logistics-SD-Master Data-Products-Material-Other Material-Create

Material:

Enter material code M123.

In SAP, the maximum number of characters for materials is fixed at 18. It is set through the session [OMSL]. Material numbering is based on the settings in the Number Ranges for Materials [MMNR]. Refer to the Appendix for more details.

Leave the field 'Material' blank if the system has to allot the material number. For external numbering, there has to be at least one character in the code.

Industry Sector:

Select Mechanical Engineering.

The industry sector that you specify here determines which screens appear and in what order. Also it decides which industry-specific fields appear on the individual screens.

Material Type:

Select Material Type FERT, Finished Product because we have done the set up only for FERT in Miscellaneous Set Up.

Refer to Attributes Of Material Types in the Miscellaneous setup for more information. Screen combinations will vary according to the combination of Industry Sector and Material Type.

Then click on the tab 'Select Views'.

Note: If the same material code already exists for any other Industry sector or Material Type, the system will pop up with the existing Organisational level to copy to the other organisational level.

If no such code exists in the system, the following screen appears to select the views

Create material [MM01] -Screen Select View.

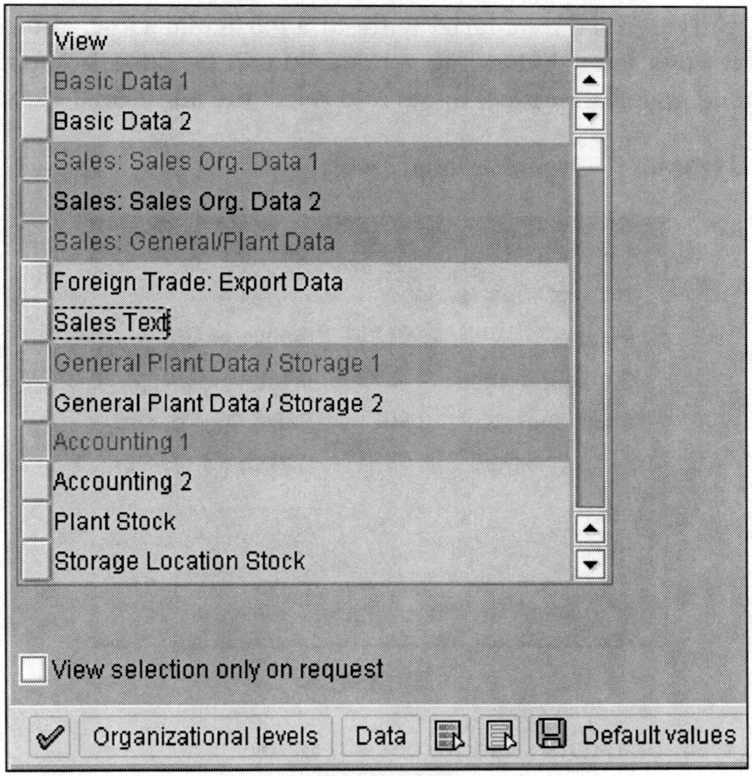

Fig:2-40

Highlight the following screen views in the above screen:

1. Basic Data 1,
2. Sales:Sales Org.Data 1,
3. Sales:Sales Org.Data 2,
4. Sales:General/ Plant Data,
5. General Plant Data /Storage 1,
6. Accounting 1.

These user departments(screens) are defaulted as per the Material Type attributes.

Click on 'Default Values' if you want to save the screen selection activity so that when you create materials again, the same set of screen selection will be defaulted.

Accept the selections by clicking on the tick mark.

Then click on the tab Organisational levels

If you have already defined a material without a particular view, you can extend the material to that view later. Extending a material can be done by using MM01 and entering the same material number again and select the additional views.

Create material [MM01] - Organisational levels

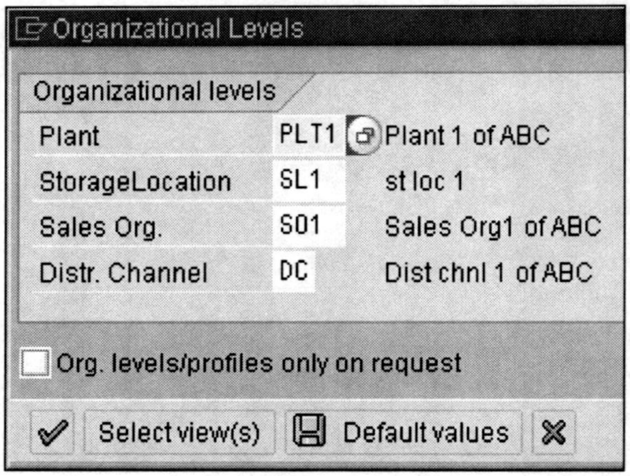

Fig:2-41

Enter our Organisational data as shown in this figure.

Note:

Organisational Units for material are:

Plant

Sales Organisation and

Distribution Channel

Or in other words:

Material is Plant/Sales Organisation/Distribution Channel dependent.

Material is not Division dependent. Plant is country dependent.

The same material can be extended to other Organisational units. That is, for example, you can create the same material code for various plants, for various Sales Organisations and for various Distribution Channels.

When you choose the Selection Views and Organisational Data, the following screen appears:

Create material [MM01] - Basic Data 1.

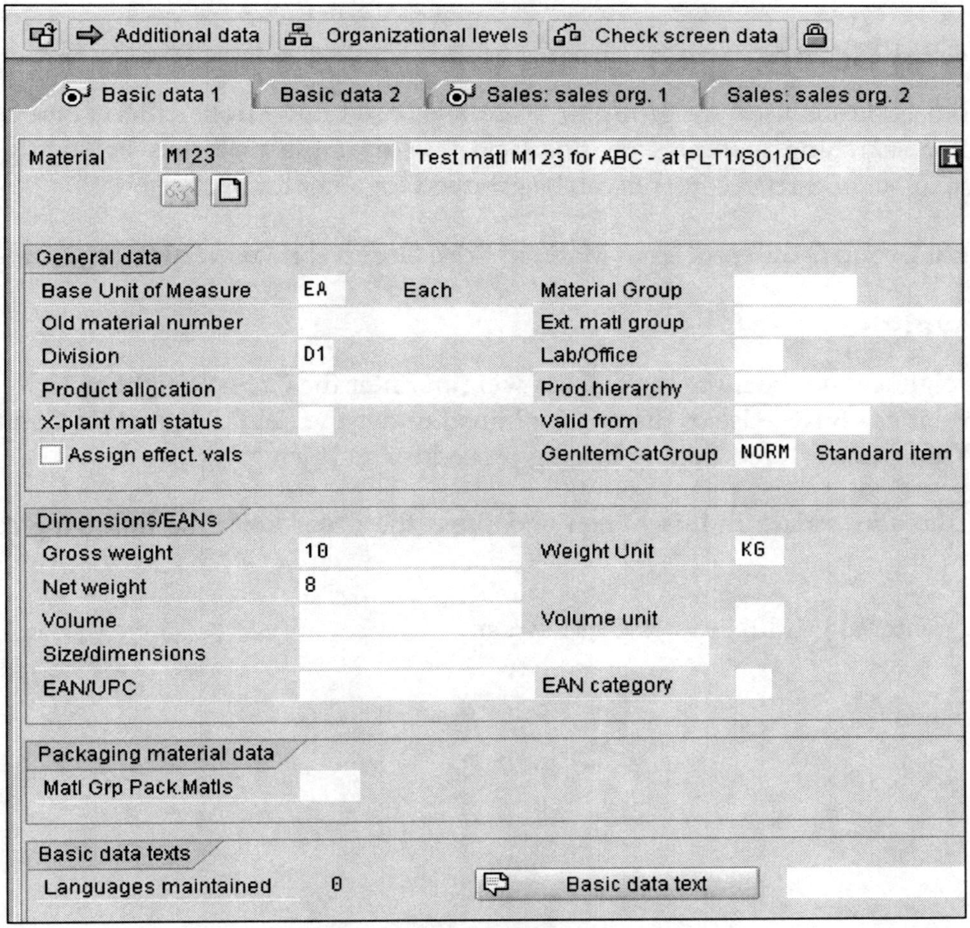

Fig:2-42

Material Description:

During your learning stage, use your name in the description field. This will help identifying the materials that are created by you.

Base unit:

The base unit in which this material is transacted.

Division:

It is the Item Division. The division determination in the Sale Order Line is decided by the field 'Item Division Y/N' in the SDT. Refer SDT(Sales Doc Type) for further information.

Material Group:

Material Group is used for grouping materials based on various criteria and can be used for searching materials on this field. For example materials belonging to a particular set of carbon contents can be grouped together for analysis.

Material Group is different from Material Price Group shown in Sales Org2 screen.

Net weight:

Net weight cannot be more than **Gross weight**. Enter the Gross Weight as 10 KG and Net weight as 8 KG. Use of these is explained under the field 'Alternative Condition Base Value' in the topic 'Setting Pricing procedure' in Pricing.

Enter the above data in this screen and press the Enter key. The following screen appears.

Create material [MM01] - Sales Org 1 screen

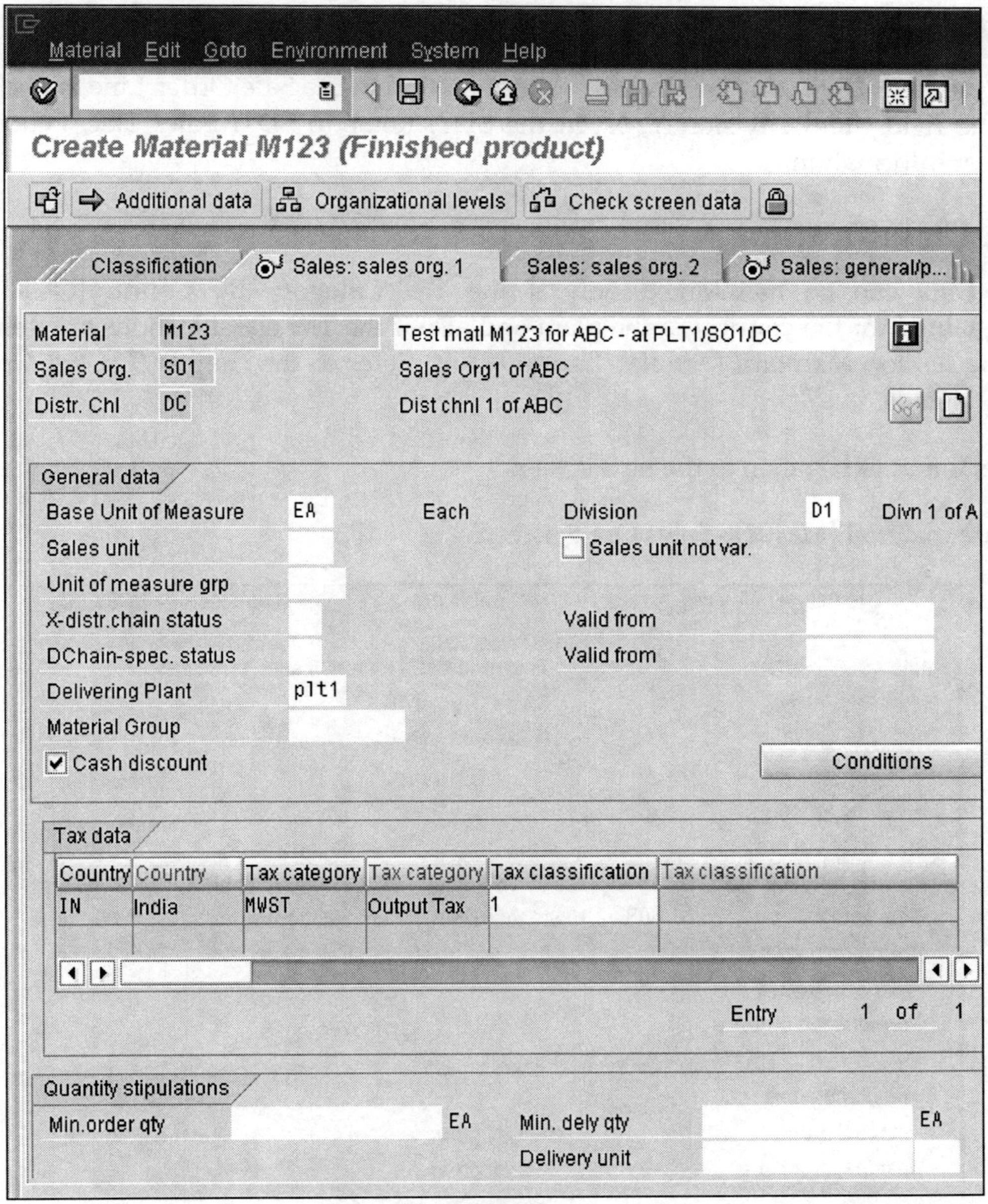

Fig:2-43

Delivering Plant:

It is an important field to identify the country of origin for determining tax.

Enter the Delivering Plant as PLT1: the plant that we created earlier.

Division:

It is the Item Division. The division determination in the Sale Order Line is decided by the field 'Item Division Y/N' in the SDT. Refer to SDT(Sales Doc Type) for further information.

Tax Classification:

Tax Data can be maintained only if the Tax Category By Country[OVK1] is maintained for the country of the plant and also if the Tax classifications are defined in the session Maintain Material Taxes[OVK4]. Refer to the chapter Tax Set Up for more details.

Press Enter, to be taken to the next screen

Create material [MM01] - Sales Org 2 screen

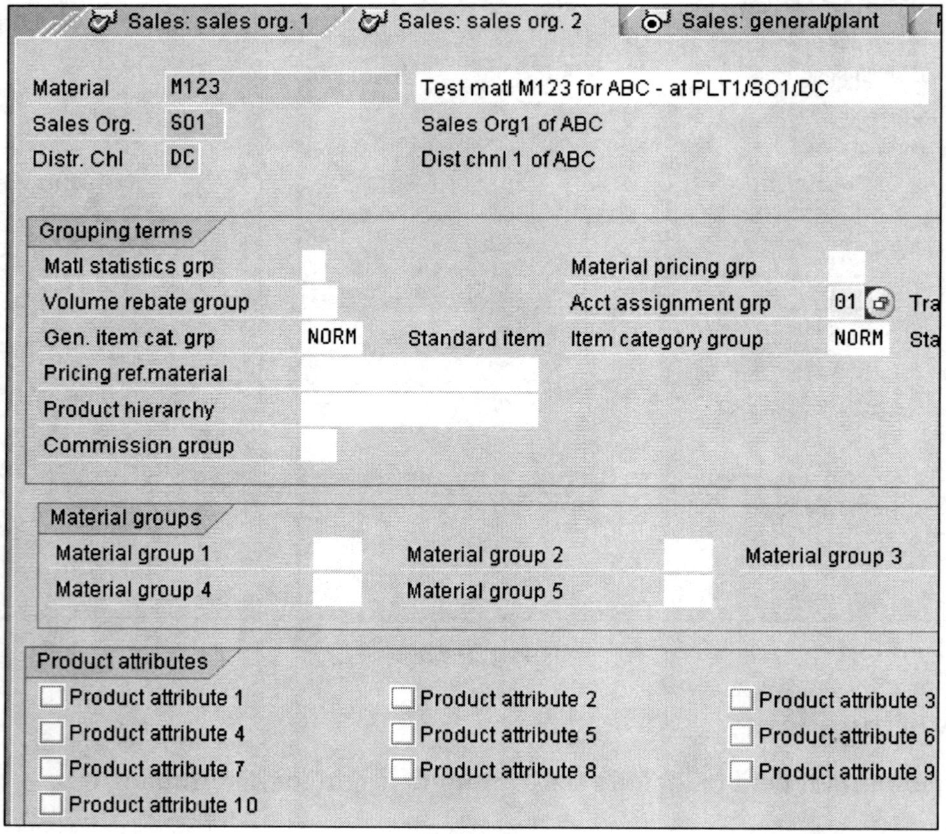

Fig:2-44

Pricing Reference Material:

It is an important field. If an existing material is entered here, the price for this material is taken from this reference material. Please note that even if you maintain the price for this material, the system always checks and takes price from this reference material only.

Material Price Group:

This field is used for grouping materials for pricing conditions. For example, you can create pricing condition records for the combination of Material Pricing Group and Material Group(from Basic data 1 screen).

Account Assignment Group :

This field is used in the Account Determination. Refer to the Determination chapter for more details.

Item Category Group(right side field):

This is a very important field. This field is used for Item Category Determination

[VOV4].

Item Category determines the Schedule Line Category. Schedule Line Category controls the delivery process.

Create material [MM01] -Sales:general / plant screen.

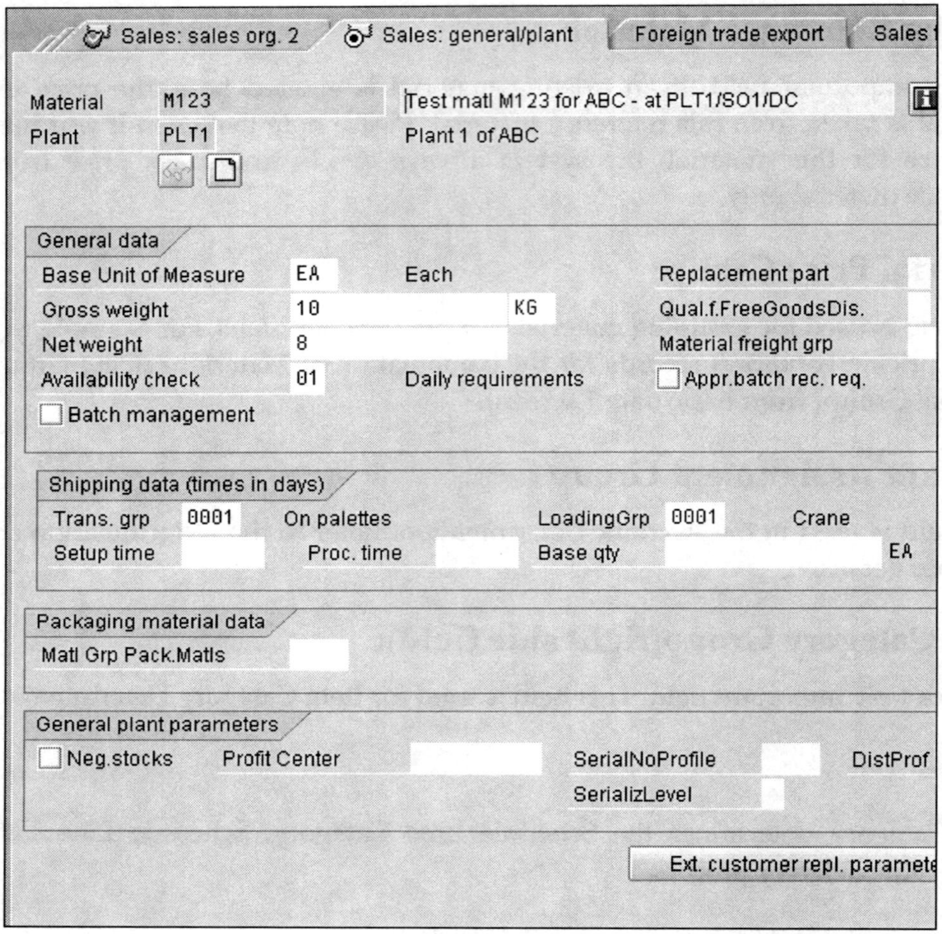

Fig:2-45

Here you enter Availability Check, Transportation Group and Loading Group.

Availability Check:

This field is used in the functionality of Availability Check. If it is mandatory, select some standard availability check which can be modified later, if needed.

Transportation Group [OVSY]:

The Path for defining Transportation Group is: IMG-Logistics Execution-Shipping-Basic Shipping Functions- Routes-Route Determination-Define Transportation Groups

Transportation Group is used in Route Determination [0VRF]. (Path for Route Determination: IMG- Sales and Distribution- Basic Functions- Routes- Route Determination- Maintain Route Determination).

Loading Group [OVSX]:

Path for defining Loading group is: IMG-Logistics Execution-Shipping- Basic Shipping Functions- Shipping Point and Goods Receiving Point Determination-Define Loading Groups.

Loading Group is used in shipping point determination [OVL2].

Press Enter to be taken to the next screen.

Create material [MM01] -Plant Data/ Storage-1 screen

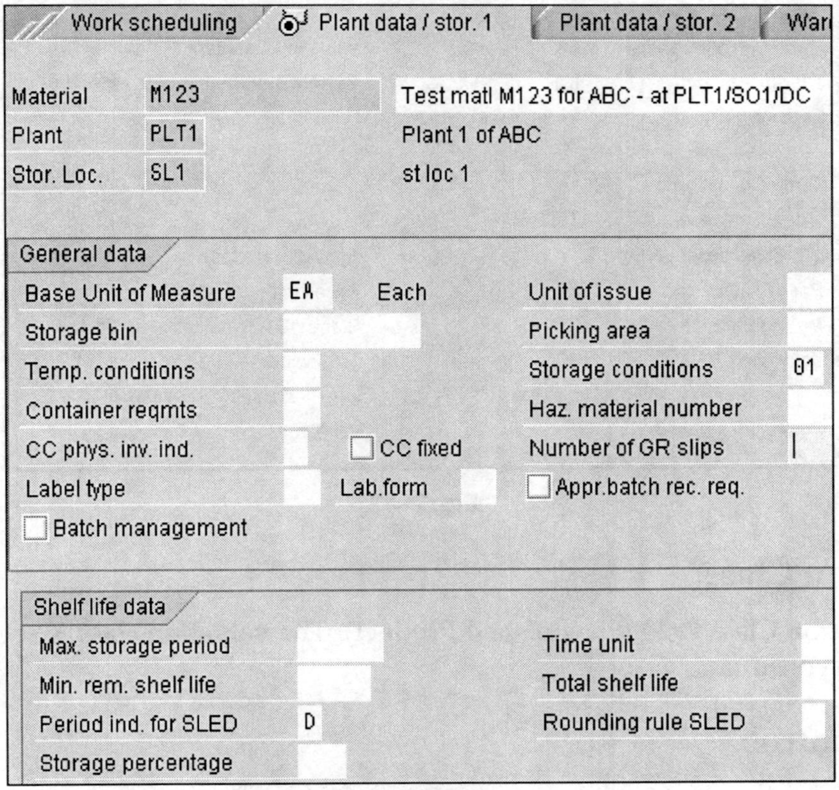

Fig:2-46

Here you have to enter only the **storage condition**.

The Path for defining the Storage Condition: IMG-Logistics Execution-Shipping-Picking- Determine Picking Location- Define Storage Conditions [OMS6]

Storage Condition + Shipping Point + Plant are used in Storage Location Determination [OVL3].

Press Enter to be taken to the next screen.

Create material [MM01] –Accounting 1 screen.

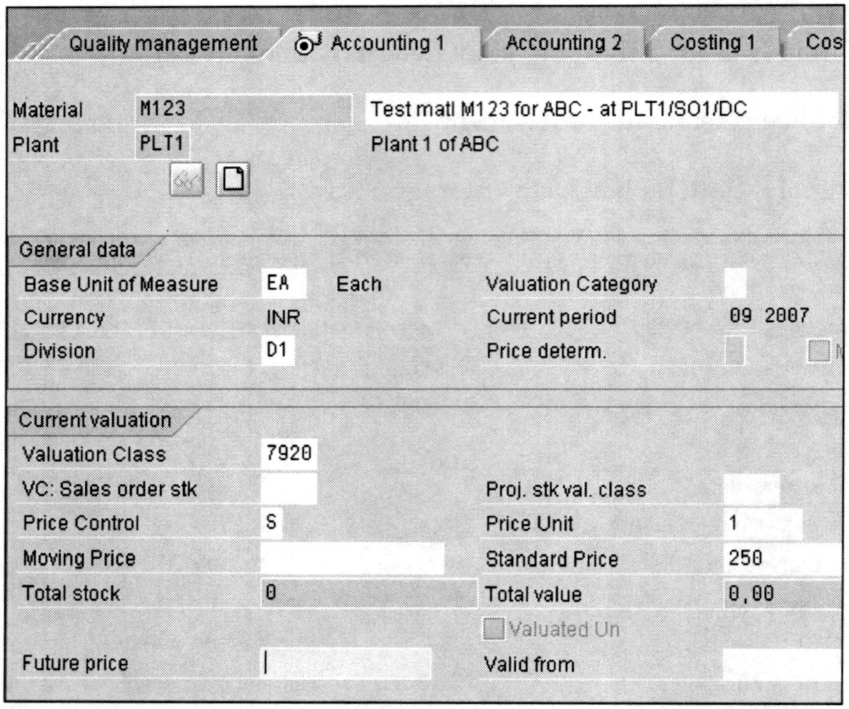

Fig:2-47

Valuation Class:

Use Valuation Class 7920 (For finished Product). The valuation class is set and used by the FIN consultant.

Price Control:

S (**Standard Price**), V(**Moving Average Price**). If you select Price control 'S', enter a value in the field 'Standard Price'. Otherwise, enter a value in the field 'Moving Price'.

Standard Price is constant whereas Moving Average Price varies according to the actual purchase prices at different times.

Then Save the material master.

Similarly create one more material M456 with Gross weight 100 KG, net weight 60 KG and Standard Price 300. We will demonstrate our Sales transactions with these two materials.

Note:

To use MRP(Material Requirement Planning), you must select one of the MRP views. In such cases you may have to define, for your plant, MRP controller(path: IMG-Production-Material Requirements Planning-Master Data-Define MRP Controllers) and Scheduling Margin Key(Path: IMG-Production-Shop Floor Control-Operations-Scheduling-Define Scheduling Margin Key.). As this is the responsibility of PP/MM consultant, MRP is not explained in this book.

Similarly, If you select warehouse management view, you must link a warehouse to the material. Warehouse can be defined in the session 'Define warehouse number' (Path: IMG-Enterprise Structure-Definition-Logistics Execution-Define, copy, delete, check warehouse number-Define warehouse number).

But if you want to use warehouse management functionality, you must link a combination of plant and a Storage location to the warehouse(path: IMG-Enterprise Structure-Assignment-Logistics Execution-Assign warehouse number to plant/storage location). If warehouse management is used for a particular combination, the delivery process of materials of that combination changes by using Transfer Orders but materials of a different combination of Plant and Storage location which are not linked to a warehouse will be processed in the normal way(without warehouse management functionality).

We do not use warehouse management functionality in this book and hence we do not use the warehouse management views while creating materials. Hence, we do not use Transfer Orders functionality in our exercises. You can go through the topic Lean Warehouse Management in the Appendix, if you want to use warehouse management functionality.

Use[SE17] or [MM17] to know data for an already created material. The table is MVKE(Sales Data for Material).

Chapter 3

PRICING

Introduction to pricing

After setting up the enterprise structure and creating all needed master data, you can set up Pricing.

Pricing is the heart of SD and hence, you must thoroughly understand the fundamentals of pricing. SAP uses Condition Technique for handling pricing.

While creating Sales Documents, the system selects automatically a Pricing Procedure based on the Pricing Procedure Determination set up in the system. Pricing Procedure contains a series of Price Condition Types(PCT) for all the pricing elements such as one Pricing Condition Type for basic price, another Price Condition Type for discounts, another Price Condition Type for rebate, another one for tax etc. Pricing values are recorded against each Price Condition Type. Certain PCTs can be set as mandatory(for example, basic price) so that before creating the sales order itself, the price records should have been entered against such PCTs. While creating the sales order, the system will pick up pricing values against each Condition Type for each line(Item)and the net price will be calculated for the entire sales order.

For each PCT, you can enter different pricing values based on various options and the system should choose one value for each condition type and the same will be assigned to the sales order lines. The System should choose only one value which it finds in the order of sequence mentioned in the Access Sequence. For example, you can enter one value based on a combination of the customer and material and another value based on just material. If the more specific value is found(based on customer and material) the system should take that value and add to the sales order line. If this specific value is not found, the system should search for the general value and the same should be added to the sales order line. This search sequence is based on the Sequences set up in the system. Because pricing values are selected based on some conditions, this method is called a Condition Technique. Condition Technique is used in many areas in SAP.

Also, you can indicate against each Condition Type whether the value is to be entered manually in the sales order; whether at least one value is to be set up compulsorily; the value entered is only for statistical purpose(not to net in the sales order pricing), etc.

You can mention a separate account key to determine unique G/L account for posting of these price values.

Procedure for setting Pricing:

1. Create Condition Tables with the required fields[V/03]
2. Create Access Sequence and assign Condition Tables to it [V/07]
3. Create Condition Type and assign Access Sequence to it [V/06].
4. Create Pricing Procedure and assign Condition Types to it [V/08]
5. Create Condition Records [VK11]
6. Set up Pricing Procedure Determination [OVKK]. This will be explained in the Determination chapter.

Each process is explained in detail in this chapter (except the Pricing Procedure Determination, which is explained in the chapter Determination).

Let us explain about the Pricing Procedure Z00001 that we are going to create later in this chapter.

[V/08] Pricing Procedure, Z00001

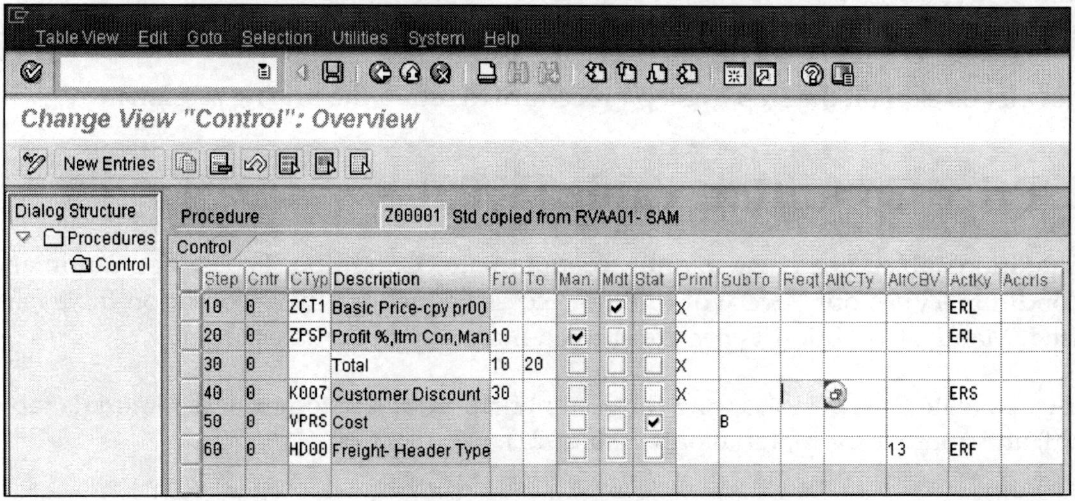

Step	Cntr	CTyp	Description	Fro	To	Man.	Mdt	Stat	Print	SubTo	Reqt	AltCTy	AltCBV	ActKy	Accrls
10	0	ZCT1	Basic Price-cpy pr00			☐	☑	☐	X					ERL	
20	0	ZPSP	Profit %,Itm Con,Man	10		☑	☐	☐	X					ERL	
30	0		Total	10	20	☐	☐	☐	X						
40	0	K007	Customer Discount	30		☐	☐	☐	X					ERS	
50	0	VPRS	Cost			☐	☐	☑		B					
60	0	HD00	Freight- Header Type			☐	☐	☐					13	ERF	

Fig:3-1

Path: IMG-Sales and Distribution- Basic Functions- Pricing- Pricing Control- Define And Assign Pricing Procedures- Maintain pricing procedures.

We are making the Condition Type ZCT1 as mandatory because ZCT1 is the basic price. Hence, if pricing records are not maintained for this Price Condition Type, sales orders cannot be created using this pricing procedure.

Condition Type ZPSP(Profit percentage on the basic price) is Manual. For manual Condition Type, we need to enter the pricing values only if we want. Entering pricing records for manual Condition Types are optional. Hence, if you want, you can enter this Price Condition Type in the sales order manually and enter prices against this condition type after creating the sales order.

Condition Type K007(Customer Discount on Total):

This condition type is used for calculating discount on step 30 (Total of Basic price and Profit)

Condition Type VPRS(Standard Cost) is for statistical purpose and hence, the value recorded against this Price Condition Type in the sales order will not be considered for net price for the sales order.

Condition Type HD00(Freight as a header condition) is used to distribute the freight values proportional to the values of all sales order lines. The header condition value is added manually to the sales order.

Now let us explain the step by step procedure to set up the pricing sessions.

1. Price Condition Table [V/03]

Condition tables are created only for automatic Condition Types. For automatic Condition Types only, we will link an Access Sequence where condition tables are used. Manual Condition Types are entered manually in the sales order.

Let us create 2 new tables, one for a combination of Customer and Material(table 920) and another for Material only(table 921).

Important: As Sales Org and Distribution Channel are 'Key fields' for Sales Document tables, first we must select these 2 fields(Sales Org and Distribution Channel)in order and then select 'Line fields'. Also the last field should be Material Number.

Let us create the condition table '920' with customer Number and Material Number.

[V/03] Creating Pricing Condition Table '920'.

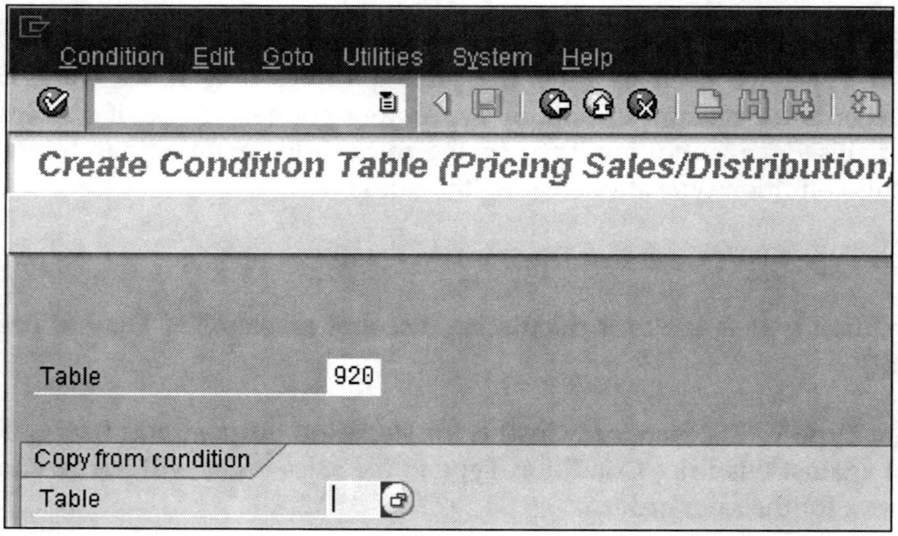

Fig:3-2

Path: IMG- Sales and Distribution- Basic Functions- Pricing- Pricing Control- Define Condition Tables- Create condition tables.

Fill up the new table code, 920 and press 'Enter'. The following screen appears:

Creating table 920 with Customer and Material fields.

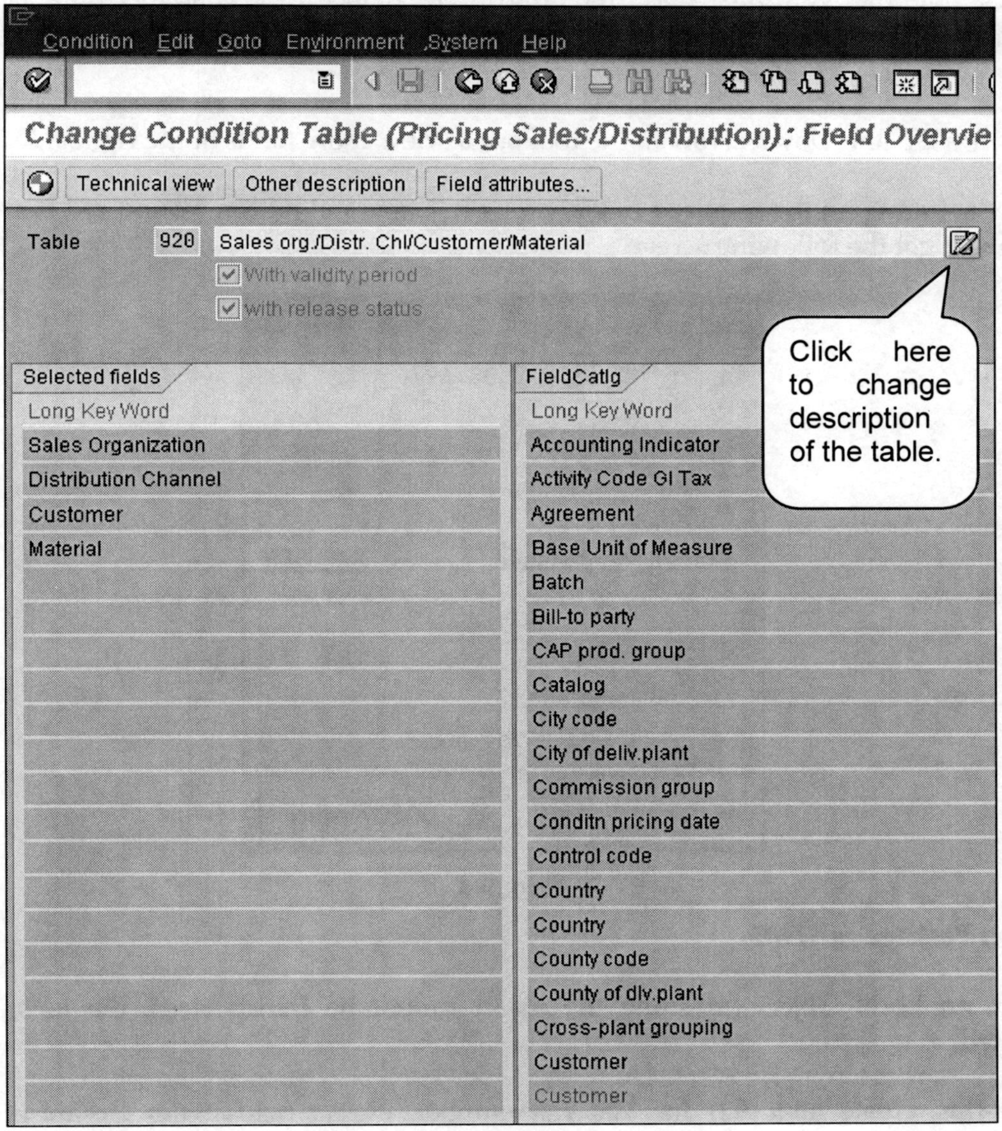

Fig: 3-3

At the right side of the screen, you will see almost all the required fields you need to create condition tables. By double clicking on the fields at the right side of the screen, the same get copied to the left side. Hence, select and copy the fields Sales Org, Distribution Channel, Customer Number and Material from the right side to the left side as shown in the screen above.

Please note that you must select the appropriate field for the customer number. To display different descriptions of the fields, click on 'Other Description' on the tool bar.

Click on Up and Down arrow in the tool bar to view more fields at the right side.

After selecting all the required fields, click on 'Generate' button (round red button). You will get the following screen

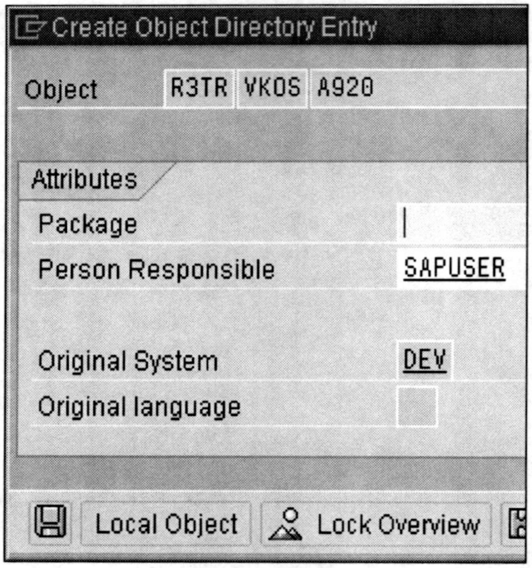

Fig:3-4

Select Package as $TMP

Click on Local Object (meaning the object cannot be transported), the table get created.

Like this, create table 921 for Material number, (Select fields Sales Organisation, Distribution Channel and Material Number).

Use V/05 to display price condition tables.

2. Price Access Sequence [V/07]

Creation of Price Access Sequence and linking of condition tables to it

Price Access Sequence is a list of Price Condition Tables arranged in a sequence with certain controls. This Access Sequence is then linked to Price Condition Types by entering the Access Sequence in the Price Condition Type.

Let us create Price Access Sequence ZABC with first access for table 920 and second access for table 921.

Creating Price Access sequence [V/07]

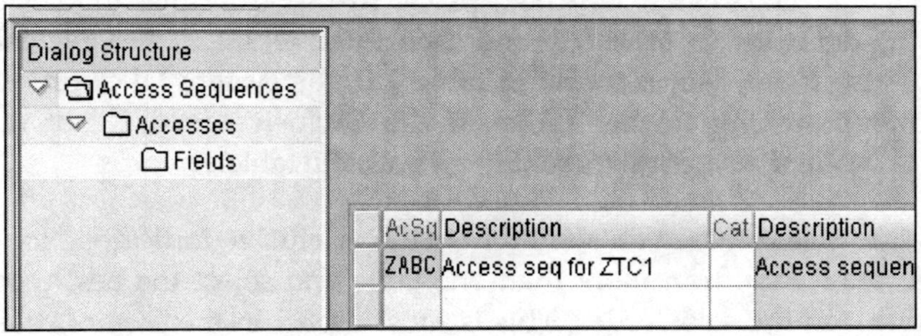

Fig:3-5

Path: Sales and Distribution- Basic Functions- Pricing- Pricing Control- Define Access Sequences- Maintain Access Sequences.

Click on New Entries, and create our Access Sequence ZABC and save.

Mark the newly created Access Sequence ZABC and link our previously created tables 920 and 921 by clicking on the left side tab 'Access'.

Linking of the tables 920 and 921 to our Access Sequence ZABC.

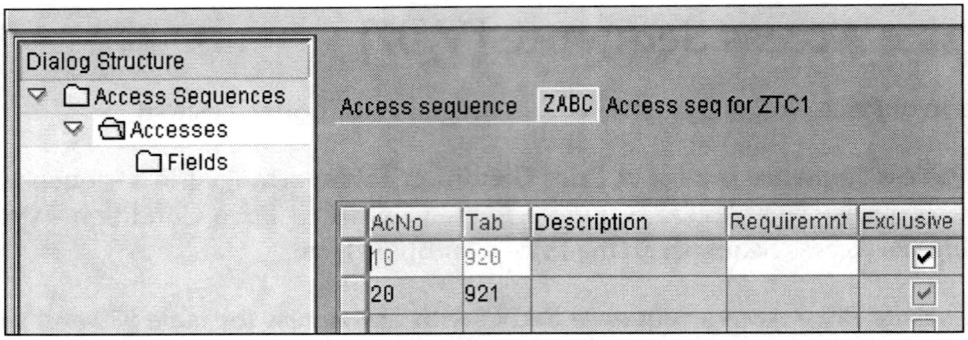

Fig:3-6

The Access Numbers (10 and 20) are important because based on this sequence number only the data search will take place. In this example, the system should search for the data first in table 920 and then in table 921. If the Exclusive field is marked and also if the data is found in table 920, the system takes price from table 920 and stops searching further tables. If the Exclusive field is not marked, the system puts data in the sales document from both the tables.

There are some cases where you should not click Exclusive indicators. for example if you want to read data from more than one table and select the best record among them and put it in the sales order. This is most useful in the case of discounts. For example, you can have many tables for various types of discounts and only one which gives maximum discount should be selected and put in the sales document. For more information about this feature, read the topic Condition Exclusions.

In Access Sequences, you must put the most specific table in the beginning and more general table at the end.

While saving the above data, you may get the message 'The field assignment has not yet been made', even if the fields were assigned. This is because the field initialisation for the new table is not done. Unless the field initialisation is done, you cannot use these tables. Ignore the message now and do the following for field assignment initialization.

Initializing the field assignment for new tables:

For using new table fields in the Access Sequence, you must initialize all the assigned fields. For this, go back and highlight the left side tab 'Access Sequence' as shown below. Then mark the Access Sequence ZABC at the right side and then directly click on the tab 'Fields' in the left window.

Fig:3-7

When you click on the tab Fields, You will get the following screen.

Field assignment initialisation.

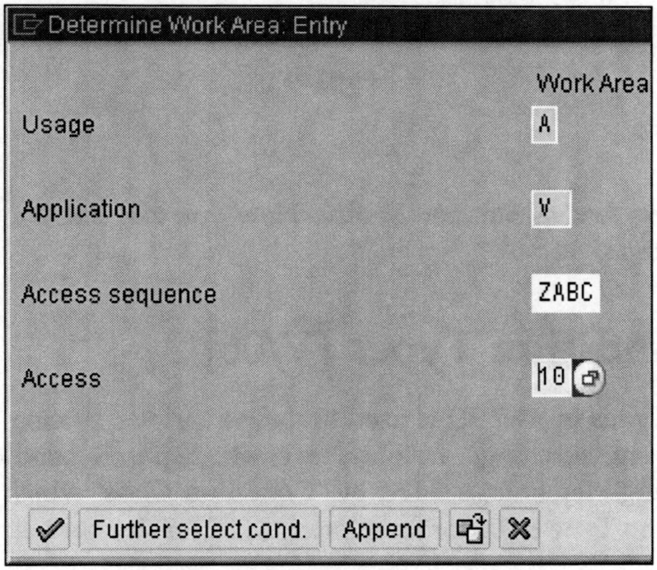

Fig:3-8

Select each Access Numbers of the table in this case 10 and click on the tick mark. The following screen appears:

Field details of the table 920 which is linked to Access Sequence ZABC at sequence no 10.

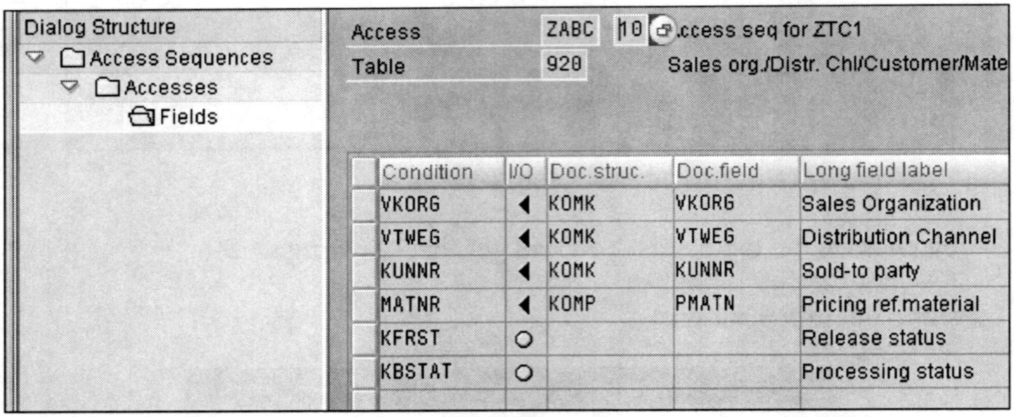

Condition	I/O	Doc.struc.	Doc.field	Long field label
VKORG	◀	KOMK	VKORG	Sales Organization
VTWEG	◀	KOMK	VTWEG	Distribution Channel
KUNNR	◀	KOMK	KUNNR	Sold-to party
MATNR	◀	KOMP	PMATN	Pricing ref.material
KFRST	○			Release status
KBSTAT	○			Processing status

Fig:3-9

Save the data.

Repeat this for the Access number 20 also. Now you can use the Access Sequence ZABC in the pricing.

3. Price Condition Types [V/06]

Price Condition Types in SAP SD is used to define various pricing elements such as basic price, discount/surcharge, freights, taxes etc. Separate condition type is used for separate pricing elements(decided by 'Condition Class' which is set by SAP). Example: Condition Type PR00 for basic price, K007 for discount etc..

Many controlling features are tuned inside the Condition Type, such as:

a) Discount is based on percentage or fixed amount ?

b) Discount values entered is sign sensitive(+ or -) ?

c) Finalized pricing value in the sales document can be modified or not? etc.

As there are many controlling features inside the condition type, it is suggested to copy an existing SAP standard condition type to your own condition type and modify the new one to your requirements. As usual, use Z as the starting letter for your own condition type as per the recommendation of SAP.

Condition Types are then lined together in 'Pricing Procedures' in a particular sequence to determine net price for the Sales Documents.

Access Sequence is assigned /linked to Condition Types inside the condition types [V/06].

If you want to use any condition type in a sales document, it should have been included in the pricing procedure. See Pricing Procedure for more details.

Creating Price Condition Types [V/06]:

Almost all types of Condition Types are already defined in the system with all the necessary links. Hence, it is recommended to create condition types by copying from SAP standard condition types.

Copy the SAP standard condition type PR00 to a new condition type ZCT1 and link our Access Sequence ZABC to it.

[V/06], Price Condition Types ZCT1.

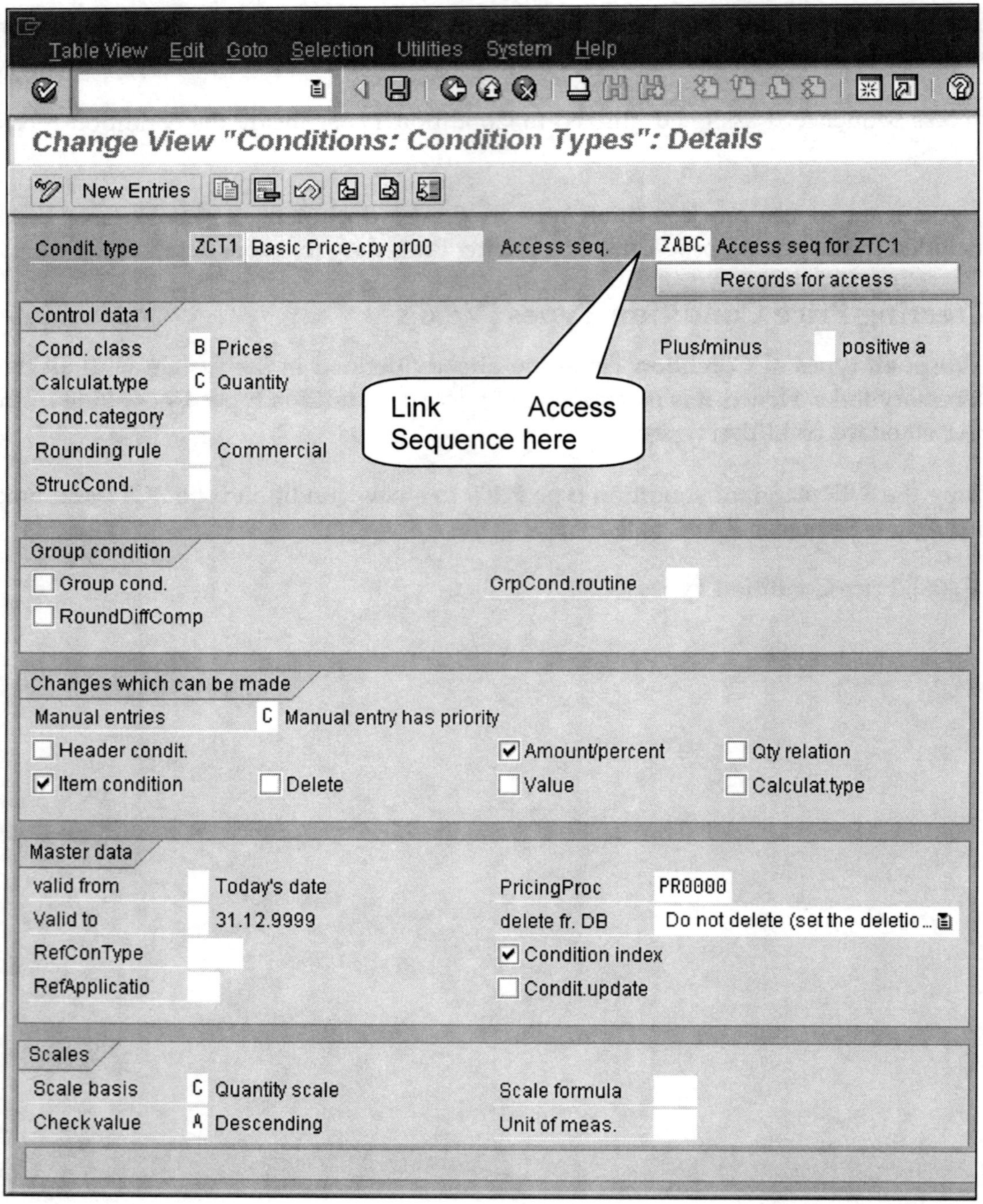

Fig:3-10

Path: IMG-Sales and Distribution- Basic Functions- Pricing- Pricing

Control- Define Condition Types.

A few important fields in the Condition Type are explained here. You are requested to take field help from the system for other fields.

Access Sequence(for automatic Condition Types):

Please note that our new Access Sequence ZABC is linked to this price condition type so that this Condition Type can be used for automatic price determination. Access Sequence can be linked to a Condition Type if it is an Item Condition only

(Refer the explanation on the field 'item condition' below). It is suggested not to link accidentally any Access Sequence to a condition type if it is to be used as a manual condition type in the Pricing Procedure. This is to avoid unnecessary search processes and slow system performance.

Condition class:

This field specifies the type of the condition type.

'A' is used for Discounts or Surcharge(eg: condition type K007, PSPR), 'B' is used for Basic prices(eg PR00), 'D' is used for taxes(eg MWST), etc.

Calculation type:

It specifies how the condition value will be calculated. 'A' for percentage, 'B' for fixed value, 'G' for formula, etc.

Condition Category:

This is another type of grouping the condition type. For example, this field is used for writing some routines such as G used for cost determination. Refer to Condition types VPRS(Cost), MWST(tax), etc.

Plus /Minus:

Blank means Positive or Negative(Meaning both are possible), 'X' for negative and 'A' for positive. Example: Discount must always be negative and Surcharge should always be positive (refer to condition type K007 and PSPR).

Group Condition:

In the case of header conditions, the group condition distributes the header condition values proportional to the line values. If it is not a group condition, the entire header value will be copied to all the lines as such.

Manual Entries:

It is an important field. It shows whether in the sales document we can alter the system calculated condition values or we can altogether enter in the document a new condition type and new values. To modify manually the system calculated values or to add new condition types in the sales documents, from the sales document overview session, select Goto-Item-Condition, or use appropriate buttons in the session.

Blank means No Limitation. For example, if you add manually in Sales Document, one more condition type in addition to the system picked same condition type, the total values of both these condition types are considered for the discounts.

'A', Free: If the condition record exists, it is as good as keeping Blank. If no record exists, you cannot enter a new condition type manually.

'B', Automatic entry has priority. If a condition record exists, the condition type cannot be entered manually. But if a record does not exist, it is as good as keeping it Blank.

'C': Manual entry has priority. When no record exists, it is as good as Blank.

When a record exists, discounts, etc are applicable for the system selected condition type. But when you enter a new condition type, the discount etc are applicable only to the manually entered condition type.

'D': Not possible to process manually. If a record exists, the system will take it. The System will not allow you to enter Condition Type manually, example condition type VPRS (Cost).

Amount/ Percentage:

If selected, you can modify the system calculated Amount and Percentage value of the condition records in the sales document.

Value:

If selected, you can modify the system calculated Condition Value in the Sales Document.

Header Conditions:

If marked, you can use the condition type in the header of the sales document. Header condition value is applicable to all line items of the sales document. To use a Header Condition Type in the sales document, go to Sales Order, select Goto-Header-Condition and then add this condition Type. Header Condition Type will work as manual Condition Type only.

You cannot link Access Sequence to a condition type if it is only a header condition. But, you can link Access Sequence to the condition type if it is a header as well as item condition.

Item condition:

If marked, you can use in the Sales Document Line items. You can link Access Sequence to an item condition only.

To use a Line Condition Type manually, go to Sales Order, select Goto-Line-Condition and then add this condition Type.

Note: In any way, if you want to use any condition type, it should have been included in the pricing procedure, refer to fig 3-12.

Reference Condition Type:

You can link here another condition type, if you want, to take the condition values from this reference condition type.

Pricing Procedure:

(PR0000): This pricing procedure is Condition Supplement Pricing Procedure. Condition supplement procedure is a group of condition types that should be applied every time this condition type is found. In this case, when the above condition type(ZCT1) is used, the system takes the prices maintained in all the condition types listed in the supplement procedure PR0000. For example, if you have a series of discounts that will be applicable for a particular material, you can use supplement procedure for easy record retrieval. While creating records [VK11] for the main parent condition type (here ZCT1), you can call the condition types listed in the supplement procedure (here PR0000) through Goto- Condition Supplements.

Condition Update:

If you select this field only you can maintain Limits for Pricing in Condition Records[VK11] by Goto- Additional Data. Refer to condition type K005. You can maintain the following limits for condition records, if you select this field:

Maximum Condition Value

Maximum number of orders

Maximum condition base value(Number of pieces/ weights etc.)

In addition to these controls, you can use OVB2(Path: IMG- Sales and Distribution- Basic Functions- Pricing- Pricing Control- Define Condition Types- Define upper/lower limits for conditions) to limit upper and lower limits for condition values.

V/06, Condition Type- Header and Line level

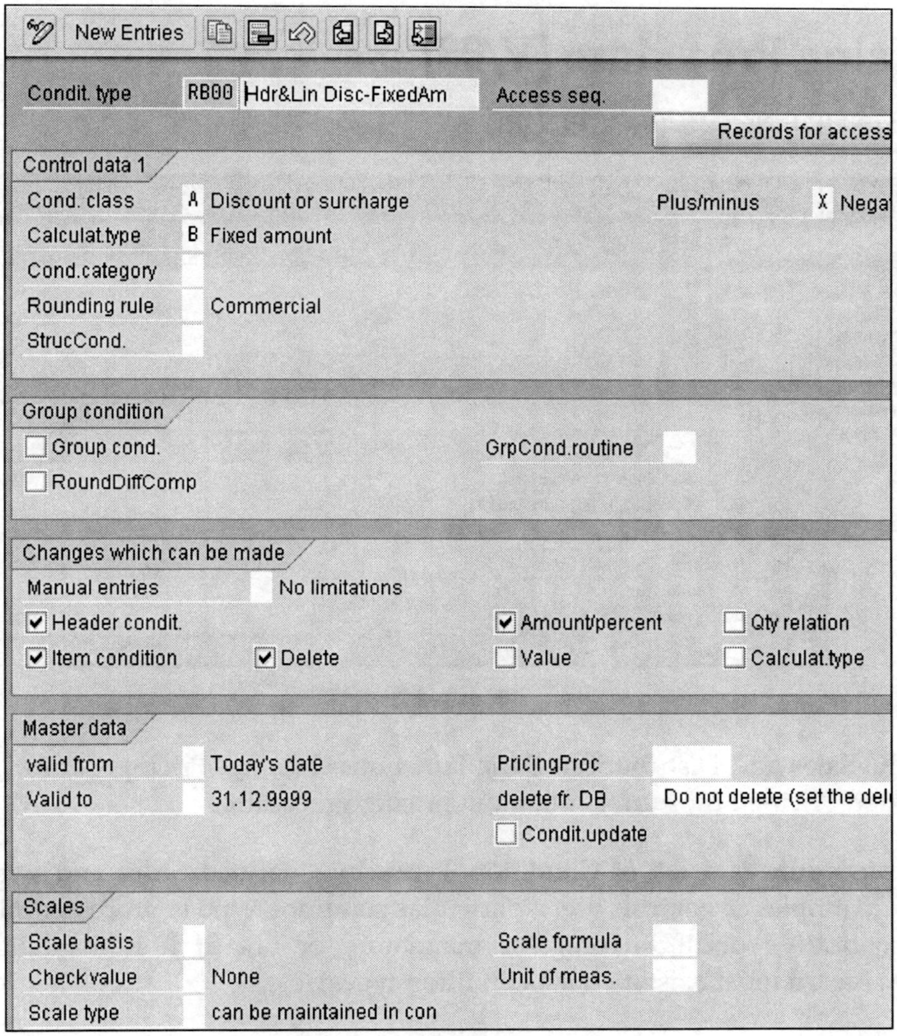

Fig:3-11

Please note that both 'Header condition' and 'Item condition' are marked for this condition type. Hence, this condition Type can be used in Header level and Item Level as well.

Now copy Condition Type PSPR to ZPSP and make it as an Item Condition for our excercise.

4. Pricing Procedure [V/08]

SETTING THE PRICING PROCEDURE.

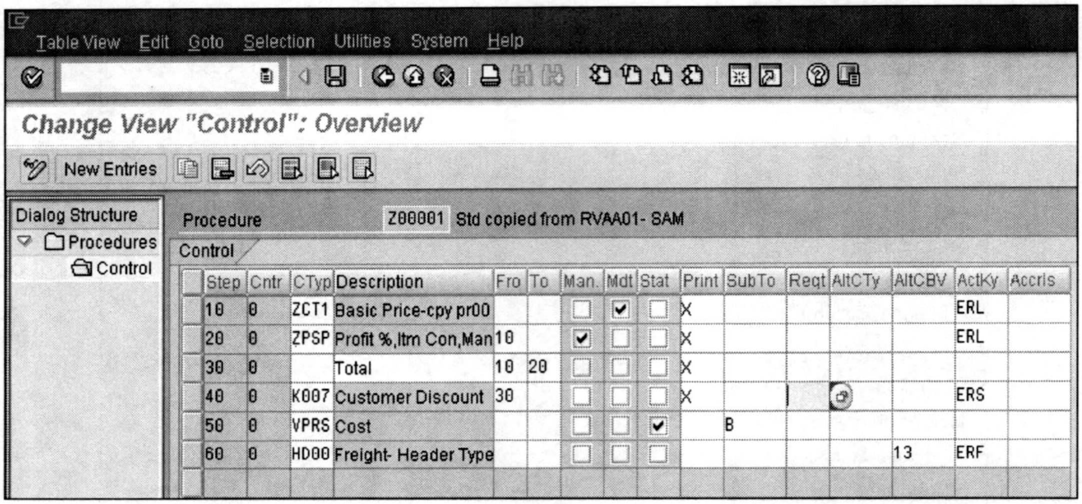

Fig:3-12

Path: IMG-Sales and Distribution- Basic Functions- Pricing- Pricing Control- Define And Assign Pricing Procedures- Maintain pricing procedures

Pricing procedure is a list of Condition Types in a defined order and with some controls. Examples of controls are: a particular condition type is processed manually or automatically, condition record is mandatory or not (if it is mandatory, the condition record must exist for such condition types), etc.

Pricing Procedure is determined by the system while creating Sales Documents. It is based on settings in the Pricing Procedure Determination which is explained in the Determination chapter.

Separate condition types are used for separate pricing elements, eg PR00 for base price, Z007 for Discounts, MWST for taxes, etc.

Remember that you can enter manually in a sales document only those condition types which are listed in the pricing procedure.

For our exercise, we will create a new Pricing Procedure Z00001 and link the following condition types to it.

Step 10.

Price Condition Type ZCT1:

This is a copy of the SAP standard condition type PR00 for basic price of the material.

This is an Item Condition Type and the Condition Class of the same is 'B', Price. To this condition type, we have already linked our Access Sequence ZABC. We will make it a mandatory condition type in our Pricing Procedure because without a basic price for the material, the sales document should not be processed.

Important: In the sales document, there should not be more than one condition types with condition class 'B' for calculating the net price.

Step 20.

Price Condition Type ZPSP:

This is a copy of SAP standard condition type PSPR and modified as an Item Condition Type. It is used as Surcharge because the sign sensitive is made as '+'. '+' is used for surcharge and '–' is used for discounts.

We will use it for adding profit percentage manually to each line item in the sales document. Since it is a manual Condition Type, we will not link any Access Sequence to it. Though it must also be set as a mandatory condition type in the Pricing Procedure, we will not make it as a mandatory Condition Type because we need to test how the manual condition type works. Generally the basic price includes the profit percentage, but to understand how the pricing conditions work, we assume that the condition type ZCT1 does not include the profit element.

Step 30.

No Condition Type:

No condition type is given for Total/ Gross etc. Just enter the description. Here we total up values of the above two condition types against this step.

Step 40.

Price Condition Type K007:

It is a SAP standard condition type for customer discount. It is an Item Condition Type. Access Sequence K007 is linked to it. Access Sequence K007 has only one condition table(with fields Sales Organisation, Distribution Channel, Division and Customer). We will use it to calculate Customer discount on total of the above 2 condition values.

Step 50.

Condition Type VPRS:

It is a SAP standard condition type for Standard Cost. It is a Line Condition Type and the system automatically adds to the sales document lines the Standard Cost from the Material Master (from Accounting 1 view). For this to happen, a programme is written against the Condition Category 'G'. We will use this condition type for our own internal reporting purposes and hence mark it as Statistics in the Pricing Procedure.

Step 60.

Price Condition Type HD00:

It is a SAP standard condition type for freight with condition class 'Discount and Surcharge' and Condition Category 'Freight'. It is a header condition type to be added at the header level with calculation type 'Gross Weight'.

Now with the above listed Condition Types, create a new Pricing Procedure Z00001 as shown in fig 3-12.

Note: While creating the above pricing procedure, the following message will appear while entering condition type VPRS.

Shown below is the message that appears when you add condition type VPRS to the above pricing procedure.

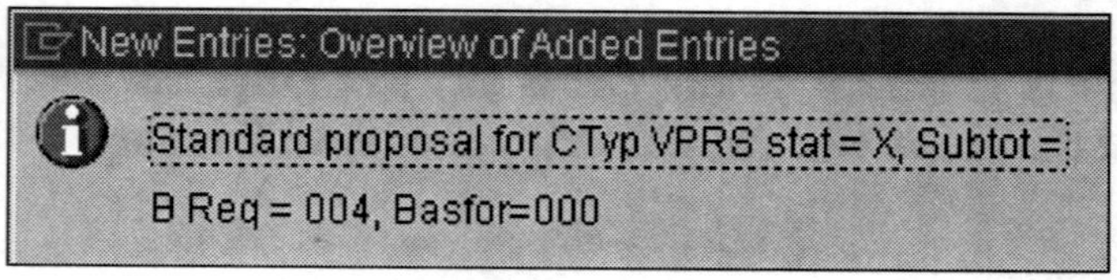

Fig: 3-13

This message is because SAP has some standard settings for some important condition types. It will be known to you during the course of this book. Ignore this message for the time being. Our aim is to understand the concept of pricing.

Field Explanations in the Pricing Procedure:

Step:

The Step Number decides in which order various condition types are to be accessed.

Counter:

The sub number under each Step Number.

From and To:

These fields refer to the step number of other condition types in the same pricing procedure.

Manual:

It indicates that this condition type is processed manually. Such condition type should not have Access Sequence linked to it. Access Sequences are linked to automatic condition types.

Mandatory:

If selected, no sales document can be created without maintaining valid pricing records for this Condition Type. Pricing Records can be maintained by the T-code VK11.

Statistical:

If marked, the value will not be considered for the net price calculation. It is used for internal statistical purposes. In our case, the standard cost is for our internal purposes.

Print:

Select X if the line details are to be printed on the order confirmations, invoices etc.

SubTotal, Requirement, Alternative Calculation Type and Alternative Condition Base Value:

These 4 fields are special fields which are used for special needs. These fields are used to create some sub-routines for special purposes. SAP has some sub-routines written against these fields and if useful for your needs, you can use it. Otherwise you can create your own programs and use them. Refer to the pricing procedure RVAA01 for more details.

Sub-Total:

In our example, condition type VPRS is linked to Sub-total B (Carry over value to KOMP-WAVWR). This indicate that the value of this condition type will be passed to some other fields which in turn can be used for statistical calculation, if needed.

Requirement:

It is used for additional needs, if needed. For example, you can specify that this Discount Condition Type is to be accessed only if the customer does not have any overdues.

Alternative Calculation Type:

If you specify an alternative formula in the field Alternative Calculation Type, this new formula will be used instead of the Calculation Type mentioned in the condition type.

Alternative Condition Base Value:

In our example, for condition type HD00, we have linked Alternative Condition Base Value as 13(Net Weight). By default, the condition base value for HD00 is Gross Weight(the field 'Calculation Type' for the condition type HD00 is Gross Weight). As the field in the Pricing Procedure has an upper hand, the system will consider the net weight of the material instead of the gross weight of the material while calculating the Freight amount.

Account key:

The account key is used to determine to which General Ledger account the value of the sale is to be posted. The key entered here is used in the Account Determination set up, a mandatory set up for pricing. If Account Determination is not set up, the

error 'G/L account Number Missing' will appear while the sales document is being created. Refer to the Account Determination in the chapter 'Determination' later.

Accrual Key:

This field is used for accruing of rebate amounts which will be settled with the customer in a phased manner. The Path for defining account key is IMG-Sales and Distribution-Basic Functions-Account Assignment/Costing-Revenue Account Determination-Define And Assign Account Keys.

Refer to the standard pricing procedure RVAA01 for more details.

5. Price Condition Record [VK11]

Let us maintain prices for all the condition types listed in the Pricing Procedure Z00001, fig 3-12

Condition Record creation.

Price Condition Records are to be maintained in condition tables for each automatic condition types (automatic means a condition type to which an Access Sequence is linked). We will use the simple process of entering condition records. For example, we will create price condition records for our price condition type ZCT1(Basic Material Price). The same method is used for all the condition types and hence, creation of condition records for ZCT1 only is explained here.

Note: If a Pricing Reference Material is linked inside the material master (refer to Sales Org 2 of the materials master), you must create the condition record for the reference material.

Create Price Condition Records.

[VK11] Creating Condition Records for Condition Type ZCT1

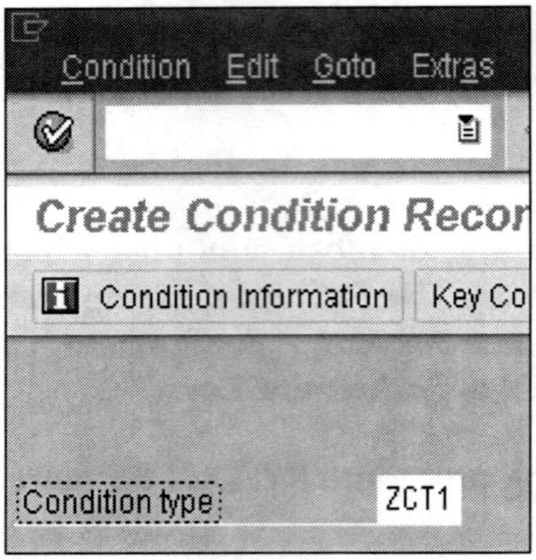

Fig:3-14

Path: Logistics- SD-Master Data-Conditions-Select Using Condition Type- Create.

On Entering the condition type as above, the following screen appears.

VK11, Options for selecting condition tables of Condition Type ZCT1.

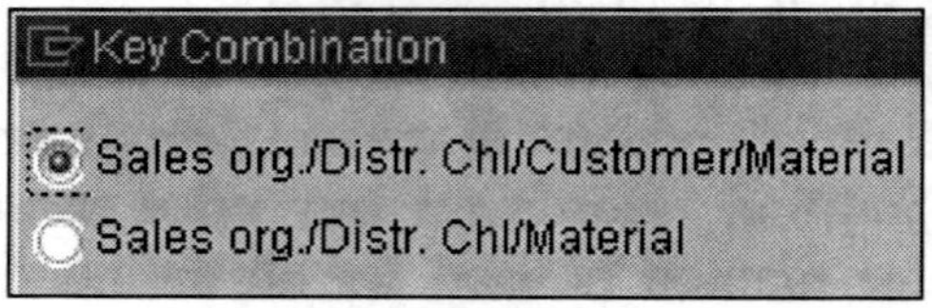

Fig:3-15

Here you are presented with 2 tables to choose from. This is because the Access Sequence linked to the Condition Type ZCT1 has the above 2 tables.

If only one condition table is linked to the access sequence, you will not be given an option for selection.

We will maintain most specific data. Hence, choose the first table(by Customer and Material). On selecting the first table, the following screen appears for entering the material price.

Let us maintain price INR 1000 for material M123 and INR 2000 for material M456.

VK11, Entering Material Prices for materials M123 and M456.

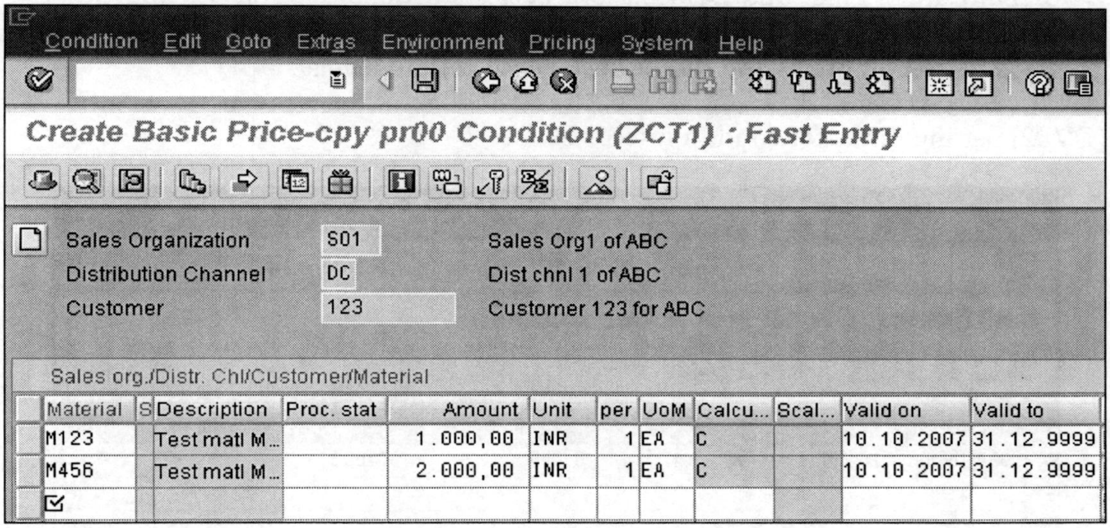

Fig:3-16

As shown above, fill up the Sales Organization, Dist Channel, customer, material codes and amounts only and press Enter. The other data gets populated automatically. Then Save the data.

Use VK12 to view and modify the data, if you want.

If you want, you can maintain records for the second table (by Material) also. But if a record is found in the first table, the system will pick the value from the first table and stop searching records in the other table because we have set Exclusive indicator in our Access Sequence ZABC.

Similarly, create condition records for the other automatic condition type K007. Give 50% discount on (Material + Profit). We will enter condition records manually in the Sales Document for manual condition types ZPSP and HD00. The System will automatically pick up condition record(standard cost)from the material master for condition type VPRS. This will be explained in the chapter Sales Transactions.

If you want to maintain records by scale values, mark the line and click on the 'scale' button in the application tool bar(Or select Goto- Scale).

Scale values are mainly used in discounts. For example 1 % discount up to order value 1000, 2 % discount up to order value 5000 etc.

You can limit the upper and lower limits for condition records through the session OVB2(Path: IMG- Sales and Distribution- Basic Functions- Pricing- Pricing Control- Define Condition Types- Define upper/lower limits for conditions) as shown below. This will help limit prices and discounts beyond certain levels.

[OVB2] Setting limits for condition records:

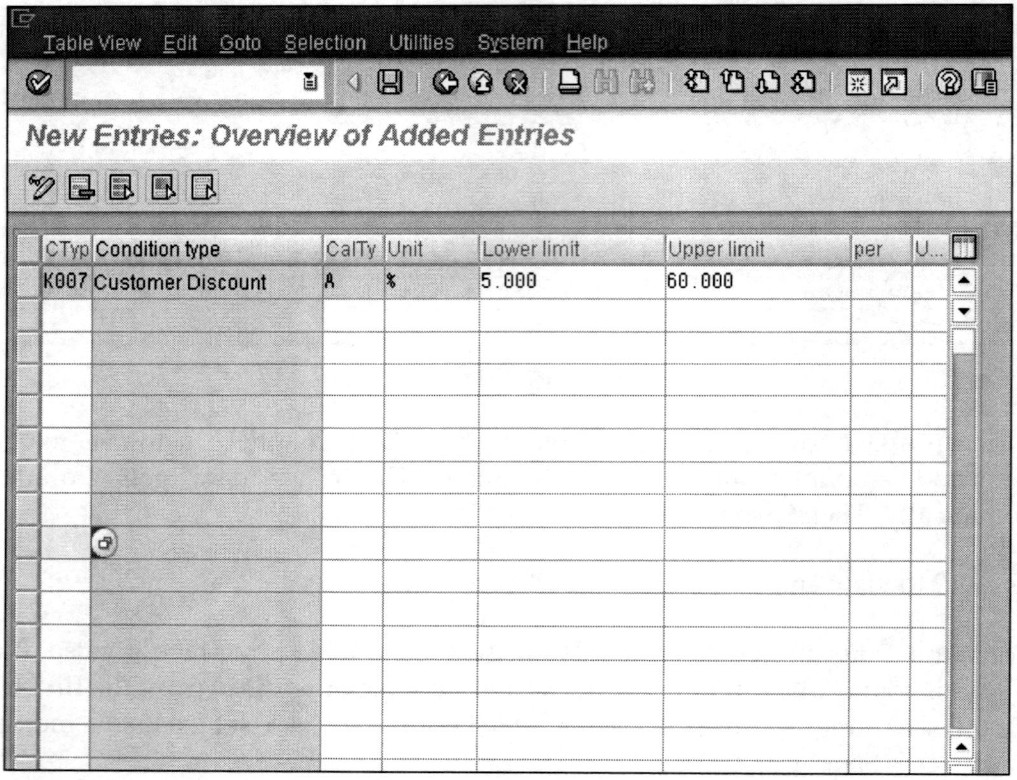

Fig:3-17

Path: IMG- Sales and Distribution- Basic Functions- Pricing- Pricing Control- Define Condition Types- Define upper/lower limits for conditions

Chapter 4

DETERMINATIONS

Introduction

Many of the master data are determined by the system and automatically picked while we do the transactions. Hence, we must set up the system for the same. This technique is used for fast and appropriate data retrieval.

For example, prices are selected by the system automatically when we create sales orders. This is bases on the Pricing Procedure Determination.

After setting the Enterprise structure, Master Data and Pricing, you can set up all the Determinations. The following are the Determinations to be set up for processing sales documents:

Mandatory Determinations:
Order Item Category Determinations [VOV4]

Delivery Item Category Determinations [0184]

Schedule Line Category Determinations [VOV5]

Pricing Procedure Determinations [OVKK]

Partner function Determinations for Customers

Account Determinations

Shipping Point Determinations [OVl2]

Optional determinations:

Picking Location/ Storage Location Determinations [OVL3]

Route Determinations [0VRF]

Order Item Category Determination [VOV4]

Based on Order Item Category Determination set up, the Order Item Category(OIC) is picked up by the system when the sales order is created. Refer to the sales order created in the chapter Sales Transactions to see the system picked Item Categories.

[VOV4], Assignment of Item Category(Determination of Order Item Category).

SaTy	ItCGr	Usg.	HLevItCa	DfltC	MltCa	MltCa	MltCa
OR	NORM			TAN	TAP	TAQ	TANN
OR	NORM		TAC	TAE			
OR	NORM		TAE	TAE			
OR	NORM		TAG	TAN			
OR	NORM		TAK	TANN	TAN		

Fig:4-1 A

Path: IMG-Sales and Distribution-Sales-Sales Documents-Sales Document Item-Define Item Categories.

In this session, you cannot make more than one records with the same combination of the first 4 fields(SDT, Item Category Group, Usage and Higher Level Item Category). With the above setup, (Sales Document Type = OR and the Item Category Group = NORM) the Item Category TAN will be picked by the system when we create the sales order. Then, if you want, you can change manually in the sales document the OIC to TAP, TAQ or TANN. Item categories listed in this session only can be used for such replacement in the sales documents.

Let us set up our OIC determination:

Now set up, if it does not exist in the system, the following OIC determination to test our sales transactions later.

[VOV4], Assignment of Item Category(Determination of Order Item Category)

SDT	ICG	Usg.	HLIC	Def IC	Man IC	Man IC	Man IC
ZOR	NORM			TAN	TAP	TAQ	TANN

Fig:4-1 B

Item Category Group(ICG):

Item category group is linked to the material master in the Sales Org 2 tab(right one).

Usage:

This field is not used in normal cases. But there are a few predefined keys such as FREE, TEXT etc for which some routines are written. Hence do not use this field if you are not sure of the routines. Refer to the figure below to understand how the Usage 'TEXT' works.

[VOV4] Explanation of the field 'Usage' in Item Category Determination.

SDT	ICG	Usg	HLIC	OIC
OR		TEXT		TATX

Fig:4-2

As per the above setup, without Material code, if you enter just a text(description) in the Description column in the Sales Order(Sales order created with SDT *OR*), the Order Item Category TATX will be selected by the system.

Higher Level Item Category(HLIC):

This field also is not used in normal cases. It is mainly used for Bill Of Material(BOM) Process, Free Goods process etc. Refer to the BOM Process in the appendix to know the functionality of HLIC.

Delivery Item Category Determination [0184]

If the Delivery is created with reference to a sales order, codes of DIC in the delivery document lines will be the codes of OIC of relevant sales order lines. For example, if 'TAN' is the OIC of a sales order line, the DIC code of the relevant Delivery Document line will be again 'TAN'.

But if you want to add one more line manually to this delivery document, the new DIC will be picked as per the Delivery Item Category determination[0184].

When you create the Order Item Category(OIC) by copying from another OIC, the DIC and DIC Determination are also created. Anyway, please check up whether the DIC determination is available in the system. Otherwise, you must set up DIC determinations for your DDTs.

DIC determination must be set up if an additional delivery line is to be added directly in the Delivery Document. For example, you may have to add packing material in the delivery document manually.

Also DIC is needed when you make delivery documents without any order reference, for example for returning of goods to the supplier. Refer to Delivery Document Type[0VLP] in the chapter Master Data for more details.

Ensure that the following DIC determination set up is available in the system. Otherwise, set up the same.

[0184] DIC Determination

DDT	ICG	Usg	HLDIC	DIC
LF	NORM			DLN

Fig:4-3

Path: IMG-Logistics Execution-Shipping-Deliveries-Define Item Category Determination in Deliveries.

Fields: (DDT)- (Item Category Group from Material)-(some free text as Usage)-(Higher Level DIC)- (DIC).

The Usage and HLDIC are not used in normal cases. Refer to the OIC determination for more details.

Schedule Line Category Determination [VOV5]

Schedule lines are created while creating Sales Orders. You can view the schedule lines in the sales order by selecting Goto- Item- Schedule Lines.

Schedule Line Category(SLC) decides finally whether the materials are to be delivered or not. The Movement Type in the SLC decides the movement of material.

Order Item Category and/or MRP Type decide Schedule Line Category (SLC) in Schedule lines.

MRP type is taken from the material master.

Make sure that our OIC *TAN* and SLC *CP* are set up as shown in the figure below.

[VOV5], Determining Schedule Line Categories.

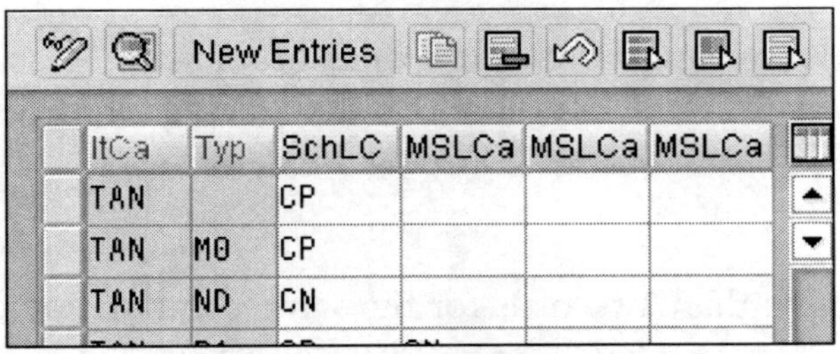

ItCa	Typ	SchLC	MSLCa	MSLCa	MSLCa
TAN		CP			
TAN	M0	CP			
TAN	ND	CN			

Fig:4-4

Path: IMG-Sales and Distribution- Sales- Sales Documents- Schedule Lines- Assign Schedule Line Categories.

Fields: (OIC) – (MRP Type from Material Master)-(SLC)-(manual SLC)

OIC in the sales order is determined by the system through OIC Determination [VOV4].

Pricing Procedure Determination [OVKK]

Pricing Procedure is automatically determined by the system while creating Sales Documents such as Sales Order, Sales Inquiry, Sales quotation etc.

The determined pricing procedure and other details can be seen in the Analysis View of the Sales Document. To view Analysis from the Sales Document, select Goto- Item-Conditions- Analysis.

[OVKK], Pricing Procedure determination.

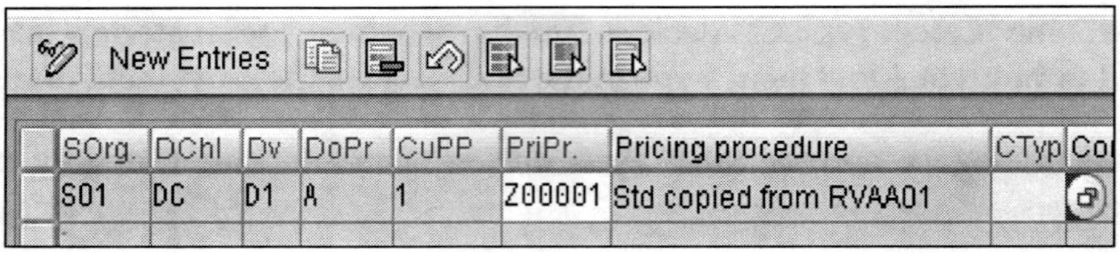

Fig:4-5

Path: IMG-Sales and Distribution- Basic Functions- Pricing- Pricing Control- Define And Assign Pricing Procedures-Define Pricing Procedure Determination.

Make the above Pricing Procedure determination set up for our exercise.

With the above setup, when you create a sales order with Sales Organisation SO1, Distribution Channel DC and Division D1, the pricing procedure Z00001 will be selected if your SDT has Document Pricing Procedure 'A' and the customer has Customer Pricing Procedure'1'

You cannot make more than 1 records for the same combination of the first 5 fields(Sales Organisation, Distribution Channel, Div, Doc pp and Cu pp)

Sales Organisation, Distribution Channel, Division, SDT and Customer are entered at the header level while creating the Sales Document.

The Document Pricing Procedure is entered in the SDT and the Customer Pricing Procedure is entered in Customer master. Refer to SDT and Customer Master in the chapter Master Data for more details.

Hence, effectively the combination of Sales Area, SDT and Customer Code decides the Pricing Procedure. The pricing procedure is decided at the header level of the sales order.

To pick up the same Pricing Procedure for your Sales Inquiry, Sales Quotation, Sales Order etc, please verify that the same Document Pricing Procedure and Customer Pricing Procedure are linked to the relevant SDT and Customer respectively.

Partner Determinations

Partners such as SP(sold to party), SH(ship to party), BU(Buyer), PY(Payer), BP(Bill to party), etc, appear in the system at various levels such as in customer, sales document header, sales document line, Delivery header, Billing header, Billing line, etc. The levels at which partner functions must exist are listed below in fig: 4-7.

When you create these master data(Account Group, SDT, OIC, DDT, BDT, etc) by copying an existing master, the partner functions also get copied.

In certain documents, certain partner functions are mandatory. For example, in sales order, partner functions SP, SH, PY and BP are mandatory.

When you assign a partner determination procedure(PDP) to an account group, the partner functions are assigned to customer masters when you create the customer masters with this account group.

Similarly when a PDP is assigned to a sales document type, the partner functions are assigned to the sales document header when this sales document type is used.

To link partner determination procedures to the account group, SDT, etc. separate sessions are used which are shown below in fig: 4-7

We explain here only the Partner Determination for Customer Master. You can explore other procedures at your own pace later.

Partner Determination Procedure AG is used for creating customers with four partner functions(SP, SH, BP and PY). AG is linked to Account Group 0001 and hence this Account Group is used to create Customer Masters with partner functions SP, SH, BP and PY. PDP specifies which partner functions are allowed ,which are mandatory and which are not modifiable, etc.

For billing documents, for example, you can specify a partner determination procedure where the sold-to party, bill-to party, and payer are mandatory but the ship-to party is not mandatory because for billing, you are more interested in who orders and pays for the goods than who receives the goods.

Let us use the existing partner determinations for our exercise.

Path for Partner Determination Procedures.

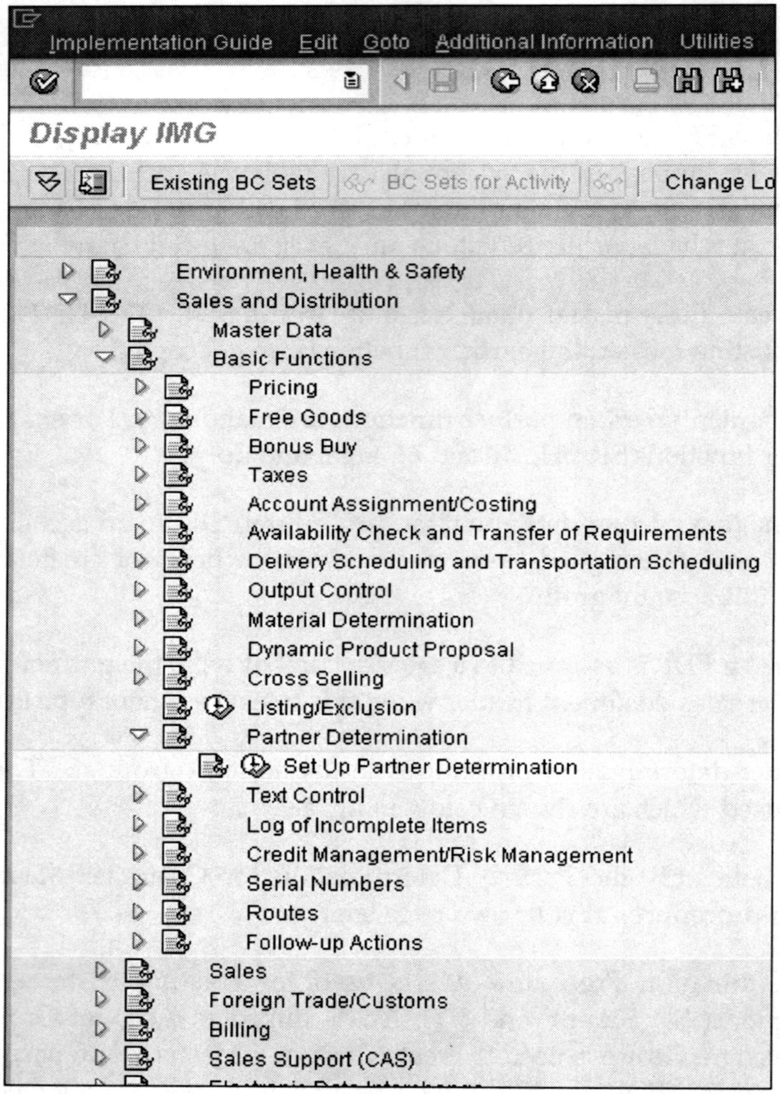

Fig:4-6

Path: IMG- SD –BF

Various sessions for Partner Determinations.

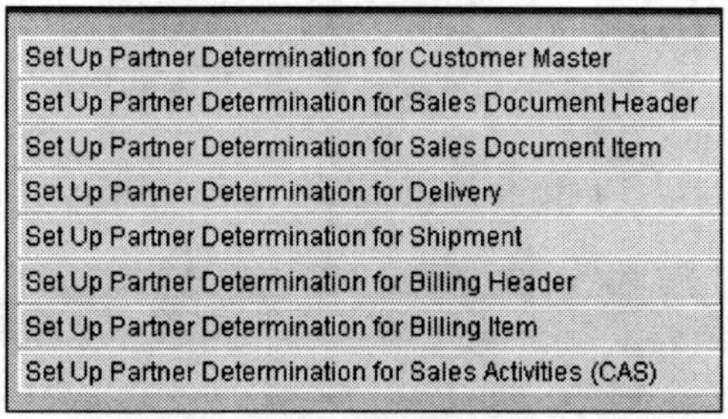

Fig:4-7

Path: IMG- SD-BF-Partner Determination-Setup Partner Determination.

Partner Determination for Customers.

Click on the first option in fig 4-7 to Set Up Partner Determination for Customers.

Set Up Partner Determination for Customer

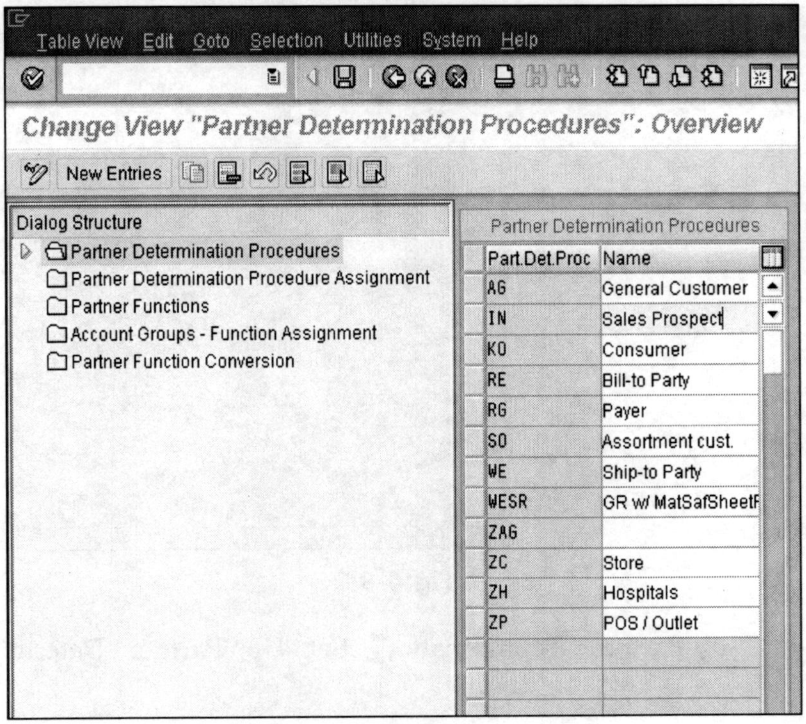

Fig:4-8

This screen shows various partner determination procedures used for creating different types of customer masters.

Select PDP *AG* and click on 'Partner Functions in Procedure' as shown below:

Maintain Partner Functions (Partner Functions in Procedure) for PDP *AG*

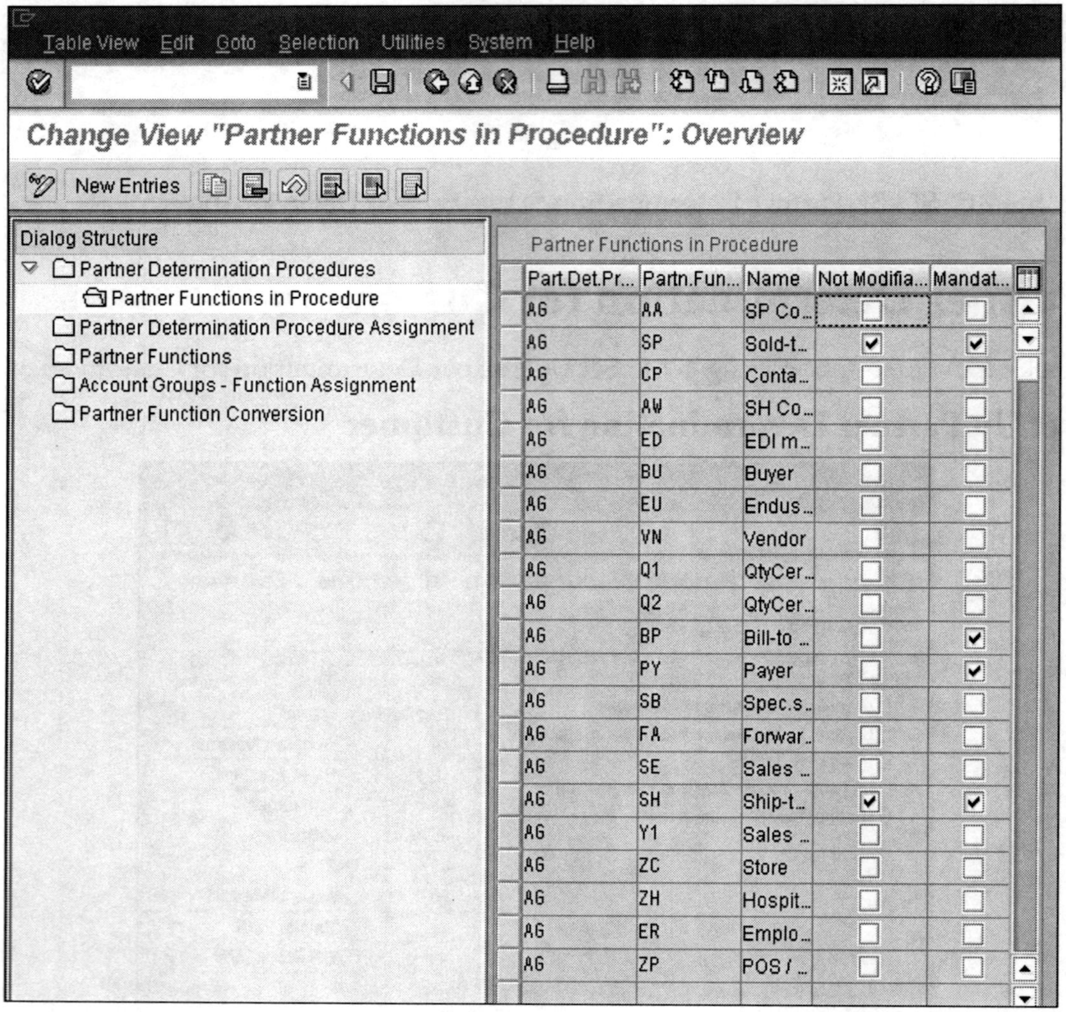

Fig:4-9

Path: IMG- SD-BF-Partner Determination- Set Up Partner Determination for Customer.

Note: Refer to fig 4-10 B below to know partner functions for PDP *WE*(Ship-to party).

The above session(fig 4-9) shows the partner functions for partner determination procedure AG.

Partner functions SP, BP, PY and SH are mandatory for AG. Hence, make these 4 partner functions as mandatory here.

The above screen shows that for Partner Determination Procedure AG, Partner functions like AA, SP, CP etc are all allowed. Two functions(SP and SH) are not modifiable in the customer master and four functions SP, BP, PY and SH are mandatory.

These mandatory partner functions must be linked to account group 0001 in the session **Account Group-Function Assignment**(shown below in fig 4-10). Then the partner functions marked Mandatory here will appear, by default, in the customer master created with the account group 0001. You can add manually in the customer master additional partner functions mentioned here. Refer to session help from the system for more information.

Maintain Mandatory Functions by Account Group 0001(Account Groups-Function Assignment)

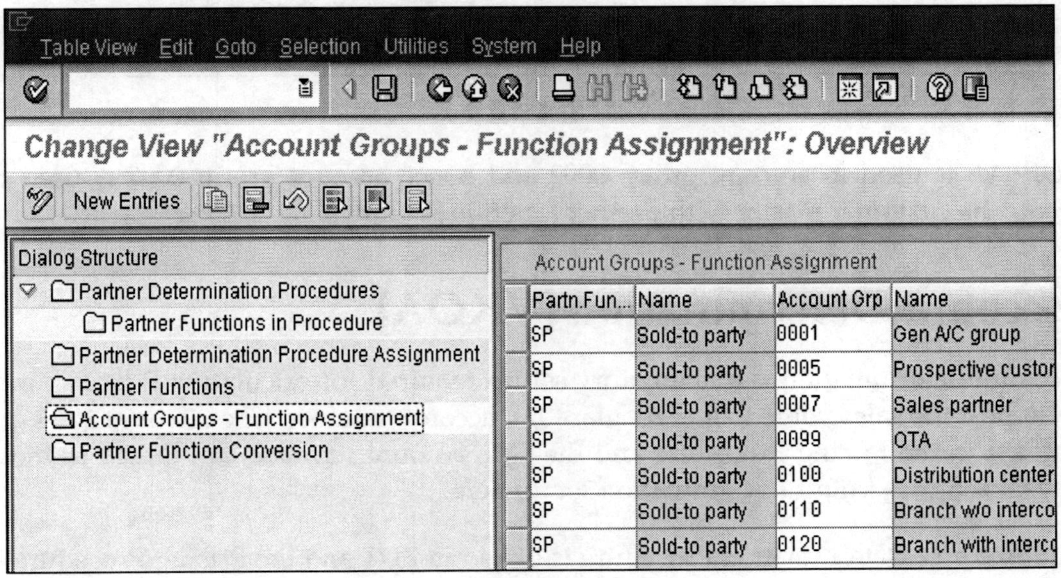

Fig:4-10

Path: IMG- SD-BF-Partner Determination- Set Up Partner Determination for Customer

In this session you must link all the Mandatory partner functions(SP,BP,PY and SH) to the A/C group 0001.

Example to show partner functions for PDP *WE*(Ship-to party).

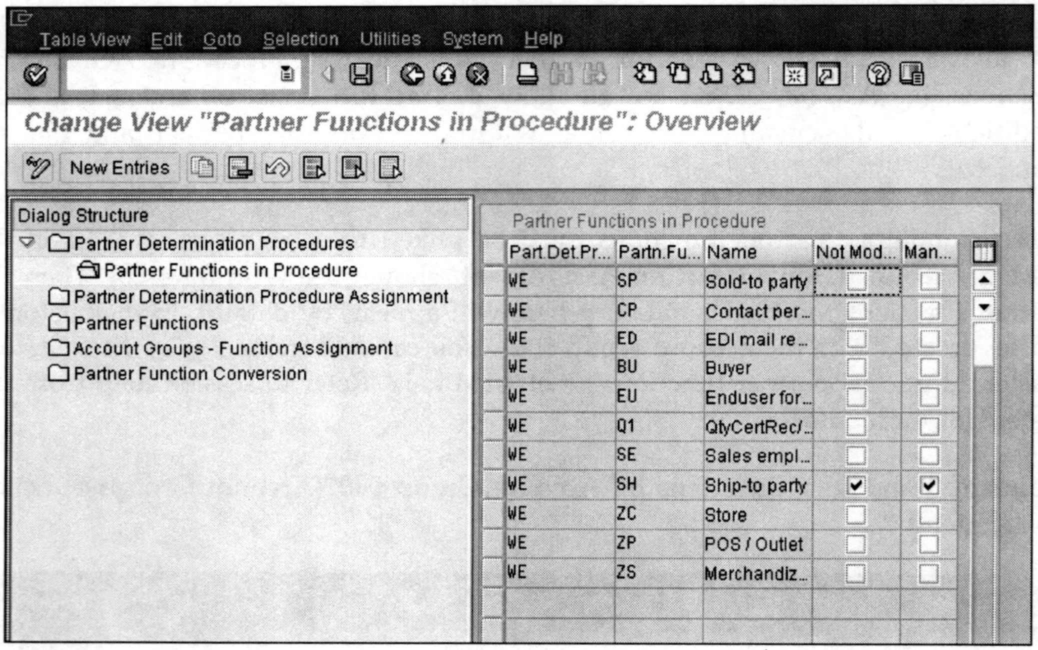

Fig 4-10 B

PDP *WE* is used in account group 0002 and hence account group 0002 is used to create the customer master with partner function SH only.

Account Determination [VKOA]

Account determination is a mandatory set up required for calculating Prices as well as to post the sales value to a particular G/L account number. The Account Keys are entered in the Pricing Procedure and the G/L account numbers are linked to those keys through Account Determination set up here.

The Account Determination Procedure is linked in BDT and the Pricing Procedure is selected by the system when the sales order is created.

Let us use the existing Account Determination set up from the system.

The following are the procedures to be followed to set up account determination:

1. Maintain Account Access Sequence and link existing Account Condition Tables to it.
2. Define the Account Condition Type and link the Access Sequence to it.
3. Define the Account Determination Procedure and link Account Condition Types to it with standard requirements
4. Assign G/L accounts to Account Condition Types and Account Keys
5. Link Account Determination Procedure to ADT.

1. Maintain Access Sequences And Account Determination Types.

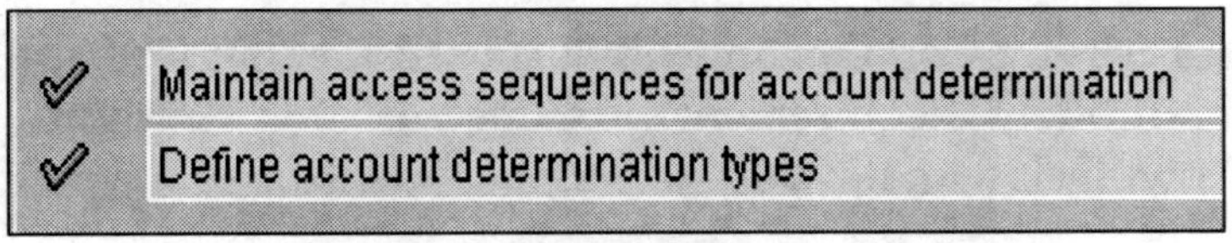

Fig:4-11

Path: IMG-Sales and Distribution-Basic Functions-Account Assignment/Costing-Revenue Account Determination-Define Access Sequences And Account Determination Types.

Choose the first option, Maintain access sequences for account determination.

Access Sequence KOFI

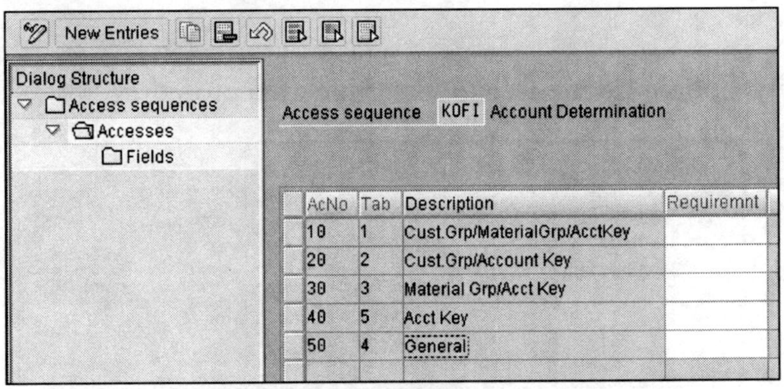

Fig:4-12

Here you are defining Access Sequence and linking existing Tables to it in the order of preference.

2. Choose the second option, Define account determination Types

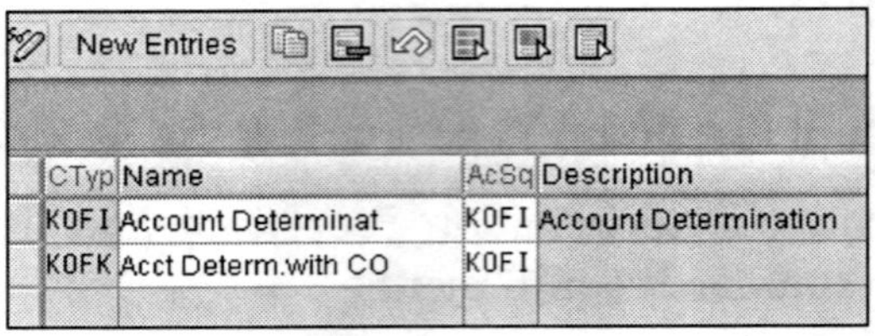

Fig:4-13

Here you define Account Determination Types(Account Condition Types) and link Access Sequence to it. Please note that the same Access Sequence KOFI is assigned to Account Condition Types KOFI and KOFK.

KOFK is used for Service Contract and KOFI is used for standard application. These are controlled through Requirement Routine in the Account Determination Procedure as shown below in fig: 4-15

3. Define and Assign Account Determination Procedures

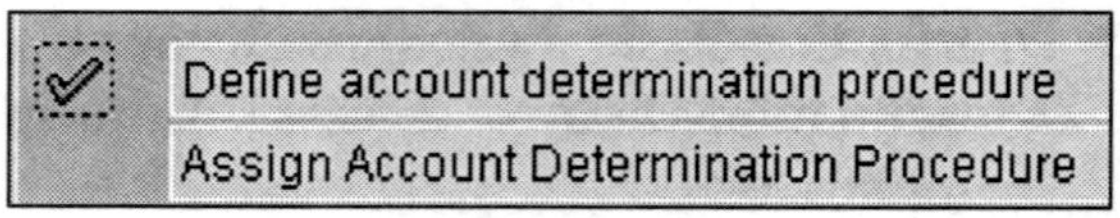

Fig:4-14

Path: IMG-Sales and Distribution-Basic Functions-Account Assignment/Costing-Revenue Account Determination- Define And Assign Account Determination Procedures.

Choose the first option, Define account determination procedure

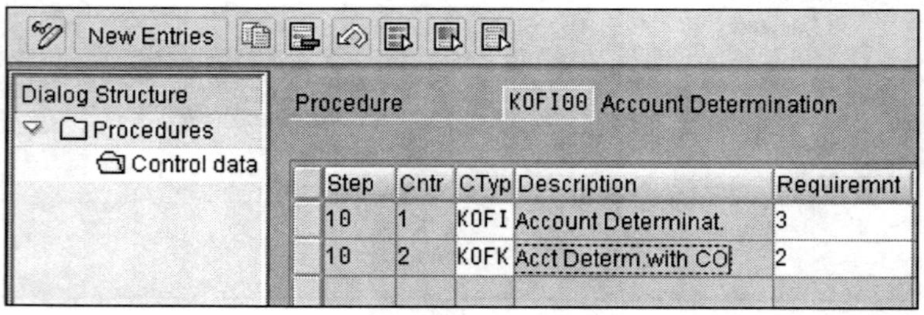

Fig:4-15

Here you define the Account Determination Procedure and link the Account Condition Types with standard Requirements.

Here the account Condition types KOFI and KOFK are linked to the procedure KOFI00.

Here the field 'Requirement' is very important. It is a routine(some formula) and in the case of service contracts, the routine 2(Account Assignment with controlling) is applicable and hence, in the case of service contracts, you must maintain account for KOFK. Otherwise you will get a message like 'G/L account Missing' while creating service contracts.

But for normal business applications, the requirement 3 is used and Account Condition Type KOFI is considered.

4. [VKOA], Assign G/L Accounts.

Assign G/L Accounts

Table	Description
001	Cust.Grp/MaterialGrp/AcctKey
002	Cust.Grp/Account Key
003	Material Grp/Acct Key
004	General
005	Acct Key
007	Vendor

Fig:4-16

Path: IMG-Sales and Distribution-Basic Functions-Account Assignment/Costing-Revenue Account Determination -Assign G/L Accounts.

This is the session where you assign various G/L accounts to the account keys you have entered in the Pricing Procedure[V/08].

To assign keys to G/L accounts, double click on any table. Let us maintain G/L accounts to most specific table 001. Hence, double click on table 001 to get the following session.

[VKOA], Assigning keys to G/L Accounts for the most specific table 001.

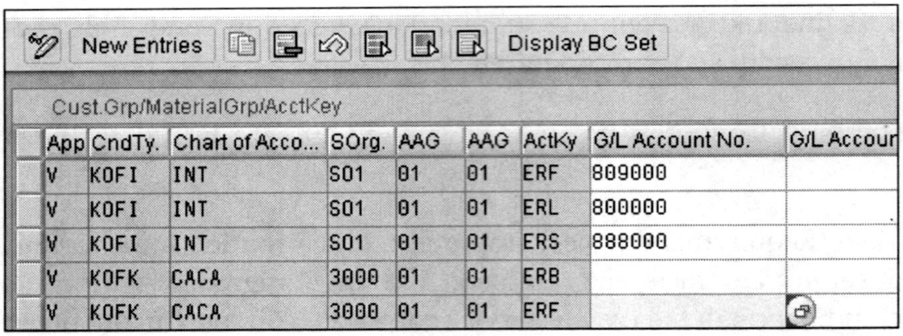

App	CndTy.	Chart of Acco...	SOrg.	AAG	AAG	ActKy	G/L Account No.	G/L Accour
V	KOFI	INT	S01	01	01	ERF	809000	
V	KOFI	INT	S01	01	01	ERL	800000	
V	KOFI	INT	S01	01	01	ERS	888000	
V	KOFK	CACA	3000	01	01	ERB		
V	KOFK	CACA	3000	01	01	ERF		

Fig:4-17

The first AAG is account assignment group for the customer and the next AAG is account assignment group for Material. These are linked in Customers and Materials respectively and if these customers and materials are used while creating sales documents, the accounts assigned here are used for posting to the finance. A chart of account for our company is linked in Value Areas in Miscellaneous set up.

If matching records are found, the G/L account for posting sales revenue is determined and the search is terminated.

For easy learning purpose, it is better to maintain records for table 005 also.

If you use Service Contracts, you must maintain in this session accounts for Account Determination Type KOFK also.

5. Please see that the proper Account Determination Procedure is assigned in your BDT.

Account Determination Procedure is assigned in the Billing Document Type(BDT) [VOFA]. Refer to BDT for more information.

Shipping Point Determination[OVL2]

Shipping point determination is a mandatory requirement for creating sales documents.

Shipping Point is automatically selected by the system when the sales document is created.

Shipping point determined by the system, can be seen in the shipping tab of sales document overview. Refer to the definition of Shipping Point in the chapter Enterprise Set up for more details.

[OVL2] Shipping Point Determination.

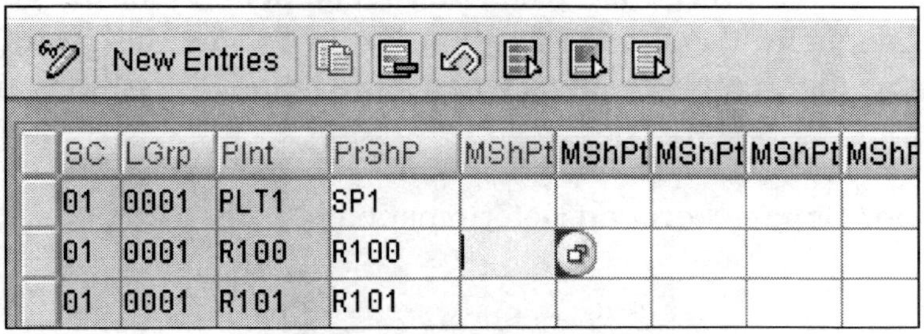

SC	LGrp	Plnt	PrShP	MShPt	MShPt	MShPt	MShPt	MShF
01	0001	PLT1	SP1					
01	0001	R100	R100					
01	0001	R101	R101					

Fig:4-18

Path: IMG- Log Exec- Shipping- Basic Shipping Function- Shipping point and Goods Receiving point determination - assign shipping points.

In this session, you assign shipping points to the desired combinations of shipping condition, loading group and Delivering plant. The Delivering plant is searched in the following order:

1. Customer- Material information [VD51]
   (Path: EA-Logistics-SD-MD-Rebate Agreements)
2. Ship to party
3. Material master.

As we are using our own plant and shipping point, set up the Shipping point Determination for the plant PLT1 and shipping point SP1 as shown in the fig above.

Set the shipping point here which should appear in the sales document's shipping line as a default shipping point. You can specify here other shipping points which you can replace manually in the sales order line.

Note: Shipping Condition is given in the customer master and Loading Group is given in the material master.

If shipping point determination is not maintained, you will get an error message **'Shipping point is not defined for this transaction'** while creating sales documents like Quotations, Sales Orders, etc.

Picking Location/ Storage Location Determination [OVL3].

This set up is not mandatory. But, if you have more than one storage locations defined for your plant, every time when you make delivery of the goods, you will have to enter manually the storage location. To overcome this, you can make the system determine the storage locations when more than one locations are defined for the same plant.

Picking Location/ Storage Location Determination.

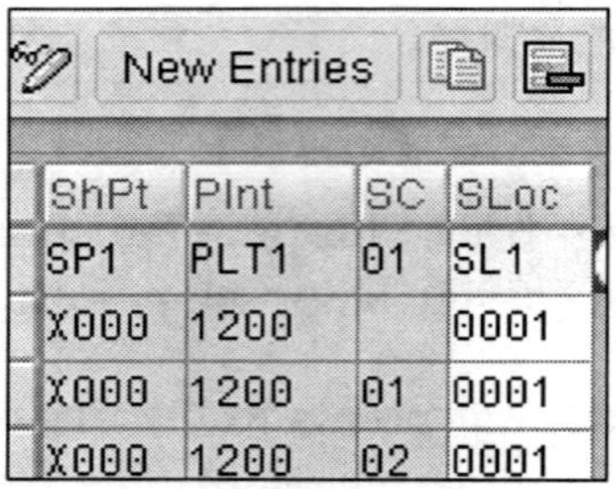

ShPt	Plnt	SC	SLoc
SP1	PLT1	01	SL1
X000	1200		0001
X000	1200	01	0001
X000	1200	02	0001

Fig:4-19

Path: IMG- Logistics Execution- Shipping- Picking- Determine Picking Location- Assign Picking Locations

The Combination of Shipping Point and Plant and Storage Condition determines the Storage Location. Storage Condition is entered in the Material master (Plant Data screen). This determination is based on the MALA rule specified in the field ' Storage Location Rule' in DDT.

Route Determination [0VRF]

This set up is not mandatory. If you want, you can set up the route determination for each item in the delivery. Route determination can be set up with Weight group or without weight group.

Route Determination without weight group [0VRF].

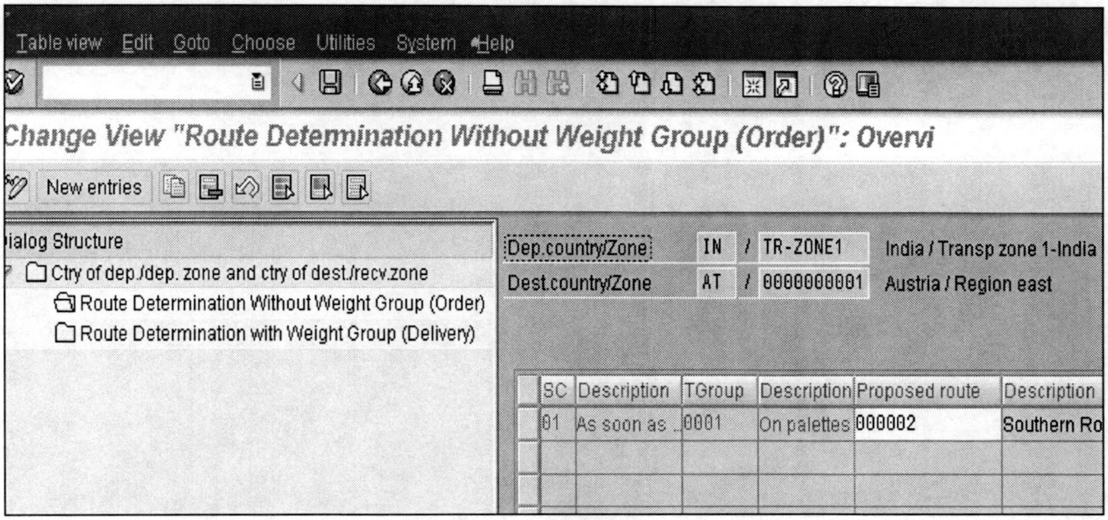

Fig:4-20

Path: IMG-Sales and Distribution-Basic Functions- Routes-Route Determination

Departure country zone + Destination country zone + Shipping Condition + Transportation group decide the Route.

Chapter 5

SALES TRANSACTIONS

Now you are ready to make the sales transactions, which are the main processes of SAP Sales and Distribution. After setting the Enterprise Structure, Master Data, Pricing and Determinations, you can create sales documents, delivery documents, billing documents and accounting documents.

The three main documents that control the entire sales processes are SDT, OIC and SLC.

The Sales process begins with your customer sending his purchase order to you. His purchase order will contain his purchase order number and his 'Requested Delivery Date' (RDD). RDD is the date that he wants the material to be delivered at his site.

If you accept his Purchase Order, you must plan your sales process to make sure that the customer is delivered the material on RDD.

Planning involves Procurement(in house production or purchasing the product from a vendor), picking, packing, shipping etc. The concept of Shipment

Scheduling/ Delivery Scheduling is used to find out when the procurement process is to start.

First, the system uses backward scheduling from the RDD to see whether material can be delivered on RDD. If not, it uses forward scheduling and recommends another date(an extended date) of delivery.

If the original RDD can be met, the system confirms that RDD as the Confirmed Delivery Date(CDD). Otherwise, the new date is fixed as CDD.

After delivering the materials to the customer, you can create billing documents

(Invoices) and send the same to customers. Then the payment will be received from the customers by our finance department based on the terms and conditions. The accounting document created in the sales process controls the payment receipts.

Introduction:

The Sales Order process is the main process in the Sales and Distribution module of SAP. As the aim of this book is to impart the basic concept of SD functions, here we explain only the following basic processes:

1. Create Sales Orders,
2. Create Delivery Documents,
3. Create Billing and/ Accounting Documents.

Once you understand these basic steps and with your real time domain experience in Sales and Marketing, you must be able to learn other functions of SD by your own efforts. Extensive online help tools are available on every SAP sessions and you can explore all the sessions one by one in the drill down menu of SAP SD.

If you have already made all the setups mentioned in the earlier chapters(Enterprise set up, Master data creations, Pricing and Determinations), you must be able to complete the sales transactions as shown in this chapter.

A sales document comprises of three levels. They are:

1. Sales Document header

Data for Sales Document header is valid for the entire document

2. Sales Document Lines.

Each line(Item) in the sales document has its own data.

3. Schedule Lines for sales order lines.

It contains Delivery Date, Delivery quantity, Schedule Line Category, Delivery blocking details, etc.

Now let us create a Sales Order.

Note: Before creating sales orders, please make sure that you have made all the following mandatory setups

1. Mandatory determinations especially Shipping Point determination[OVL2], Account Determination[VKOA] and Pricing Procedure Determinations [OVKK]
2. Mandatory Pricing records [VK11]
3. Periods are closed till the current period [OMSY] and [MMPV]
4. Sufficient stock is available for the materials[MB1C] and [MMBE]
5. Number ranges are maintained for accounting documents and stocks [FBN1]

(Period closing, Stock creation and Number ranges are explained in the Appendix).

Graphical view of Path for Logistic Sessions to create Sales Order

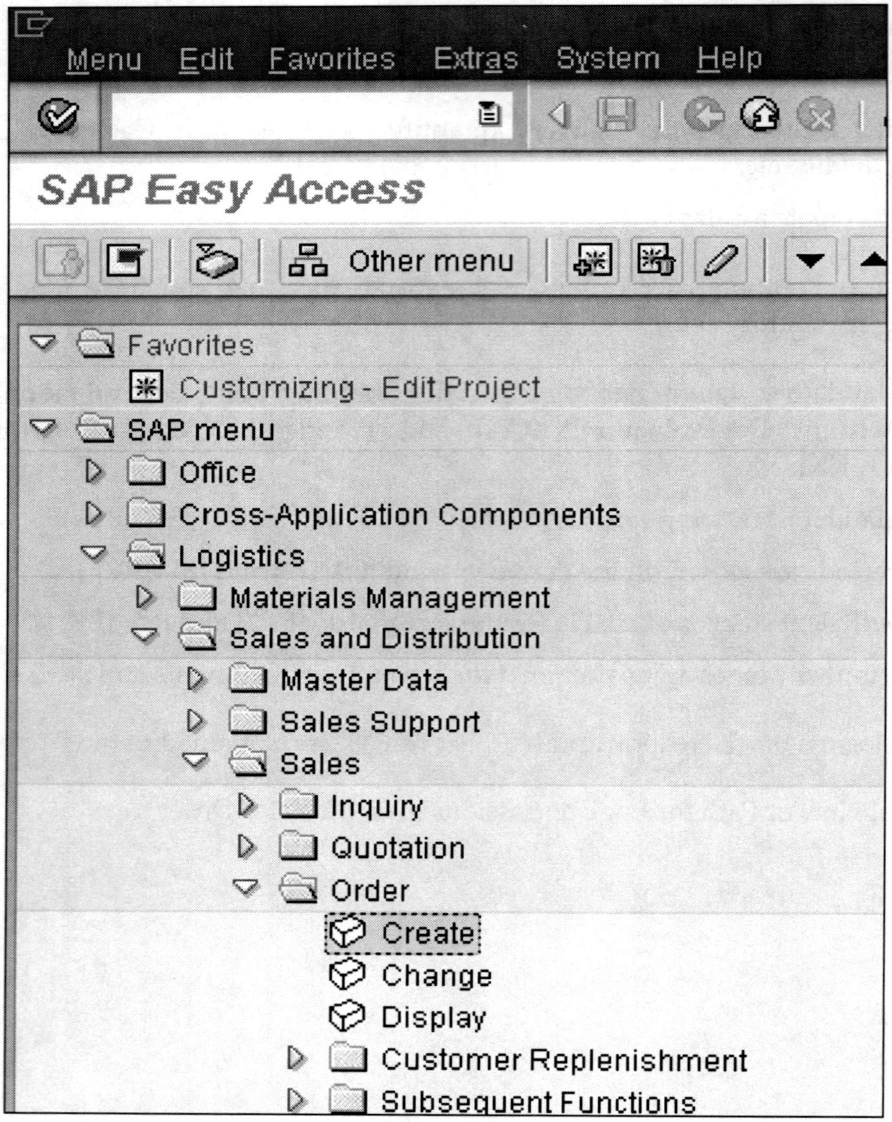
Menu Edit Favorites Extras System Help
SAP Easy Access
Other menu
Favorites
Customizing - Edit Project
SAP menu
Office
Cross-Application Components
Logistics
Materials Management
Sales and Distribution
Master Data
Sales Support
Sales
Inquiry
Quotation
Order
Create
Change
Display
Customer Replenishment
Subsequent Functions

Fig:5-1

Sales Order Creation [VA01]

[VA01], Creating Sales Order with our SDT '*ZOR*'.

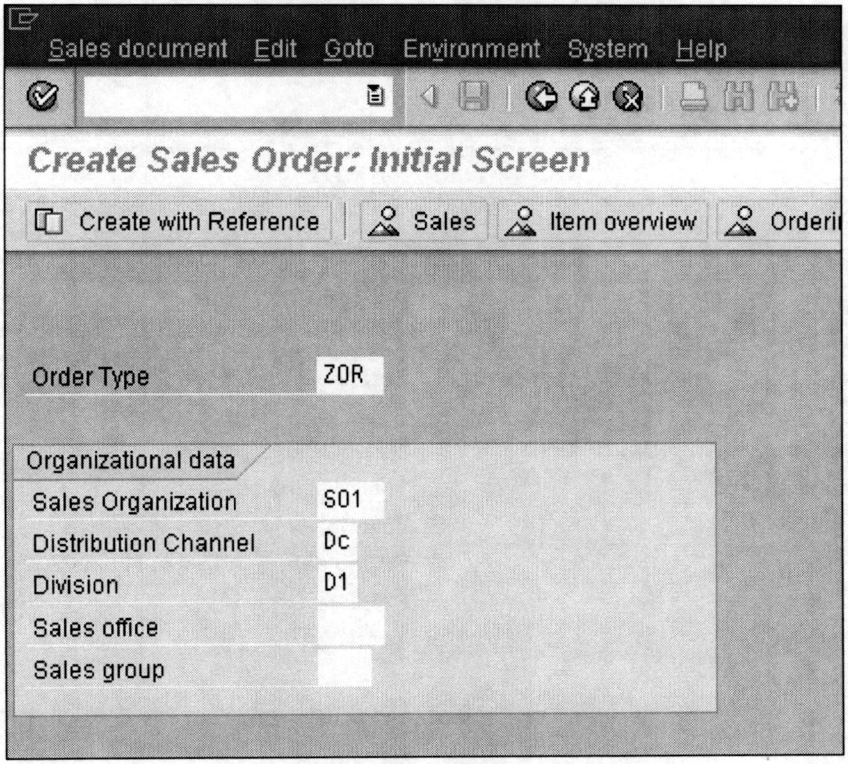

Fig:5-2

Path: Logistics-Sales and Distribution-Sales-Order-Create.

This is the Initial screen of Sales Order creation.

In this screen you enter the Sales Order header data: SDT and Sales Area.

When you enter the SDT *ZOR*, the system checks the field 'SD Document Category' of the SDT and the system brings in appropriate screens. In this case, the system come up with a screen for creating normal sales order(Standard order). If you enter the SDT *CS*, the system will come up with a different screen to create Cash Sales Order.

After entering the above data, press Enter. The following Sales Order Overview screen appears:

[VA01], Sales Order Overview screen.

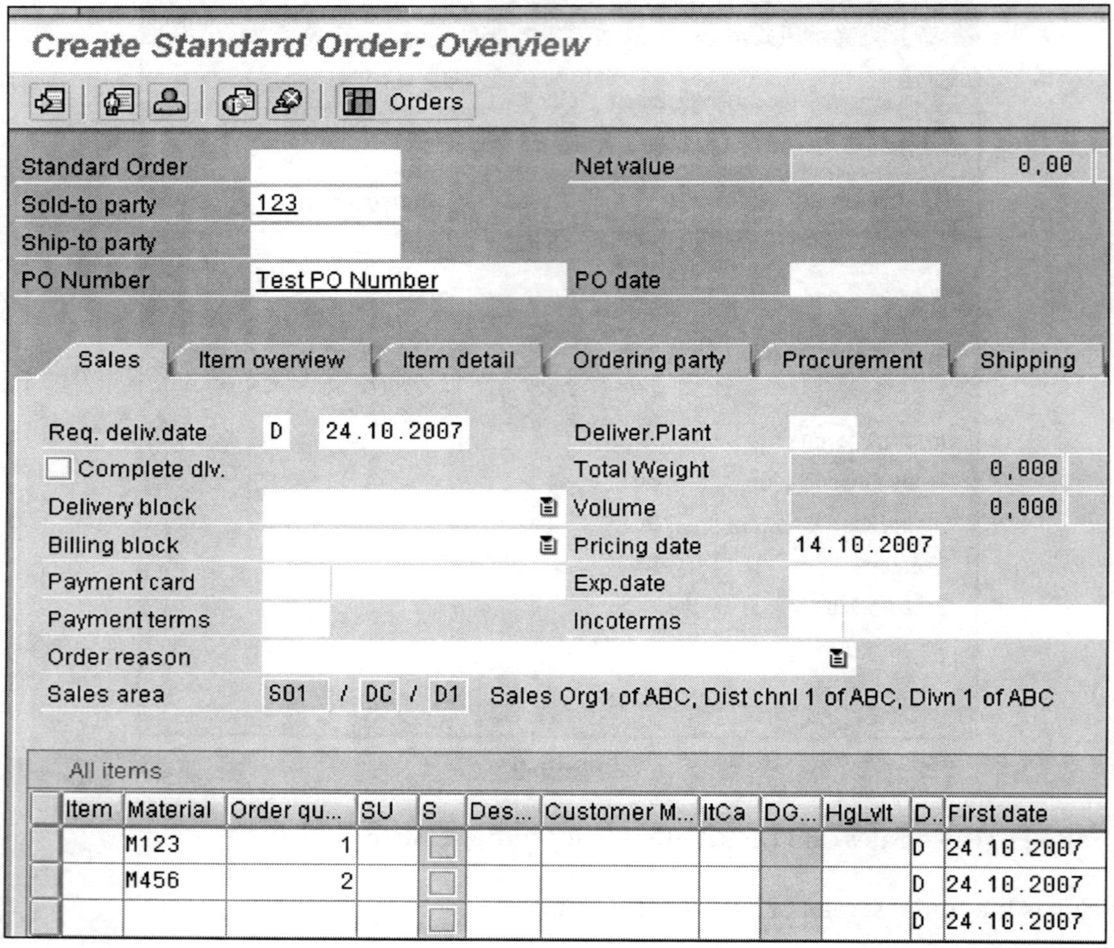

Fig:5-3

'Standard Order', 'Sold- to Party(Customer)', 'Ship-to Party', 'PO number(Customer's PO Number)', etc. shown in the upper portion of this screen are header data.

'Material', 'Order quantity' etc are line data.

The System determines Pricing Procedure when you finish entering the Sales Area , SDT and the Customer.

Important fields:

Standard Order: If you want to create SO with external numbering, you enter here the Sales Order number as per number series given in the SDT. Otherwise, the system will issue a number as per the internal number series. Number ranges are maintained in the session [VN01]. Let us create a sales order with internal numbering. Hence, leave this field empty.

Sold-to Party: Here you enter our customer number 123. For creating the sales order, the customer number should have all 4 mandatory partner functions(SP, SH, BP and PY).

Ship-to Party: It is an optional field. Instead of entering Sold-to party above, you can enter Ship-to Party here and the system will take the Sold-to Party from it. Let us leave it blank

PO Number:

Here you enter the customer's PO number. This PO number is a search criterion for our sales orders. Hence, during your learning stage, enter here your name so that you can easily search the sales orders created by you. You can use wild character (*) while searching.

Requested Delivery Date(RDD): It is the date at which the customer wants the goods to be delivered at his premise. If you leave it blank, the system will take the current date.

Fill up only the above data(Sold-to Party, PO number, Materials and their quantities) and then press Enter. The data gets populated as shown in the screen below.

[VA01], Sales Order Overview screen.

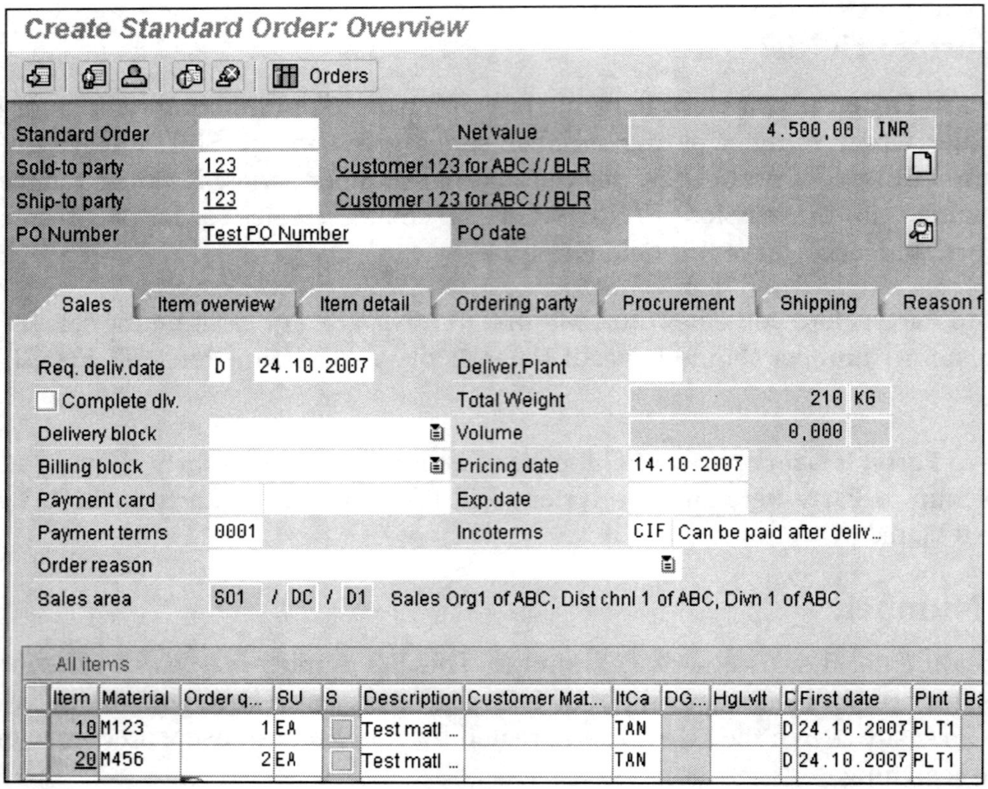

Fig:5-4

Note: If Pricing Reference Material is entered inside the Material Master, you may have to maintain Prices for the reference material.

Net Value: Net value of the SO(total of all the lines) is shown as INR 4500 at the top.

First date: This is the system proposed first Delivery Date. The System has proposed the date as 24.10.2007. This is based on various factors such as Lead Time mentioned in SDT, next working day, customer's Requested Delivery Date (RDD), Availability Check set up('Availability Check' functionality is out of scope of this book) etc. If sufficient stock is available and the Lead Time in SDT is 0, then the system would have proposed the first delivery date as the current date or the next working day. For more details, refer to the Delivery Process.

Note that the system has taken the Item Category TAN automatically based on the Item Category Determination. Item Category decides whether Pricing is applicable,

Billing can be done, Delivery can be made, Break Down is to be done to it's components(in the case of BOM) etc. For OIC *TAN*, delivery, billing, etc are applicable and hence, for this sales order line you can print delivery document and billing document, etc. But if you change this item category to TAP(for which delivery, billing, etc are not applicable), you cannot print delivery document, billing document, etc. This way by using proper OIC(whose Delivery = 'Yes' and Billing = 'No'), you can manage gift items (Free Goods) to the customers along with normal sales order items.

Save the sales order and note down the order number(8225) for further process. For testing purposes, you can modify the First date in the sales order line as current date and you can create Delivery Document.

Go to change mode by [VA02] and review your SO. You can find status of the SO by clicking on button Document Flow in the tool bar.

In the change mode, select Goto-Header-Conditions and add your header condition HD00. Go back and see how this header value is distributed against each line item.

Schedule Line created for line 10 is shown below.

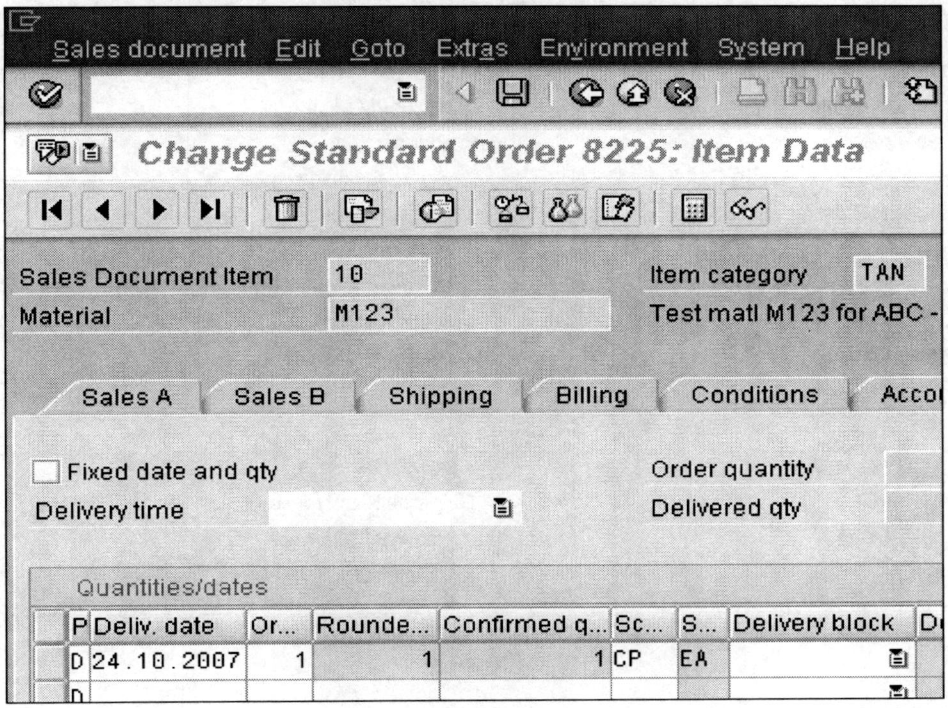

Fig:5-5

To see the Schedule line from the Sales Order overview session, select Goto-Item-Schedule lines.

Note that the Schedule Line Category CP is selected based on the Schedule Line Category Determination[VOV5].

Shipping Overview of the sales order line 10

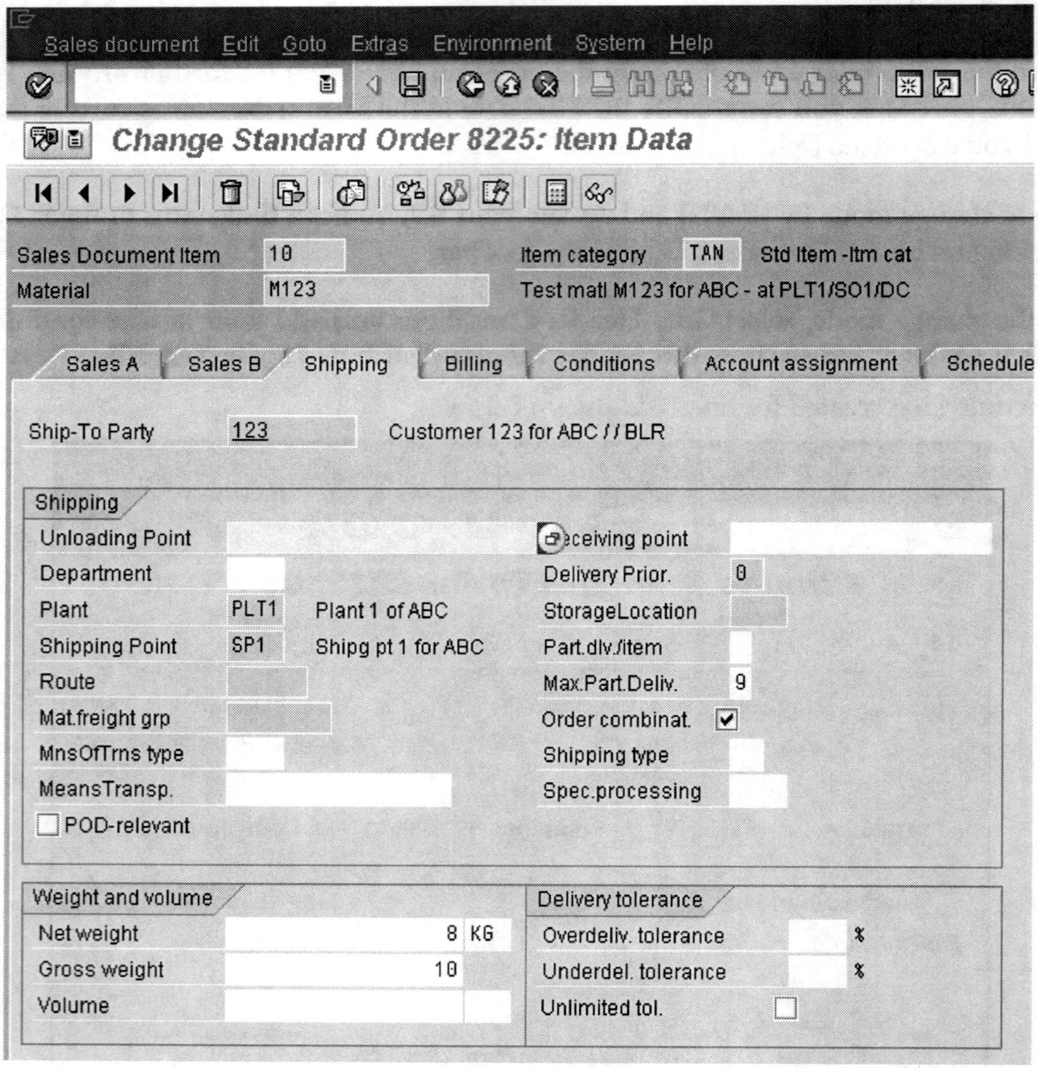

Fig:5-6

Shipping overview can be seen for a line by Goto – Item – Shipping.

Note that the shipping point SP1 is selected by the system automatically.

Pricing Details of SO 8225 for line10, Material M123.

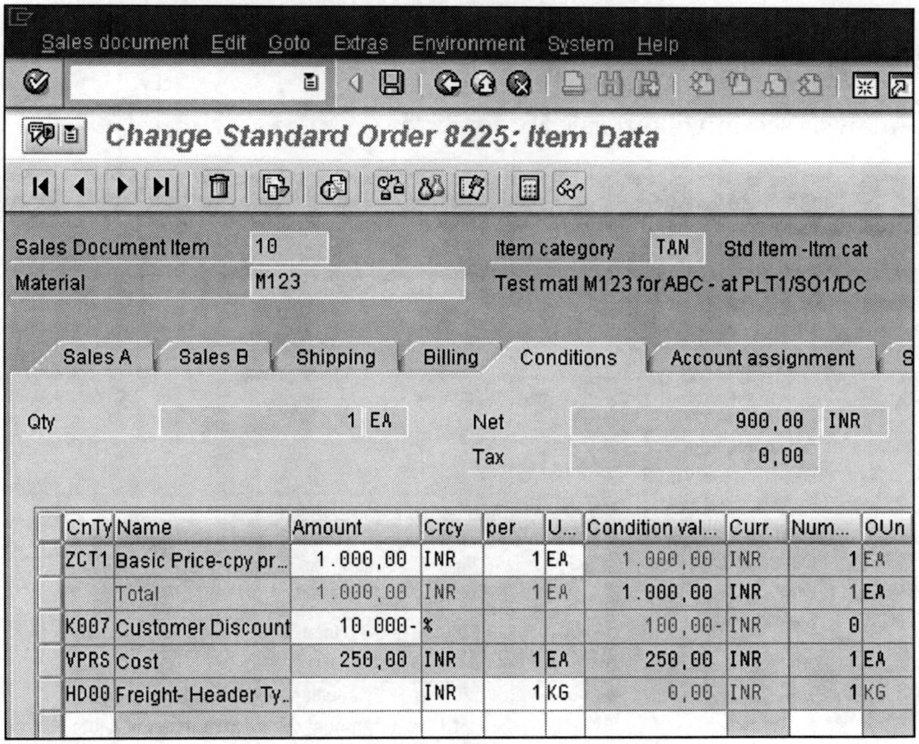

Fig:5-7

Pricing Details for each line can be seen by selecting Goto-Item-Conditions.

Columns are re arranged by pulling the column by mouse to the desired positions.

Note that the net price for the line 10 is INR 900. All the above values are taken by the system as per the condition records we have created in the chapter Pricing.

In this view, if you want, you can add your manual Item Condition ZPSP, (Refer to our Pricing Procedure). Then the pricing details change accordingly.

Pricing Analysis.

Pricing analysis can be used to know various pricing details of the sales order.

Pricing Analysis:

Pricing Analysis session of our sales order 8225.

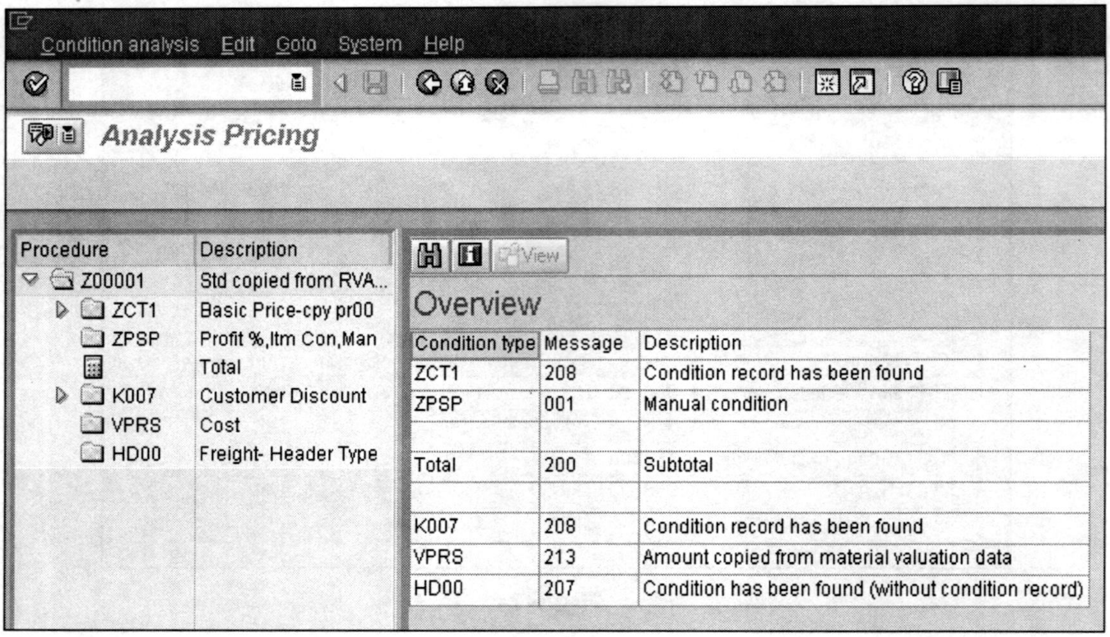

Fig:5-8

To view pricing analysis for a particular item, select an item(line) in the sales order overview and then Goto-Item-Conditions and then click on the button 'Analysis' at the bottom of the screen. In this session, you can find out which Pricing Procedure, which condition type etc. are picked by the system.

Delivery Document Creation [VL01N]

Sales Delivery process

Sales Delivery Documents can be created with a reference to a sales order or without reference to a sales order. Example for delivery without reference to an order is the case of return of goods to the supplier. Separate sessions are used for these purposes. Use [VL01N] for delivery with order reference and [VL01NO] for Delivery without reference. Sales Delivery can be processed for individual orders and collective orders.

If the delivery document is created with reference to a sales order, the DDT of the delivery document will be taken from SDT. But if you create the delivery document without a sales order reference, you will have to enter DDT while creating the delivery document. You can see the DDT from the delivery document by clicking on Goto-Header-Administration.

Please see that stock is available in the plant before creating Delivery. Stock can be created through the session [MB1C]. Refer to the Appendix for stock creation.

If created with reference, Copy Control must exist for the same. If you are not able to create delivery, the main reason could be that copy control is not maintained. Unlike Sales Documents, Delivery Documents do not contain schedule lines. The schedule line in the sales document becomes a line in the delivery document.

Note: If warehouse management is implemented, the transfer order is created for those delivery lines for which physical picking is applicable(Refer DIC).

You can create delivery documents for a single order in 2 ways:

a) By calling the sales order through [VA02] and then choose Deliver in the drop down menu.

b) Use transaction VL01N.

[VL01N], Create Delivery for single order with reference to an order.

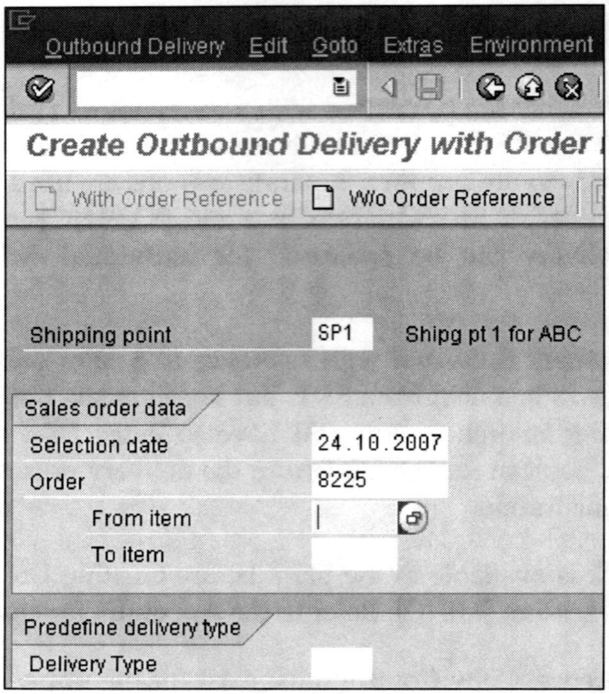

Fig:5-9

Path: Logistics- Sales and Distribution- Shipping and Transportation -Outbound Delivery- Create- Single Document- With Reference to Sales Order.

Selection Date:

It is an important field. This date is the date up to which the deliveries are applicable. Give a date equal to or later than the 'First Date' of the sales order lines. Give a future date if you face a problem. Take field help on this field for more details.

Note: If DIC is not available, you will get the **error message 'Item Category xxx is not available'** while creating delivery document. Do not panic: it indicates that DIC is deleted even if OIC is available. Use [0VLP] to create DIC.

Fill up Shipping Point, Selection date and Sales Order number and then press Enter.

Please note that the Selection Date given is 24.10.2007(which is the 'First Date' in SO). If you had given a date before 24.10.2007, the following message would have appeared:

Type	SD Doc.	Item	Message Text	LTxt
△	8213	10	No schedule lines due for delivery up to the selected date	?
△	8213	20	No schedule lines due for delivery up to the selected date	?

Fig:5-10

The above message may come for other reasons also like if stock is not available as on the selection date, materials are already delivered, etc.

[VL01N], Delivery Overview screen

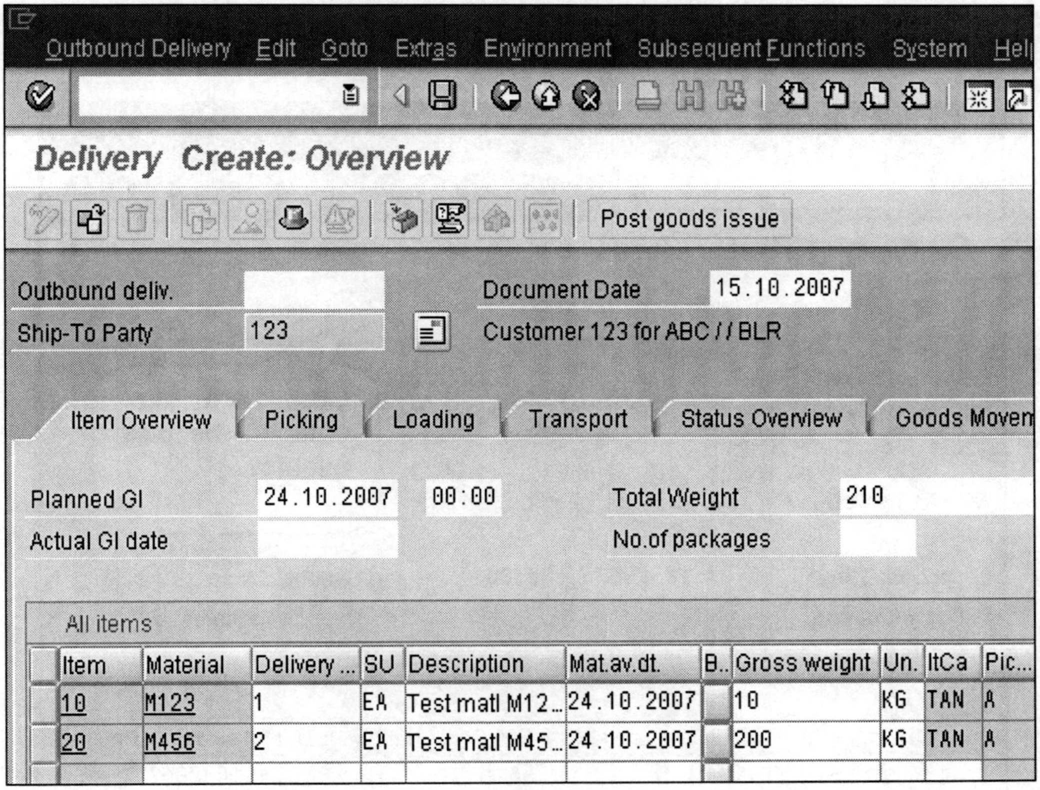

Fig:5-11

Note: The Item Category TAN that you see in this Delivery Document is DIC and it is copied from the Sales Document lines. But, in this session, if you enter another line manually, the item category will be Delivery Item Category as per the set up done in the Delivery Item Category determination. Refer to the chapter Determinations for more information.

Click on 'Picking' tab and enter the ordered quantity at the field 'Delivery quantity' as shown below. If the storage location is not filled up, fill up that also.

Pick tab will be active only if the field 'Relevant for delivery' in DIC is selected.

If Warehouse Management is implemented, Picking / PGI will be active only after processing the Transfer Orders. If Warehouse Management is implemented, save the delivery document, complete the Transfer order and then call the delivery document for further processing.

[VL01N], Delivery and Goods-Issue.

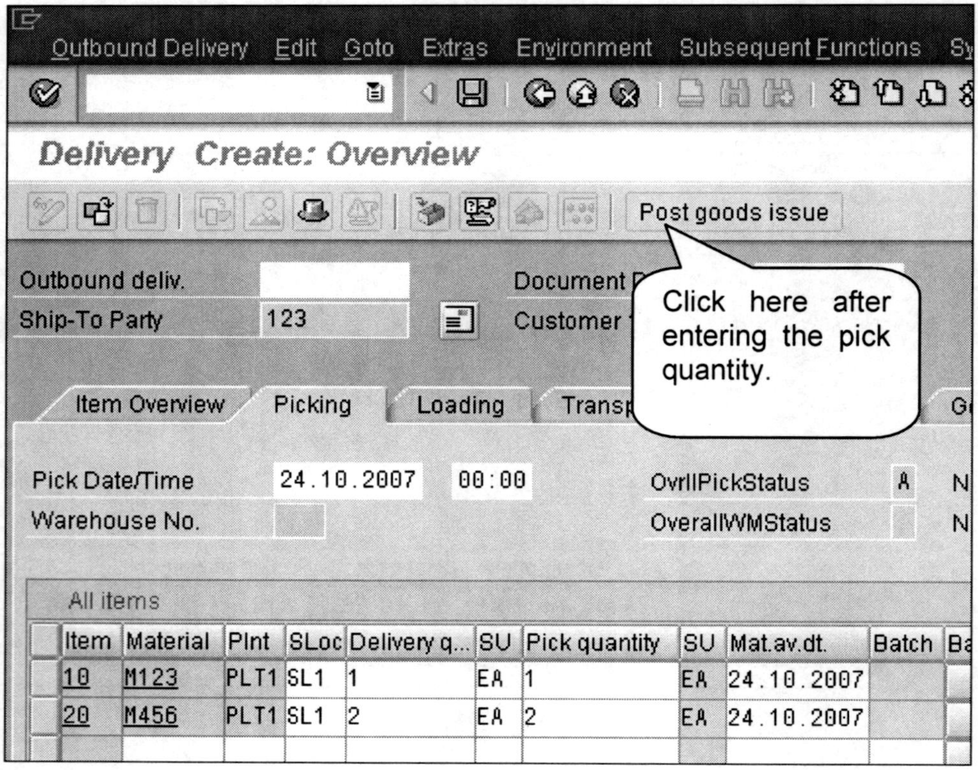

Fig: 5-12

After entering the pick quantity, click on PGI(Post Goods-Issue). If delivery is proper, you will get the message 'Delivery xxx has been saved'. Note down the Delivery Document number to process the Billing Document.

If Storage Location is not filled, you will get the **error message 'Storage location not defined for delivery item xx'**. If more than one storage location is defined for the plant, you may have to enter it manually or you must maintain Storage Location Determination.

You can see the Document Flow to know the status of the process by clicking on Environment- Display document flow.

If you do not want to issue goods now, you can save this delivery document without clicking on PGI and later you can call up this delivery document and issue goods by clicking on PGI(Post Goods- Issue).

You post the goods- issue only when the material leaves the Organisation. When Goods- issue is posted, stock in the inventory comes down and all the related tables are updated.

The following tables are updated when goods issue is posted:

1. Stock quantity is updated
2. Values are updated in inventory accounting
3. Accounting documents are updated in controlling
4. Billing index is updated so that the system will allow to generate billing documents
5. Statuses in relevant sales documents are updated.

The Number Series for Delivery Document is taken from Delivery Document Type(DDT) that is linked in the Sales Document Type(SDT).

If the number range is not maintained for delivery for the current year, you may get the **error message 'Number Range interval 49 does not exist FBN1'**. Refer to the appendix for maintaining number ranges.

Billing and Accounting Document Creation [VF01].

The Billing Document creates an external document Invoice. The Accounting document creates an internal document used for accounting purpose.

Billing and accounting documents are created after delivery of the goods.

Billing and accounting documents can be created together or separately. This depends on the field 'Posting Block' in BDT. If the posting block is selected, the accounting document must be created separately.

When you save the billing document, the system carries out debit posting on the customer receivables and credit posting on revenue accounts.

[VF01], Create Billing Document(Invoicing)

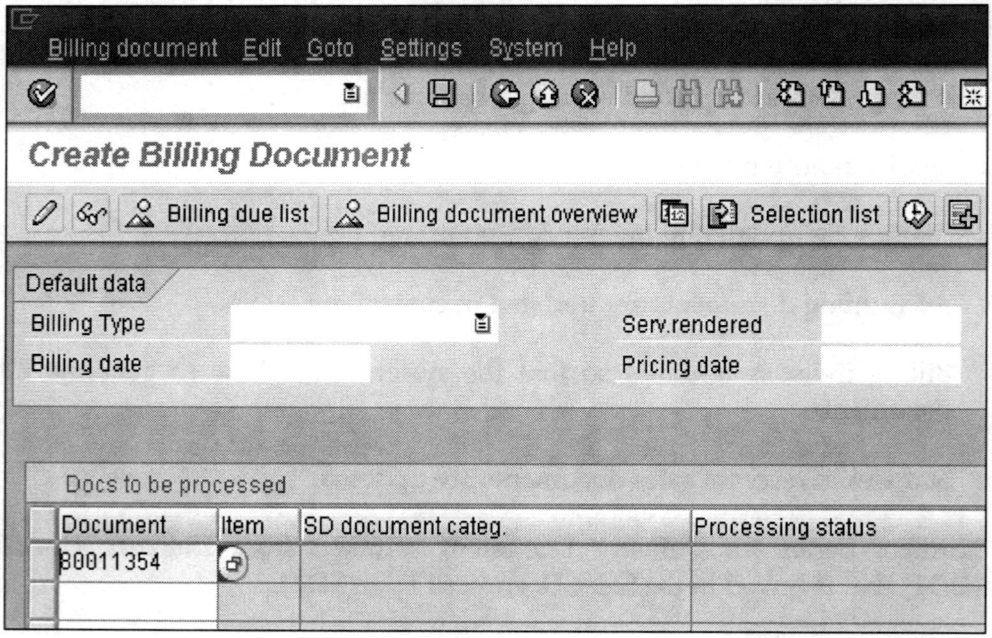

Fig: 5-13

Path: Logistics- Sales and Distribution- Billing- Billing Document- Create

Fields:

Billing Type(Billing Document Type):

If you do not enter anything here, the system takes the BDT from SDT. If you want to use a specific BDT, you can enter the same here. Please note that the Account Determination Procedure is based on this BDT.

Document:

You can enter either the Sales Order number or Delivery Document number here. This depends on the field 'Billing Relevance' in OIC. Refer to the field 'Billing Document Type' in SDT for more details.

Our item is of delivery related billing type and hence, fill up the Delivery Document number in the field 'Document' and press Enter. You will get the following screen.

[VF01], Create Billing Document(Invoicing)

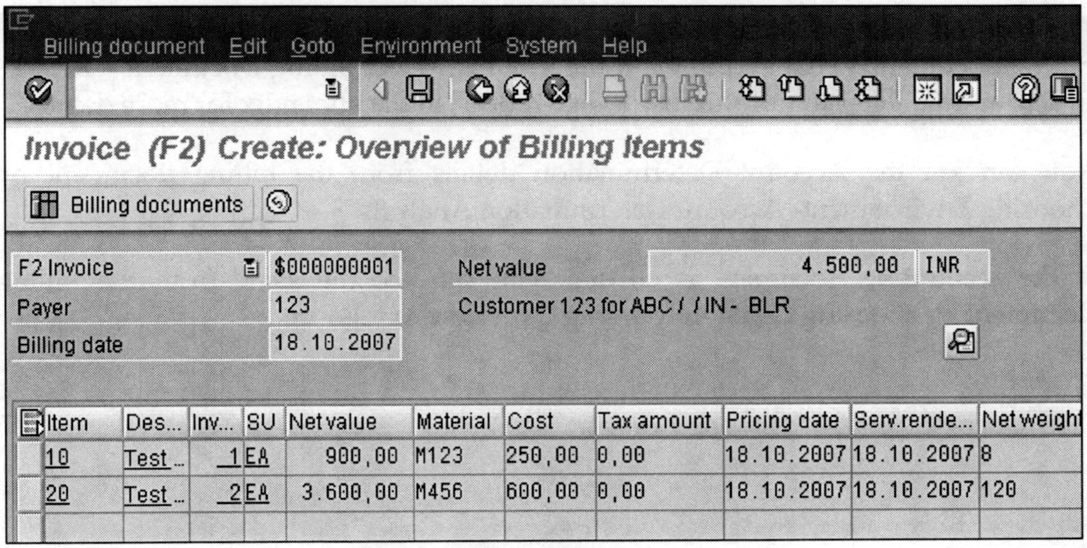

Fig: 5-14

Save the Billing Document (Invoice). While saving, if the accounting document is also generated, you will get the message 'Document yyy has been saved'. It shows the completion of the Sales Transaction showing that the accounting document is also generated.

If you get the message, while saving the billing document, 'Document yyy saved(no accounting document generated)', it indicates that the accounting document is not generated, but the billing document is generated. In this case the status of the billing document will show as 'Open'.

Accounting Documents will not be created because of the following reasons:

--The field 'Posting Block' in the Billing Document Type is selected.

--The account determination is not done properly.

--The number series mentioned in the Accounting Document Type is not available for the current year in the session Number Ranges for Accounting Documents.

Please check the accounting document type *RV* in the session [OBA7]. The number range for accounting document is maintained in the session [FBN1]. Note that the total number range available is to be split into various series for the current year. Otherwise you may get the **error message 'Enter intervals without overlap'**.

The blocked billing document can be released by going to the change mode of the billing document[VF02] and then, in the tool bar, select Billing Document - Release to accounting. Refer to the Number Range [FBN1] in the appendix for more details.

You can see the Account Determination details from the billing document by choosing Environment- Account Determination Analysis.

If the accounting document is created, you can see the same from the Billing document by choosing Goto- Accounting Overview as follows:

Viewing Accounting Document:

[VF03] Display Billing Document.

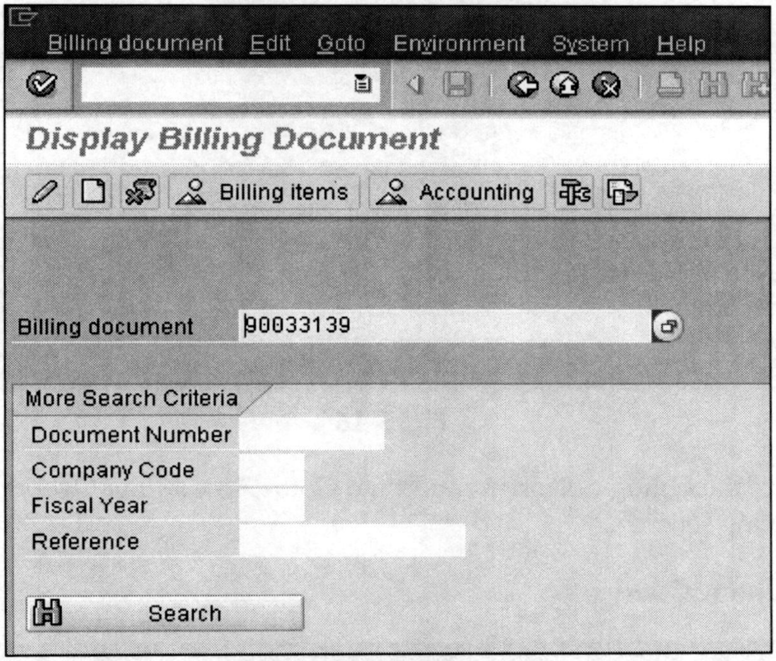

Fig:5-15

Enter the Billing document number and click on the tick mark. The following screen appears:

[VF03] Billing Document- to view the accounting document

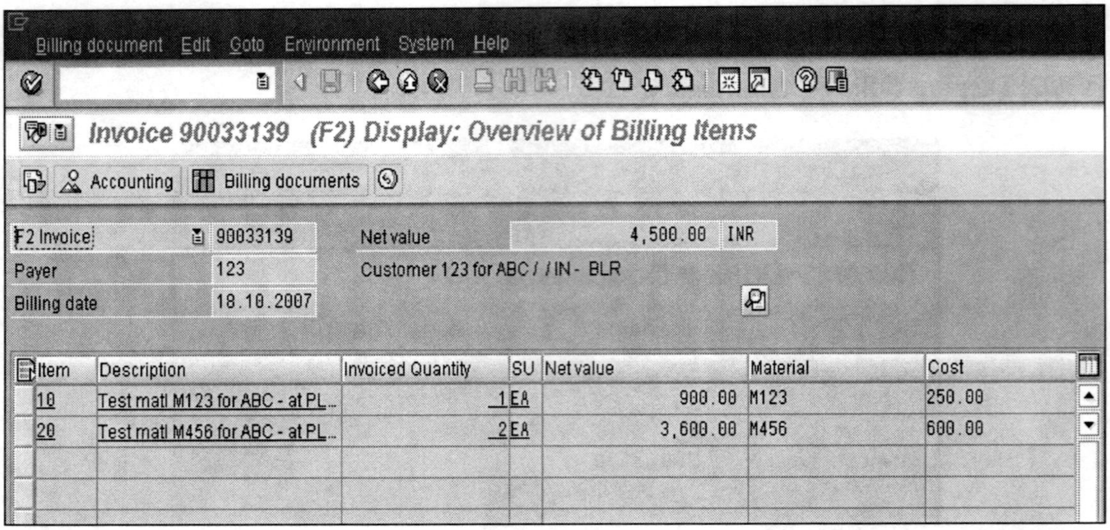

Fig:5-16

Select a line in the billing document and then Goto- Accounting Overview. You will see the following screen:

[VF03] Accounting Overview

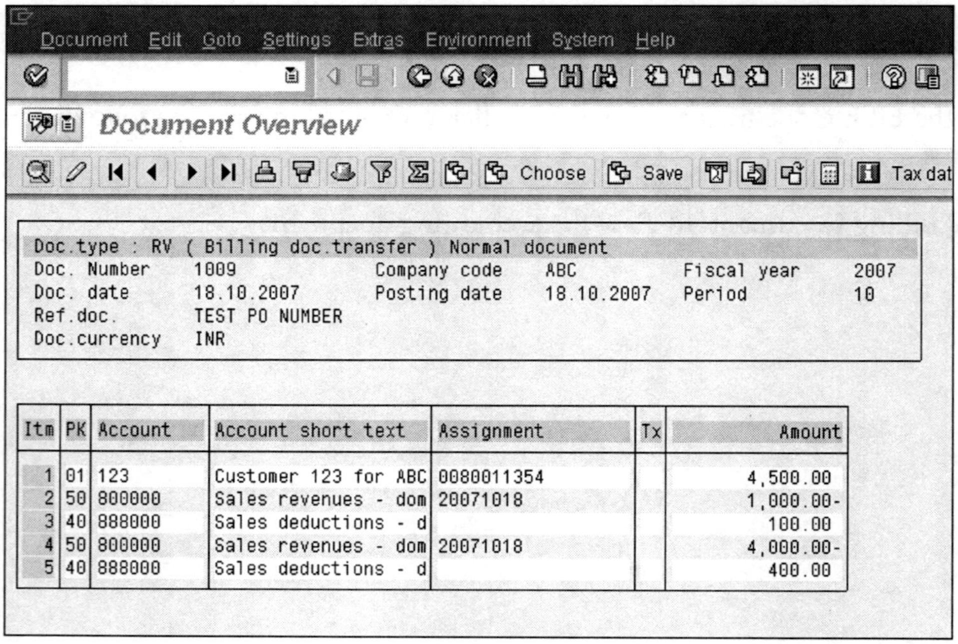

Fig:5-17

Here you can see the Accounting Document Type, Accounting Document number, Reference document, G/L accounts to which the revenues are posted, etc.

Here the reference document is PO number. Copy control (Delivery to Billing-VTFL) decides which document number is to be copied to the accounting document as reference document. Refer to [VTFL] at the header level for more information.

If you know the accounting document number, you can use [FB03] to see the accounting document details.

Sales Order Status

To know the document status from sales order creation onwards, go to change mode of the Sales Order [VA02] and click on the button Display Document Flow or select Environment- Display Document Flow in the Toolbar.

Document status for the sales order 8225

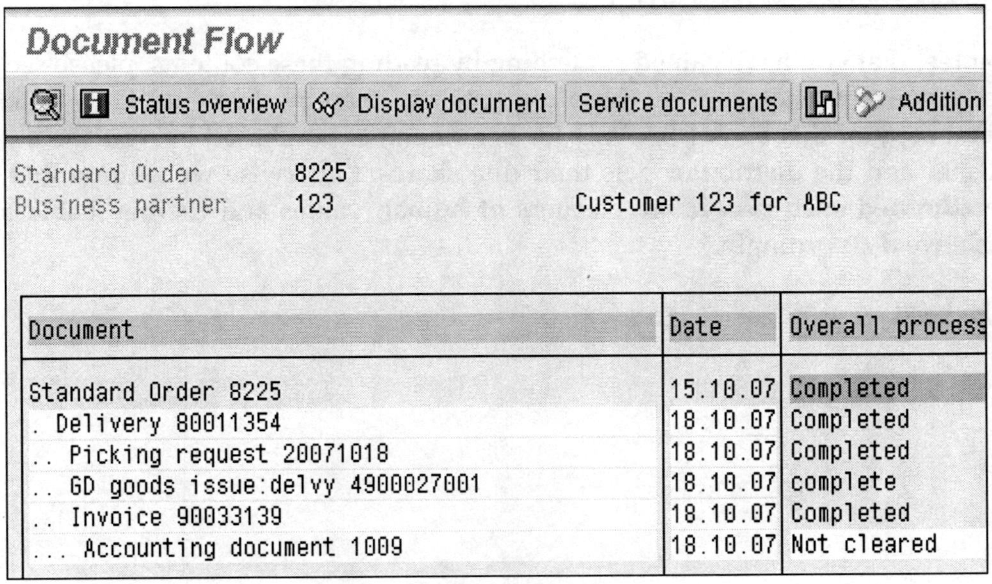

Fig: 5-18

The above status shows that the Sales Order 8225 is complete in the SD perspective.

If you receive the payment through the session [F-28], the status of the accounting document will be 'Cleared'. Receipt of payment is the function of FIN consultants.

CONGRATULATIONS !!!

If you could make a sales order with the above status, you can boast that you now know the fundamentals of SAP SD.

Now create another sales order with reference to this sales order.

Note: Click on the tab 'Create With reference' in the initial screen and choose the tab 'Order'- Refer Fig 5-2.

But remember it does not end here. Learning is never ending. You can learn other functions of SAP SD by going through other menus, books, SAP sessions and field help tools at your own pace.

Note that this knowledge is not sufficient for getting certified in SAP SD. You need to go for a formal training and learn other auxiliary functions of SD. If you have mastered these fundamentals, you can easily follow fast track training and pass the certification examination easily.

If you feel that you have gained something by reading these contents, please see that nobody makes a photocopy of these contents and thereby cheats us. Only when an original copy of this book (SAP SD for beginners) is purchased by you the author, publisher and the distributor gets their due shares. Otherwise we assume that you have admitted such people are cheaters of human values and thereby liable to be punishewe d accordingly.

All the best!

Chapter

6

APPENDIX

Period closing [MMPV]

You will have to close the periods for material postings every month end. Unless you close periods properly, you cannot transact with materials properly. Period closing has to be done at the end of every month(assuming that the calendar month is defined as periods).

The following session shows the status of period closing.
Maintain Company Codes for Materials Management[OMSY]

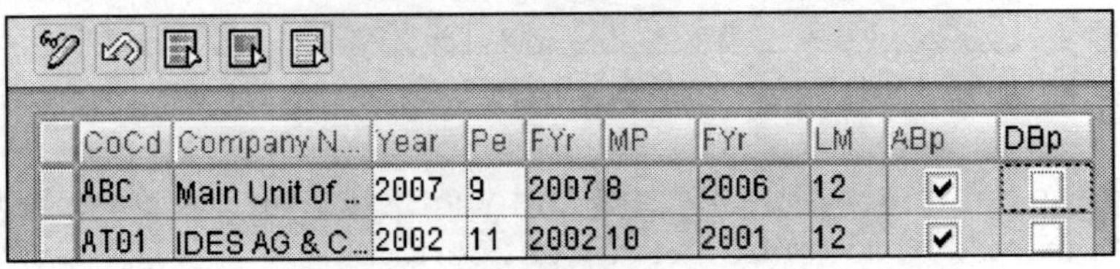

CoCd	Company N...	Year	Pe	FYr	MP	FYr	LM	ABp	DBp
ABC	Main Unit of ...	2007	9	2007	8	2006	12	☑	☐
AT01	IDES AG & C...	2002	11	2002	10	2001	12	☑	☐

Fig: 6-1

Path: IMG-Logistics General-Material Master-Basic Settings-Maintain Company Codes for Materials Management

Here for the company ABC, 2007/9 is the current posting period, 2007/8 is the previous period, 2006/12 is the last period of the last year. ABp indicates that the system will allow back posting to the last period.

Note: You can close a period, if the previous period is closed. Hence, you may have to close all the previous periods till the current period. Use [MMPV] for closing periods.

[MMPV],Period closing.

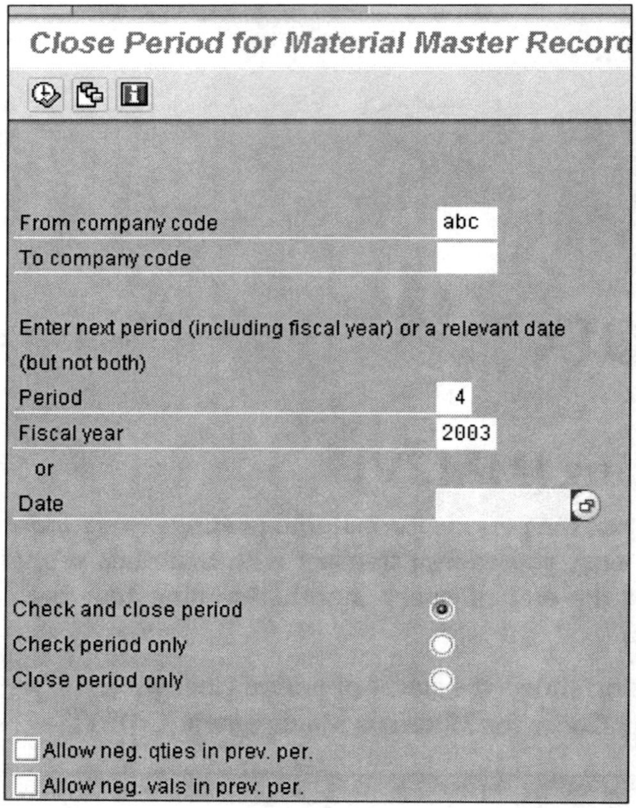

Fig: 6-2

After entering the company code, period and year, click on the Execute button. Then close the next period and so on till the current period.

Incorrect closing of period

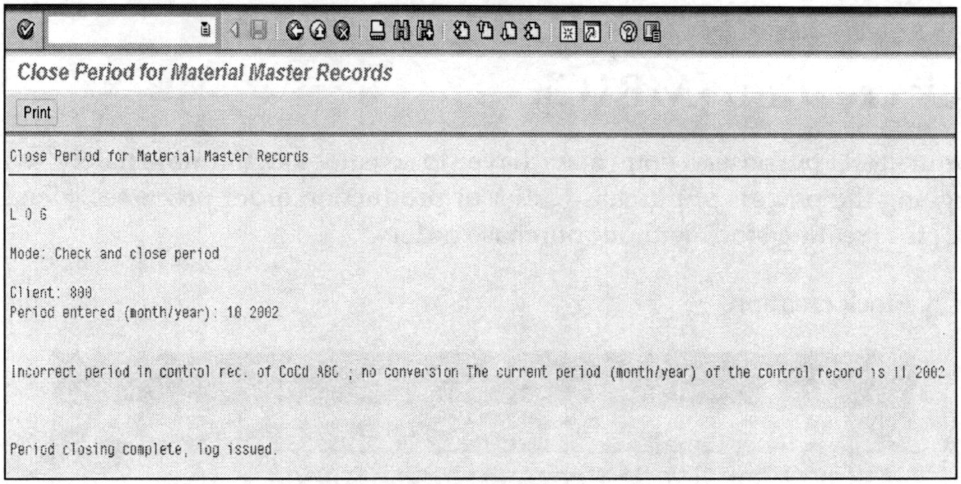

Fig:6-3

The above message shows that period 11/2002 is already closed and now you have to close period 12/2002 onwards.

Period closed successfully

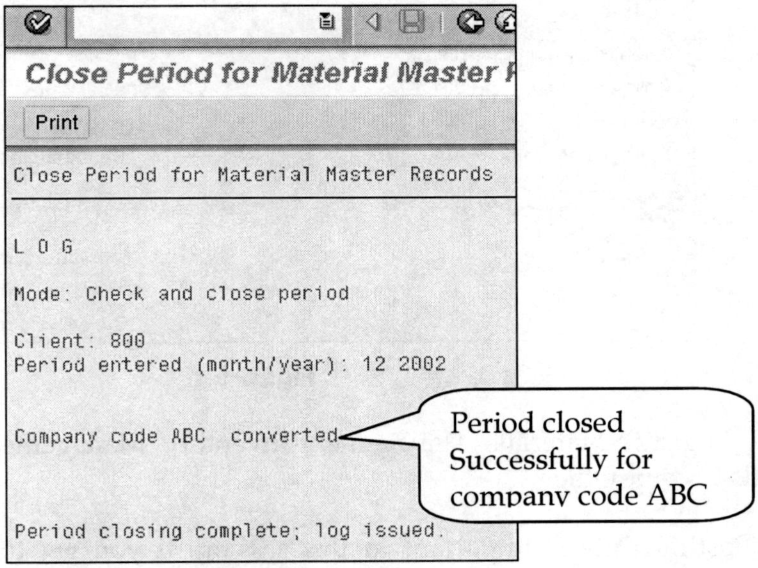

Fig:6-4

If period is closed successfully, you will get a message like "Company code xxx converted.

Stock creation [MB1C].

For your test purposes, you may have to create stock immediately without undergoing the process of purchase order or production order processes. Hence, use [MB1C] for creating stock without purchase orders.

[MB1C], Stock creation.

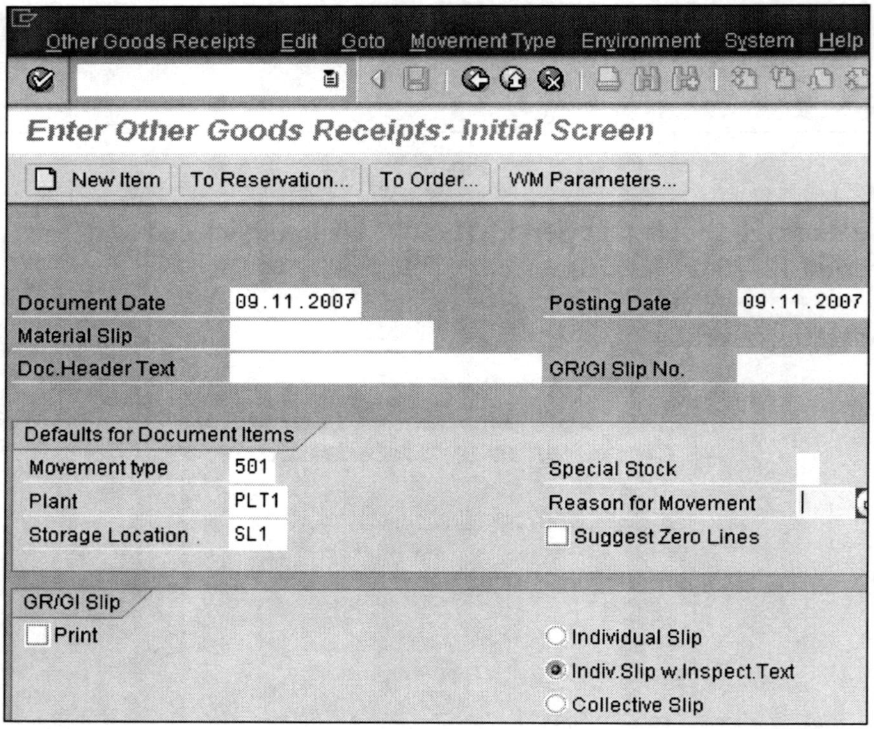

Fig: 6-5

Path: Logistics-Materials Management-Inventory Management-Goods Movement-Goods Receipt-Other

The Posting Date is important in this session. If you get the **error message like "Posting only possible in periods 2007/08 and 2007/07 in company code ABC"** , the reasons could be the following:

Generally after creating a new company code, the posting period set by the Finance Department will be the current period(as per the above screen, month 09. 2007). It is the responsibility of the FINANCE department to close periods properly every month. If it is not done so, the above error will appear and you will not be able to proceed.

In the above case, if you enter the posting period either as 08.2007 or 07.2007, the system will allow you to proceed. The System will allow posting in the current period(09.2007) if you close the period 2007/09.

Note: You can close a period, if the previous period is closed. Hence, you may have to close all the previous periods till the current period. Use MMPV for closing periods.

Use movement type 501 or 561(Receipt without purchase order into warehouse). Also enter Plant and Storage location of the plant. On Entering the following screen appears:

[MB1C], Stock creation.

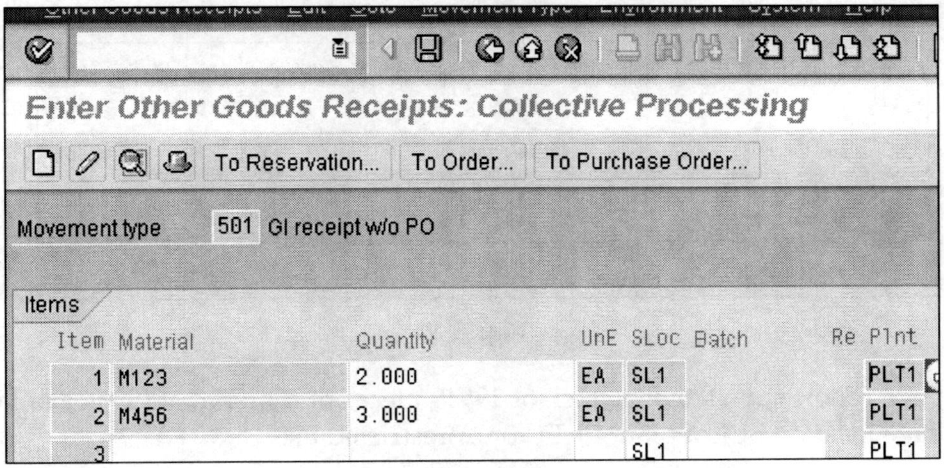

Fig: 6-6

Fill up material codes and quantities and then press the Enter key.

On Saving, the quantity gets Posted. If you get the error message **'Number range 49 does not exist',** create the number range through [FBN1].

If you get the error message, **'Material belongs to a Material Type whose stocks are not managed on a quantity basis'**, check the 'quantity/value updating for material types' in the session Define Attributes of Material Type as explained under the Miscellaneous setup.

Stock viewing [MMBE]

Use MMBE or MM03 to see the stock overview. For consignment stock overview, use [MB58].

MMBE, Viewing stock of material M123.

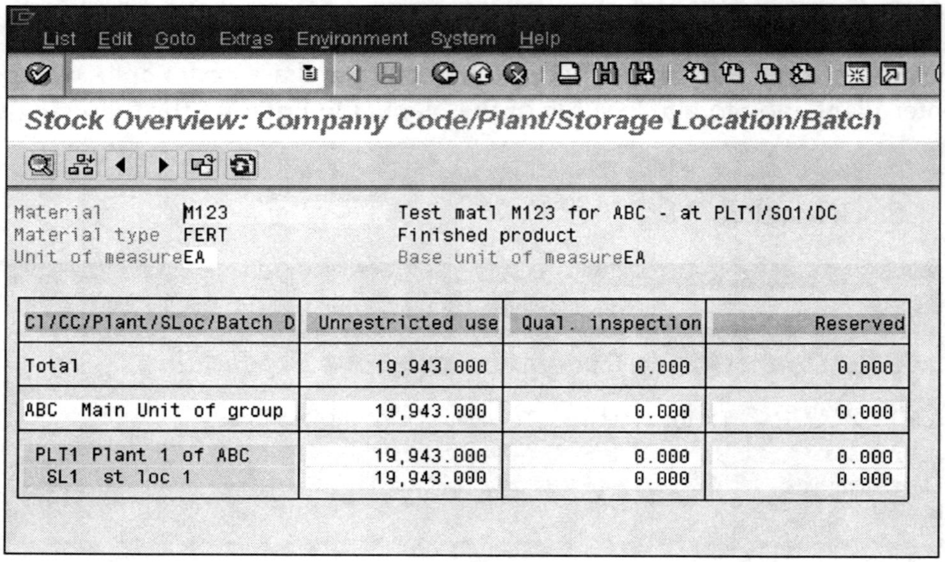

Fig: 6-7

The Above report shows that a stock of 19943 pieces of Material M123 is available at the storage location SL1 of plant PLT1 for unrestricted use.

Tax Calculation

If you want to calculate taxes in your sales documents, you must maintain condition records for taxes against price condition types[V/06] of condition class D(tax). Standard condition type MWST is available in the system for the same.

In addition to the basic settings done for tax in the chapter Master Data, you must set up tax codes for calculating and displaying taxes in the sales document.

As tax rules are different for different countries, for most of the countries, SAP has developed tax sessions separately. Some are developed by SAP and some are developed by third party vendors. Any way, the standard way of calculating tax is mentioned here. If this standard method is not suitable for your country, you can opt for other methods.

Various sessions used for Tax Calculation are shown in the figure 6-8.

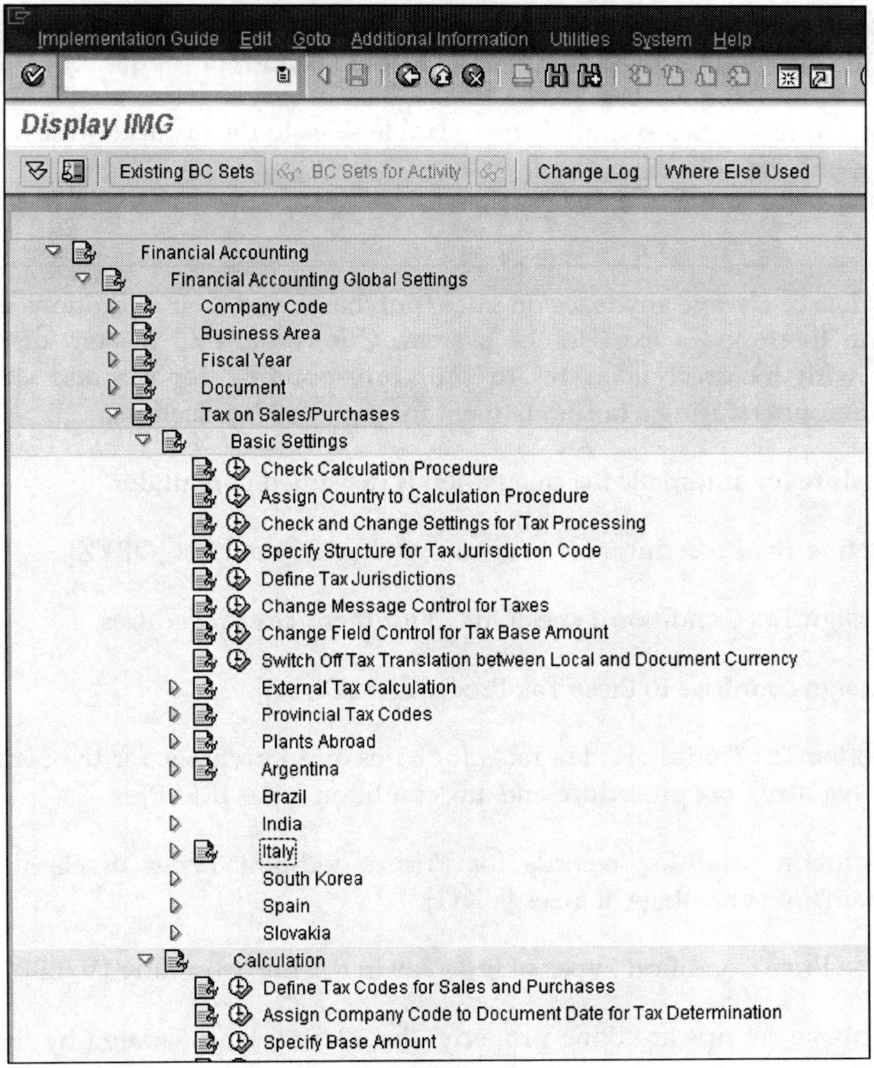

Fig: 6-8

Path: IMG-Financial Accounting- …

You can define one or more tax categories for each country. During sales order processing, the system applies the tax category according to the country of the delivering plant and location of the customer receiving the goods.

SAP supplies a tax calculation procedure for each country. Most of the procedure comprises a list of all common Tax Condition Types.

You have to define separate Tax Codes for sales/purchases for each country in which one of your company codes is located. Each tax code contains one or more tax rates for the different tax condition types(Output tax and/or Input tax).

If you have to report tax-exempt or non-taxable sales to the tax authorities, you need to define a tax rate with the value 0.

Note:

Do not delete or change any taxes on sales/purchases and their definitions as long as items with these codes exist in the system. Otherwise, R/3 System displays tax amounts with incorrect tax rates in the corresponding reports and determines incorrect amounts during a tax adjustment for payment transactions.

The procedure for automatic tax calculation is explained here under.

1. Define Tax Procedures for countries, if they do not exist [OBYZ].

2. Assign Tax Condition Types[OBYZ] for these Tax Procedures.

3. Assign countries to these Tax Procedures [OBBG].

4. Define Tax Codes and tax rates for Sales and Purchases for the combination of country/ tax procedure and tax condition types [FTXP].

5. Maintain condition records for Price Condition Types of class 'taxes' = Maintain percentage of taxes [VK11].

6. Use Price Condition Types of type Tax in Pricing Procedure [V/08].

If all the above set ups are done properly, the tax will be calculated by the system while creating the sales documents.

1. Defining Procedure for tax calculations. [OBYZ]

Define the Tax Procedure, ZTAXIN(Indian Tax)

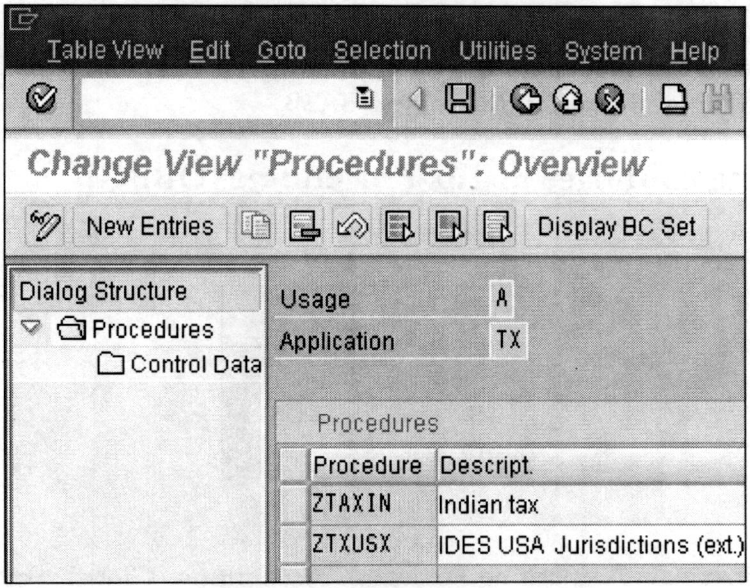

Fig: 6-9

Path: IMG-Financial Accounting-Financial Accounting Global Settings-Tax on Sales/Purchases-Basic Settings-Check Calculation Procedure-Define Procedures

2. Assign Tax Condition Types[OBYZ] to Tax Procedure

Select the Tax Procedure and enter Tax Condition Types for the above tax procedure as shown below.

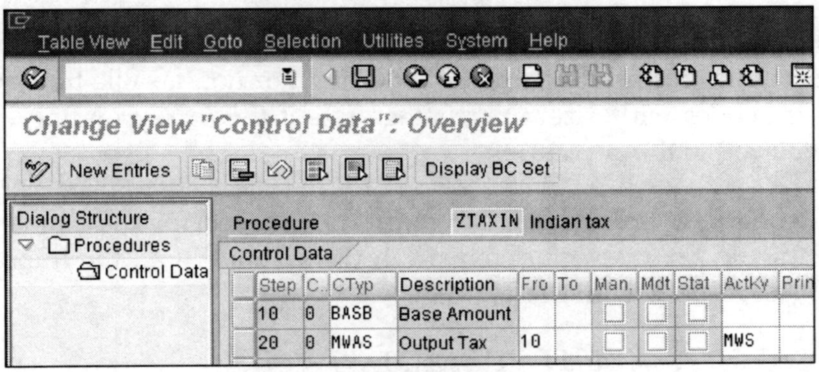

Fig: 6-10

Note

1. These Tax Condition Types[OBYZ] are different from Price Condition Types[V/06].
2. The tax is calculated on the base amount. This is controlled by Condition Category of the Tax Condition Type BASB.

3. Assigning countries to Tax Procedures [OBBG]

Assign Country to Tax Calculation Procedure

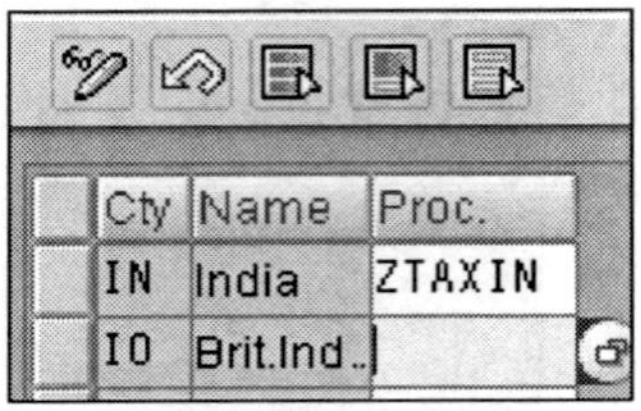

Cty	Name	Proc.
IN	India	ZTAXIN
IO	Brit.Ind..	

Fig: 6-11

Path: IMG-Financial Accounting-Financial Accounting Global Settings-Tax on Sales/Purchases-Basic Settings-Assign Country to Calculation Procedure

Here you assign a Tax Procedure for tax calculation to every country with which your company has business dealings.

4. Define Tax Codes and tax rates [FTXP]

Tax codes are unique per country and the tax rate calculation set ups and other features are stored in a separate table against each tax code.

The tax code represents a tax type which must be considered while making tax returns to tax authorities and hence, for tax-exempt or non-taxable transactions, you should use tax codes with a zero percentage rate if the corresponding transactions are to be displayed in the tax returns.

You must define new tax codes if tax rates are changed for the country. The old codes with the old tax rates must remain in the system till all the transactions are completed in all respects with this tax code.

Define Tax Codes for Sales and Purchases[FTXP]

Fig: 6-12

Path: IMG-Financial Accounting-Financial Accounting Global Settings-Tax on Sales/Purchases- Calculation- Define Tax Codes for Sales and Purchases

Enter the country code to which the tax code is to be maintained. The following screen appears to maintain the Tax Code:

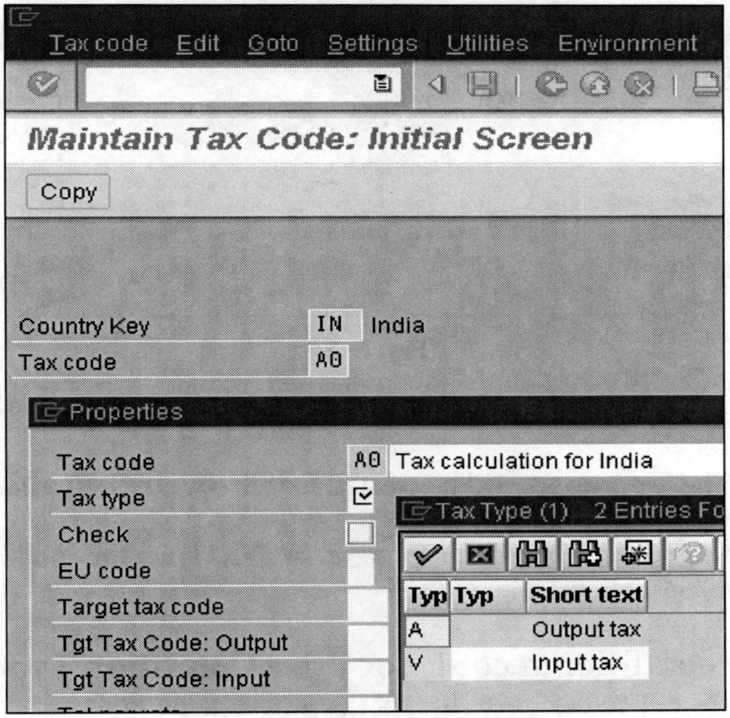

Fig: 6-13

Enter the Tax code. When you enter a new tax code(say A0) here, you will be prompted with a sub window as shown here for selecting the tax type. You have two standard options A(Output Tax) and V(Input Tax).

On selecting 'A(Output tax)' for the field 'Tax Type', the following screen appears to maintain the tax percentage.

Maintain the percentage of tax at the field Tax Percentage, say 12, as shown below in Fig 6-14.

Maintaining tax percentage for the combination of country code, Tax Code(Tax Code is with respect to a tax type) and Tax Procedure.

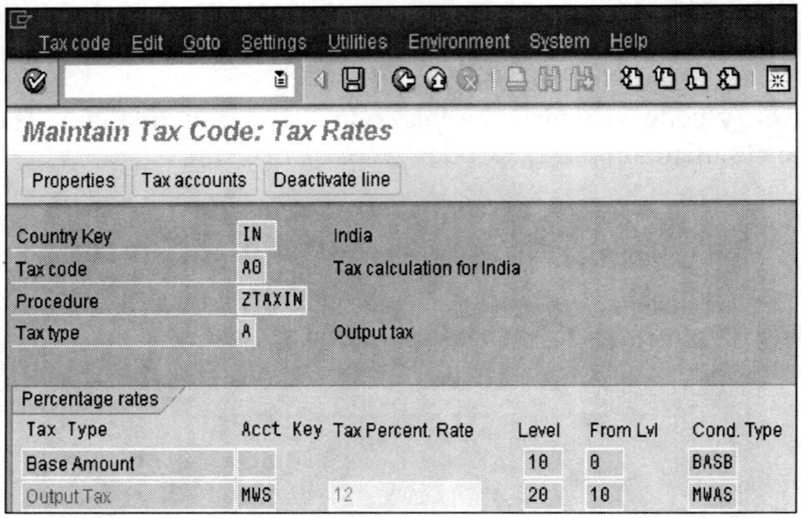

Fig: 6-14

You will have access to only one field here, viz Tax Percentage Rate.

Save the data. The tax code A0 will be created for the country IN(India).

Now you can enter condition records for taxes by [VK11] for the combination of each customer and material in pricing.

5. Maintain condition records for Price Condition Types of class 'taxes' = Maintain percentage of taxes

Use [VK11] to create condition records for price condition type MWST

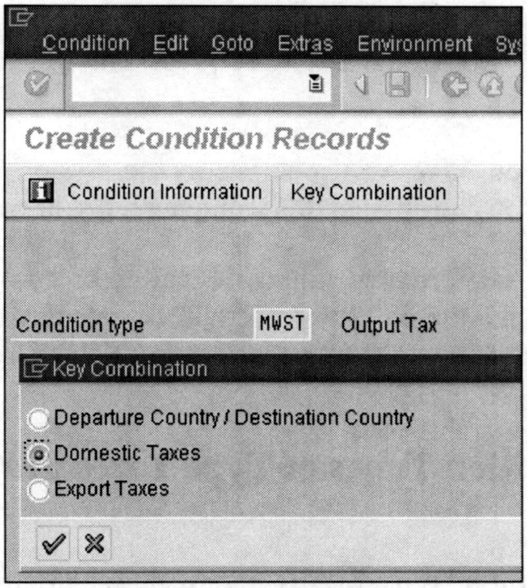

Fig: 6-15

Here we used the existing standard price condition type MWST for inputting the Domestic Tax. This condition type MWST is linked with price access sequence MWST. As this access sequence MWST is linked with 3 tables, the above 3 table options are displayed for inputting condition records. For our example, select Domestic Taxes.

[VK11] creating records for Price Condition Type MWST

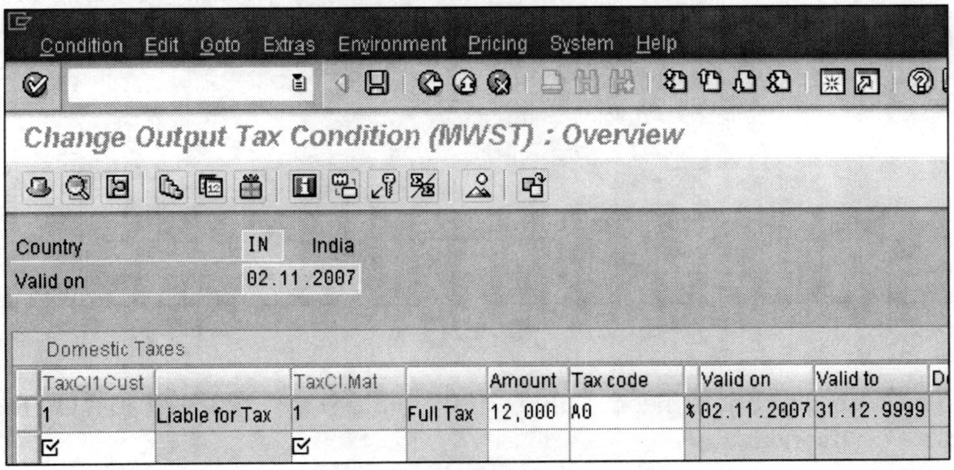

Fig:6-16

Fill up relevant County code, Customer Tax Classification code , Material Tax classification code and Tax Code and then press Enter. The system pops up the Amount

(in percentage) that you have set up earlier in the session 'Define Tax Codes for Sales and Purchases'. You can change this value here, if you want.

Now, when you create sale order for the combination of this customer tax class and this material tax class, the tax of 12 percent will be calculated by the system. Refer 'Billing Document' tab of the customer master and 'Sales Org1' tab of the Material Master for more details.

6. Use Price Condition Types of Type Taxes in Pricing Procedure [V/08]

[V/08], Enter price condition type, MWST in our sample pricing procedure

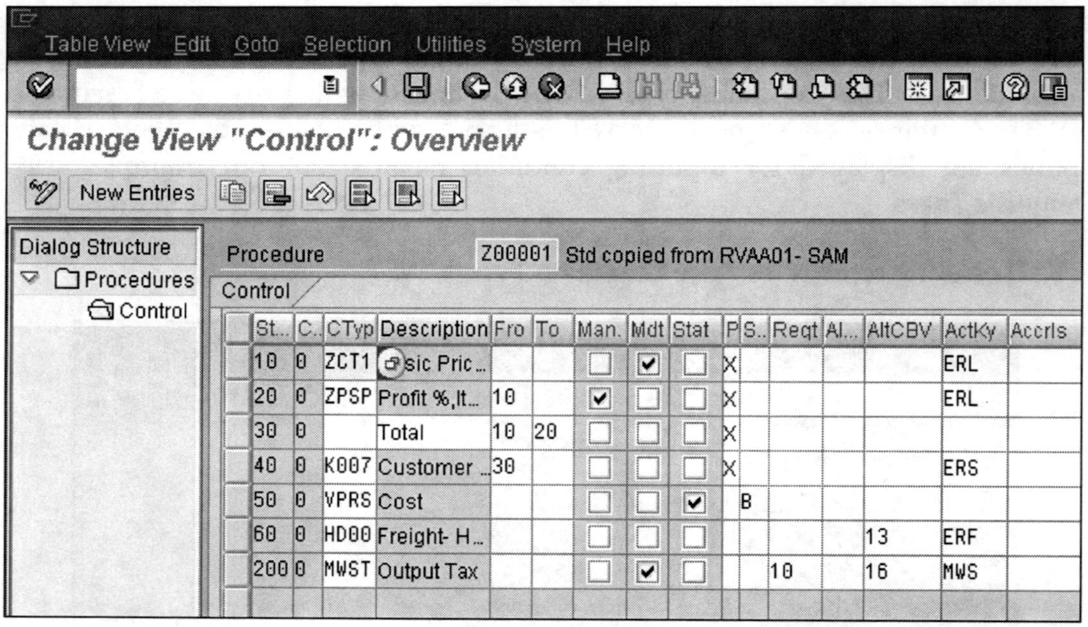

Fig: 6-17

Imp: The Alt condition Base Value, 16(Netvalue+XWORKSD) makes the tax applicable on the net value.

If you are marking the condition type MWST as mandatory, you must maintain records for the tax.

Taxes in Sales Documents

Now see the Item Condition, shown in Fig 6-18, for a sample Sales Order created through[VA01].

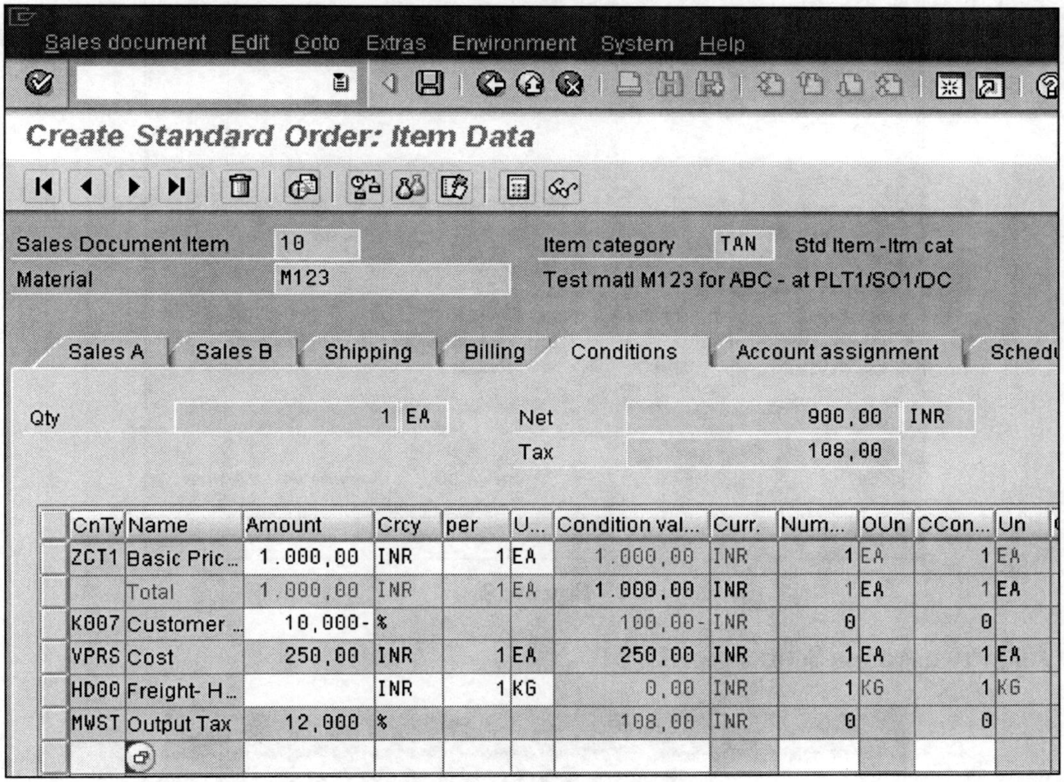

Fig: 6-18

Note: The Price Condition Type(tax) MWST has applied 12 percent tax on the net value of INR 900.

The Following are some of the master data used in the tax calculation procedures.

[V/06], Price Condition Type MWST

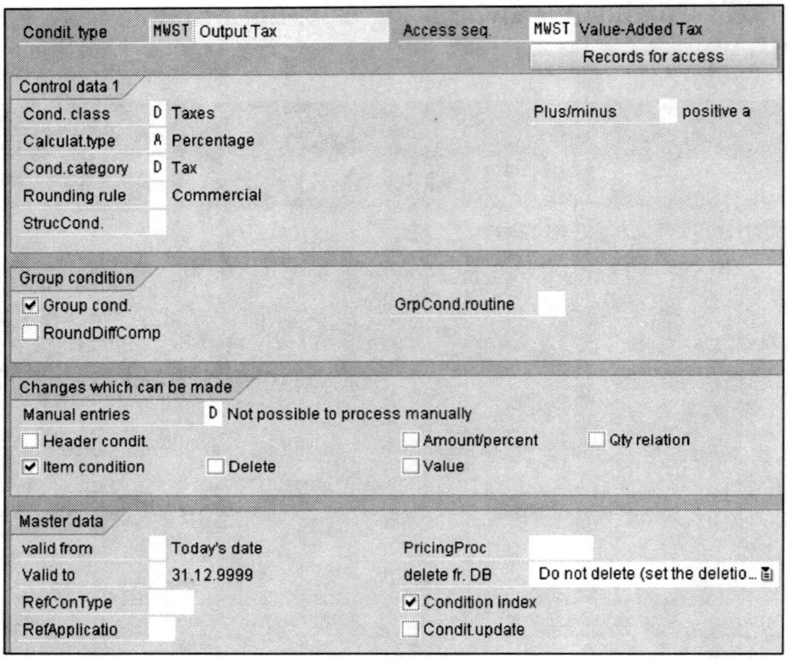

Fig:6-19

[V/07] Price Access Sequence, MWST

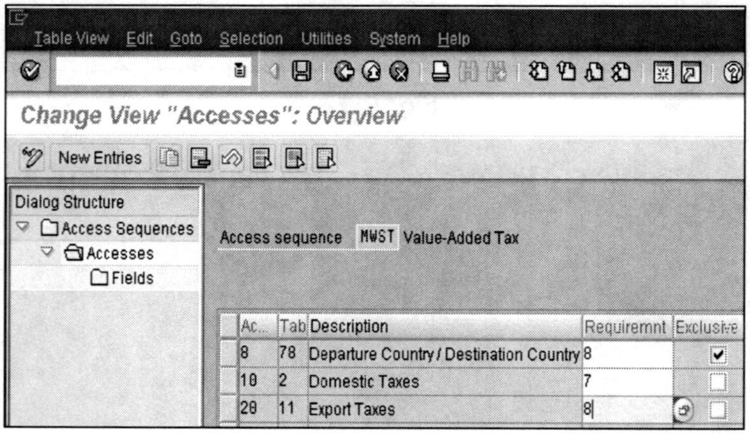

Fig: 6-20

This is the SAP standard Price Access Sequence for taxes.

[OBYZ]Tax Condition Type, BASB

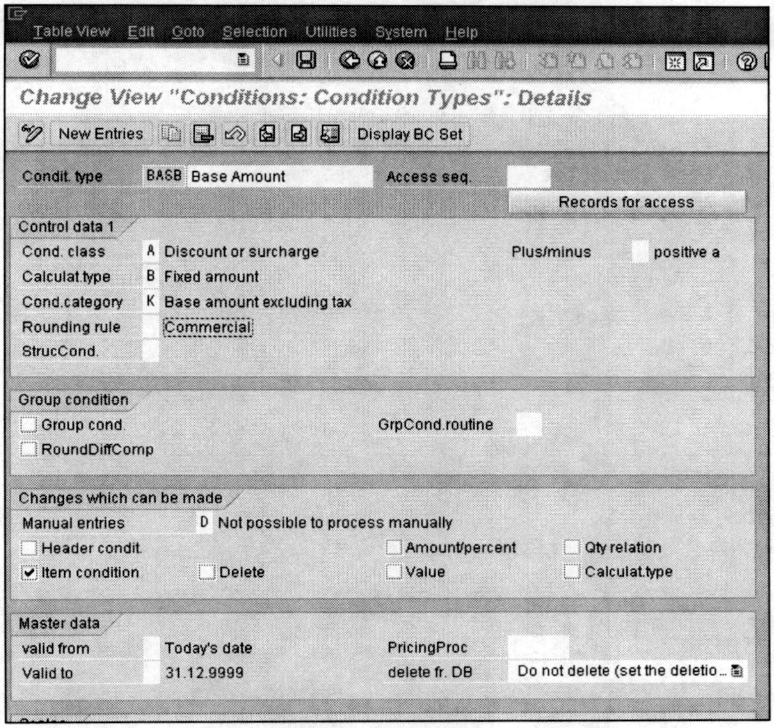

Fig: 6-21

Path: IMG-Financial Accounting-Financial Accounting Global Settings-Tax on Sales/Purchases-Basic Settings-Check Calculation Procedure-Define Condition Types.

Tax Condition Type, MWAS

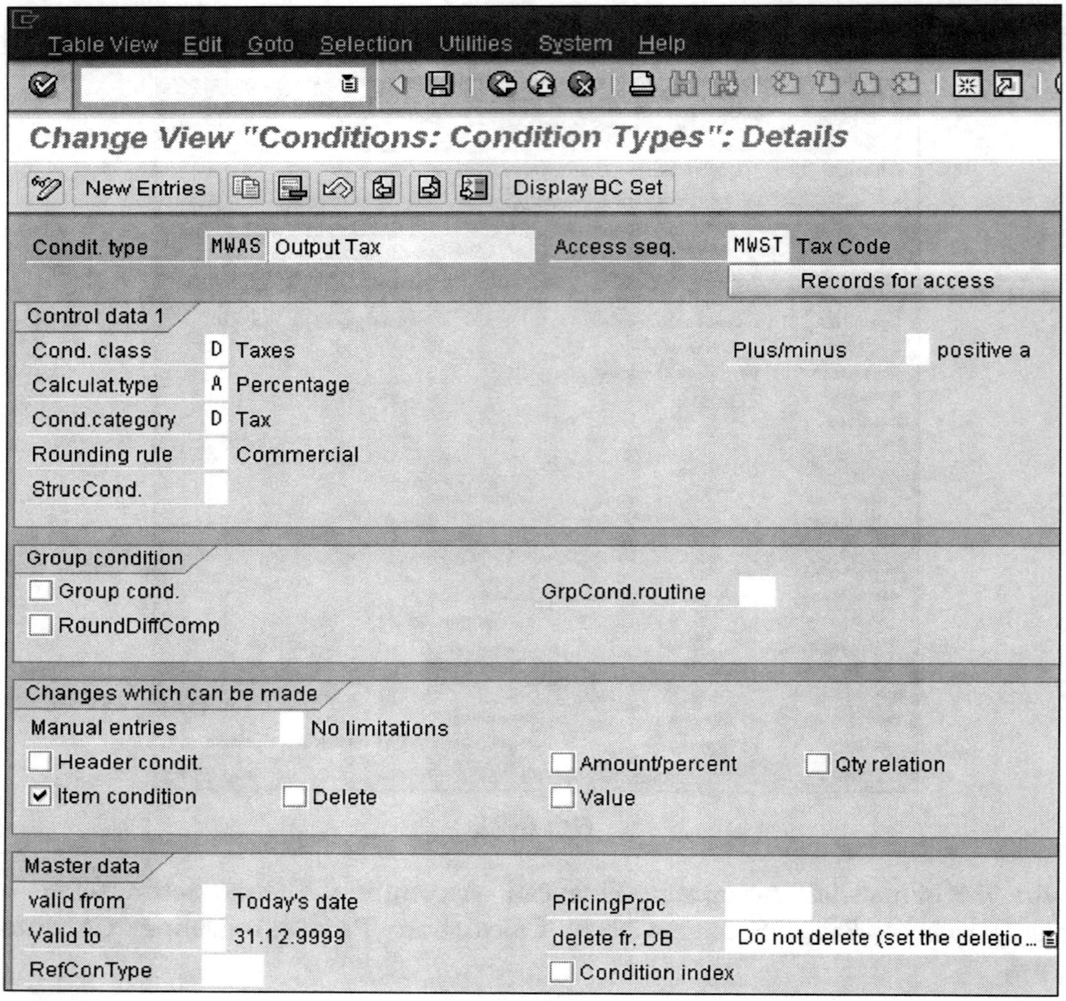

Fig: 6-22

Path: IMG-Financial Accounting-Financial Accounting Global Settings-Tax on Sales/Purchases-Basic Settings-Check Calculation Procedure-Define Condition Types.

Note: In this Tax Condition Type MWAS, Tax Access Sequence MWST is linked.

[OBYZ] Tax Access Sequence, MWST

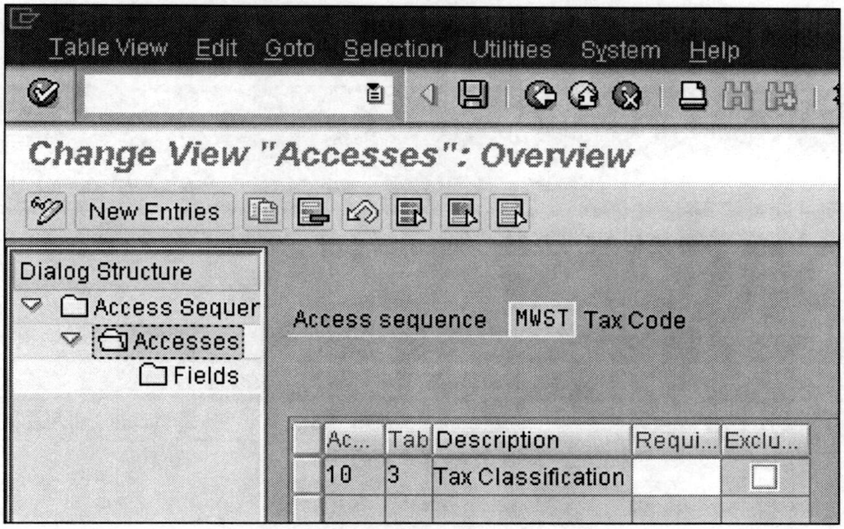

Fig: 6-23

Path: IMG-Financial Accounting-Financial Accounting Global Settings-Tax on Sales/Purchases-Basic Settings-Check Calculation Procedure- Access Sequences.

Fields of Tax Access Sequence, MWST.

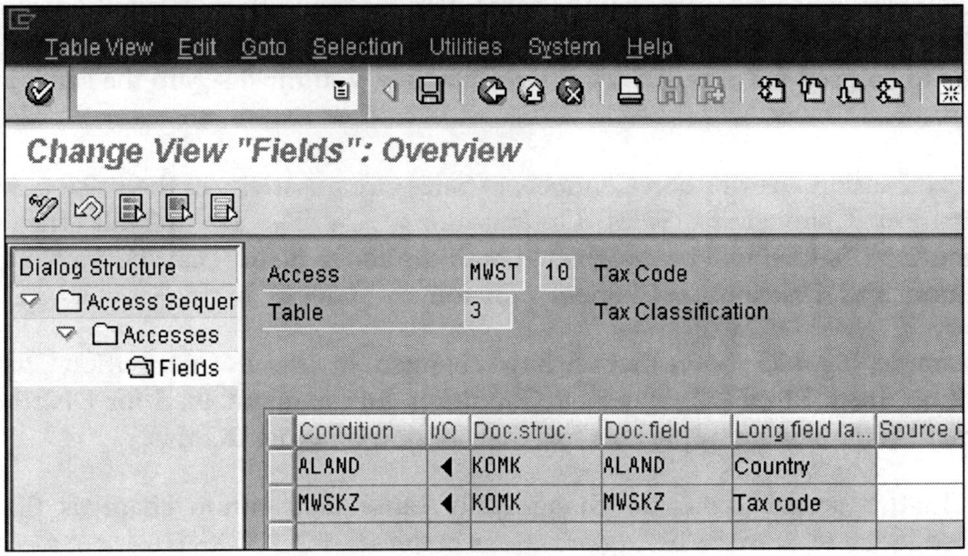

Fig:6-24

Note: Country code and Tax code are the 2 fields used in this table 3.

Defining Common Distribution Channels [VOR1]

Define Common Distribution Channels [VOR1]

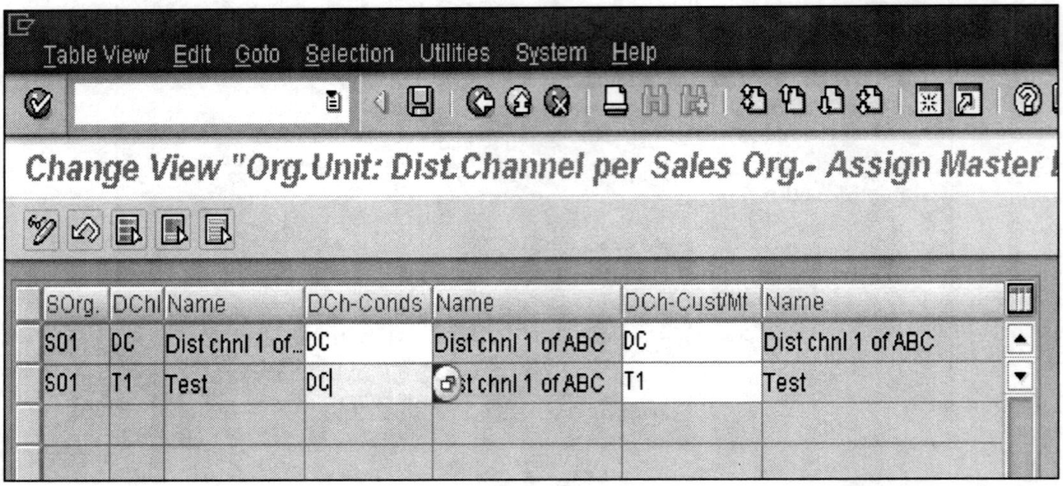

Fig: 6-25

Path: IMG-SD-MD

Price Condition Records for materials are maintained for a particular Distribution Channel. Hence, if you try to sell the same item through other distribution channel, the same price will not be picked up by system. Hence, if you want the same price records to be used for other Distribution Channels, you must set up the same in this session.

When you assign Distribution Channels to Sales Organisations in the session Assign Distribution Channel to Sales Organisations [OVXK], by default the same Distribution Channel will be assigned at both the above fields 'Distribution Channel-Condition' and 'Distribution Channel – Customer/Material' in this session.

For example, Fig 6-25 shows that we have changed, in line 2, 'Distribution Channel-Condition' from T1 to DC. Hence, if Condition data is maintained for Distribution Channel T1, the same is applicable for Distribution Channel DC also.

Note: In this session you can change only those distribution channels that are assigned to the relevant Sales Organisations in the session [OVXK].

Similarly Customer-Material master data is also maintained separately for each Distribution Channel.

Hence, in this session you can specify one distribution channel as the source of Customer- Material master data for other distribution channels. Thus you need to maintain data in one place only.

Defining Common Divisions[VOR2]

Define Common Division [VOR2]

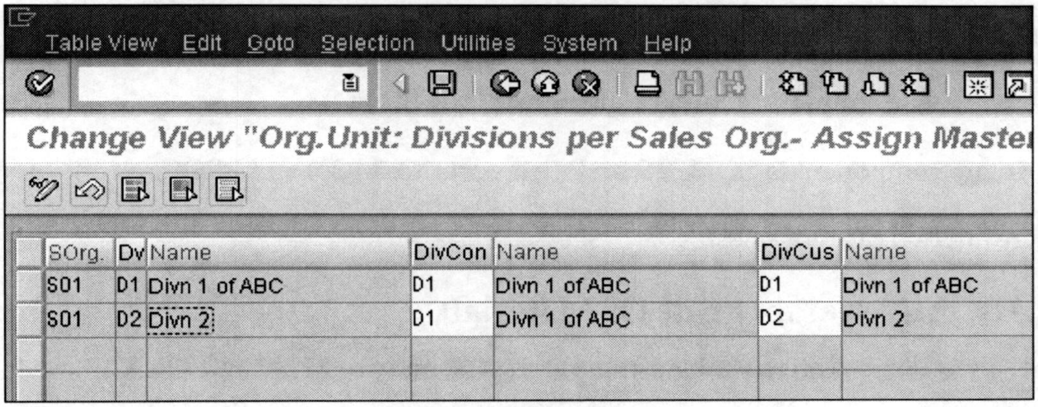

Fig: 6-26

Path: IMG-SD-MD

Customer Master Data is maintained for a particular Division. Hence, if you want to use the same customer in other Divisions, you must set up the same in this session.

When you assign Divisions to Sales Organisations in the session Assign Divisions to Sales Organisations [OVXA], by default the same Division will be assigned at both the above fields 'Division- Condition' and 'Division- Customer' in this session.

Note: In this session you can change only those Divisions that are already assigned to the relevant Sales Organisations in the session [OVXA].

BOM Process in SD

In SAP, we create BOMs(Bill Of Materials) separately for separate purposes. BOM can be created in SD only for sales purposes. BOM Usage 5 is used for the same. For production, BOM Usage is 1 and for Costing, it is 6. See below for BOM usage.

Two types of BOM processes are used in Sales and Distribution. They are ABOM and KBOM.

Example: In the case of computer sales, there are two scenarios. In one scenario, we sell the parts together as an assembled bundle and in that case the pricing is done for the bundle and not based on the individual parts. But in another scenario, parts of the computers are sold separately in a kit and the pricing is done based on the parts and their quantities.

Let us define three materials COMPTR, PROC(Processor) and MON(Monitor).

Let us create a simple structure for demonstrating SD BOM.

The main component is COMPTR and their parts are MON and PROC.

There are two cases of sales:

1. ABOM(Assembly Bill Of Material)

The sale is done as an assembled computer(Assembly of MON and PROC).

For selling the assembled computer, Pricing, Inventory, Delivery, etc are done at the parent level (COMPTR) and not to be done at the component level.

How to setup ABOM is explained in detail below.

2. KBOM(Kit Bill Of Material)

The sales are done as separate components for MON and PROC

The sale are done as separate components in a kit(without assembly) in which the Pricing, Inventory, Delivery, etc are done at component level and not to be done at parent level. How to setup KBOM is also explained in details below.

These controls are done at the OIC level.

Separate Order Item Categories are used for parent item and components. Item category and Higher Level Item Category in Order Item category Determination decides how these BOMs work.

Demonstration of ABOM:

To demonstrate ABOM, we will use Item Category Group ERLA for the parent item and Item Category Group NORM for components. We will link OIC *TAQ* to the parent item through Order Item Category Determination. Billing, Pricing, Delivery, Structure Breakdown etc are applicable to TAQ.

Similarly we will link OIC *ZTAE* for components. For ZTAE billing, Pricing, Delivery, Structure Breakdown, etc must not be applicable. The components will act like a text in the sales document. Hence when we make delivery, stock of the parent item will come down and stock of components will not come down. Billing can be generated only for the parent item.

Demonstration of KBOM:

To demonstrate KBOM, we will use Item Category Group LUMF for the parent item and Item Category Group NORM for components. We will link OIC *ZTAP* to the parent item through Order Item Category Determination. Billing, Pricing, Delivery, etc are not applicable for parent item but Structure Breakdown is applicable to the parent item.

We will link OIC *TAN* for components. For TAN, billing, Pricing and Delivery are applicable but Structure Breakdown is not be applicable.

For KBOM, the parent will act like a text in the sales document. Hence, when we make delivery, stock of the components will come down and stock of the parent will not come down. Billing can be generated only for component item.

Order Item Categories and Order Item Category Determinations are shown below for more information.

Hence, create 3 materials COMPTR, MON and PROC through the session MM01.

Create sufficient stocks for these materials through MB1C.

Also maintain prices through [VK11] for all of them.

The set up required for these scenarios(ABOM and KBOM) are explained hereunder.

Create SD BOM through the session [CS01].

[CS01]Creating SD BOM

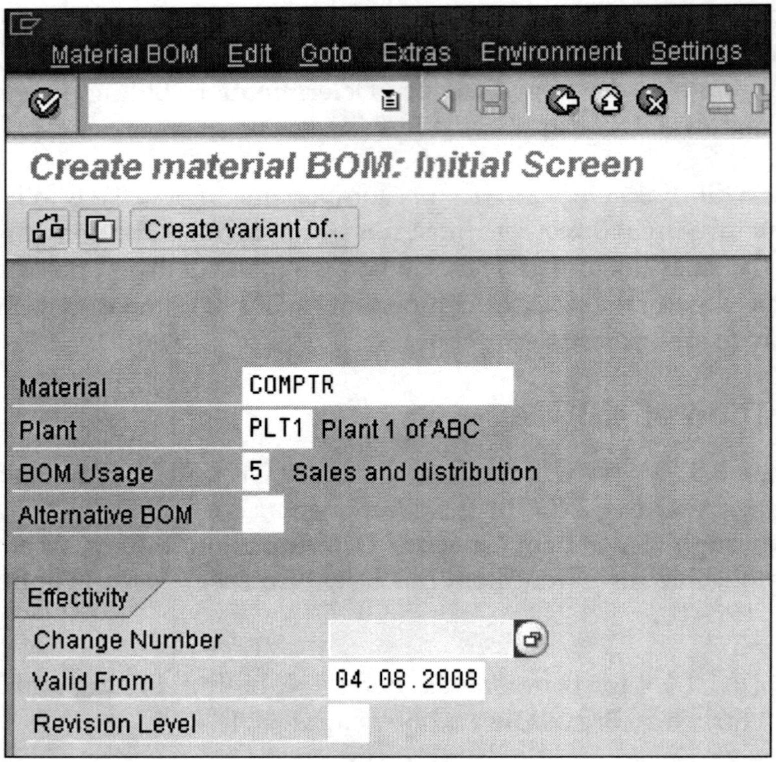

Fig: 6-27

Path: Logistics-Materials Management-Customer Service-Management of Technical Objects-BOM-Material BOM-Create

Important: For SD, select the BOM Usage 5.

For the same combination of Material, Plant and BOM Usage, we can create more than one BOM. This is controlled by the field 'Alternative BOM'.

On pressing the Enter key, you will get the following screen:

[CS01]Creating SD BOM.

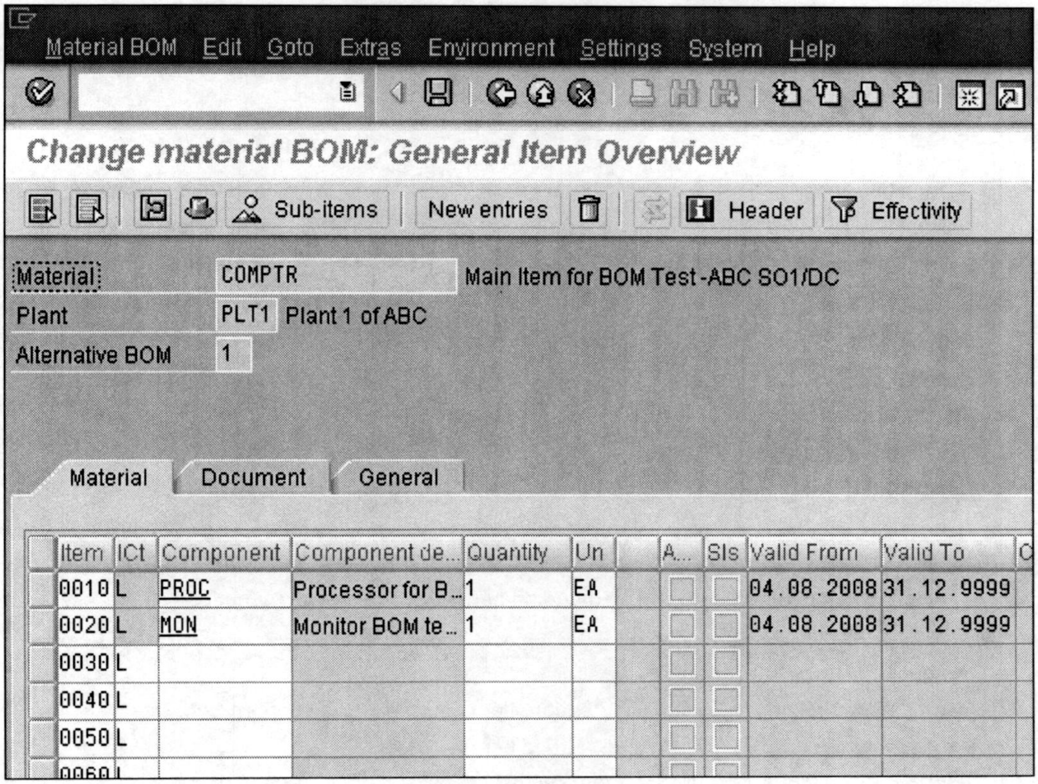

Fig: 6-28

Path: Logistics-Materials Management-Customer Service-Management of Technical Objects-BOM-Material BOM-Create.

Enter the components PROC and MON and their quantities and then save.

Now set up the following Order Item Categories:

[VOV7]. Order Item Category, TAQ for parent item for ABOM testing.

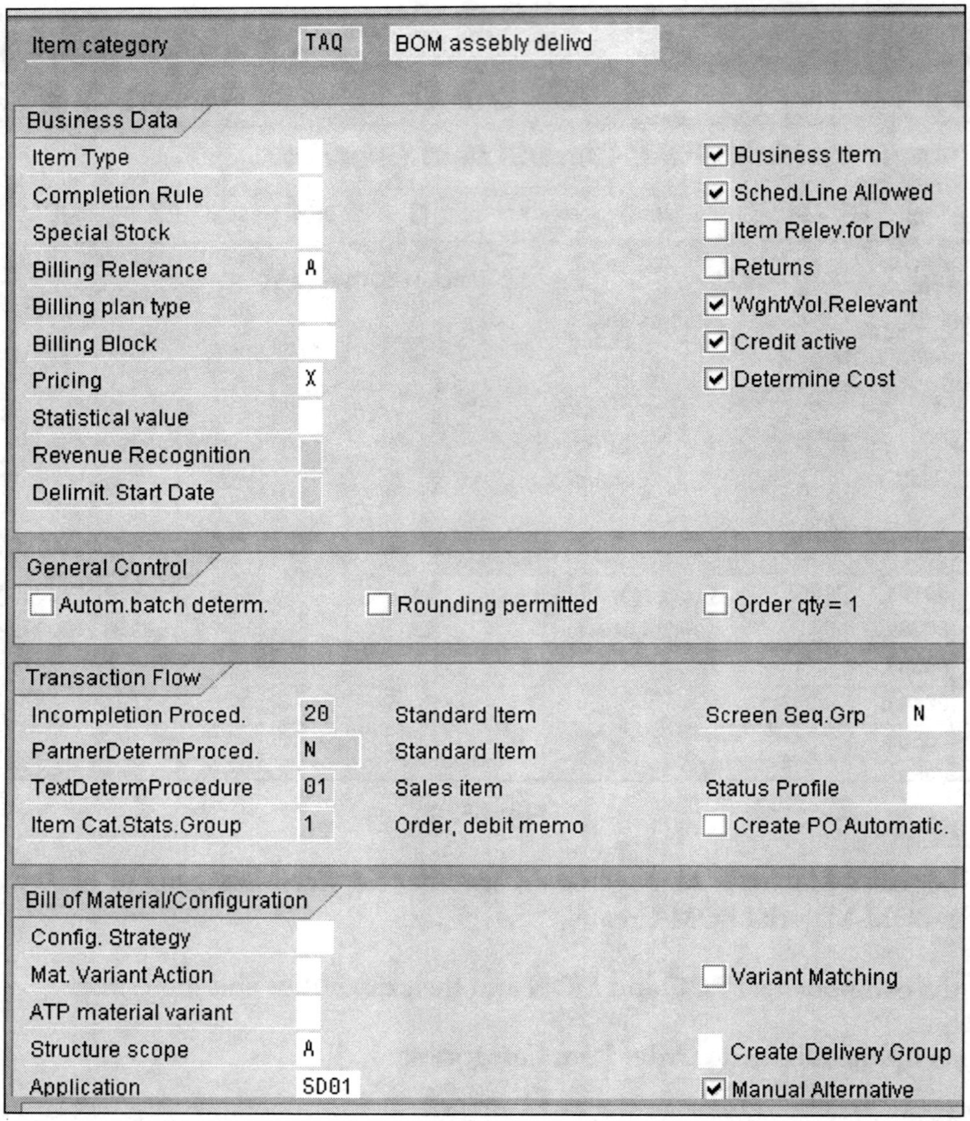

Fig: 6-29

Path: IMG- SD- SLS- SLS DOCS- SLS DOC ITEMS- Define Item Categories.

Note: the above given OIC is a SAP standard OIC. In this OIC; Billing, Pricing, Delivery(Schedule Line), Structure Break Down, etc are applicable.

The structure scope A means the components are to be exploded to a single level. Refer to OIC in the chapter Master Data for more information.

[VOV7]. Order Item Category TAE for components for ABOM testing.

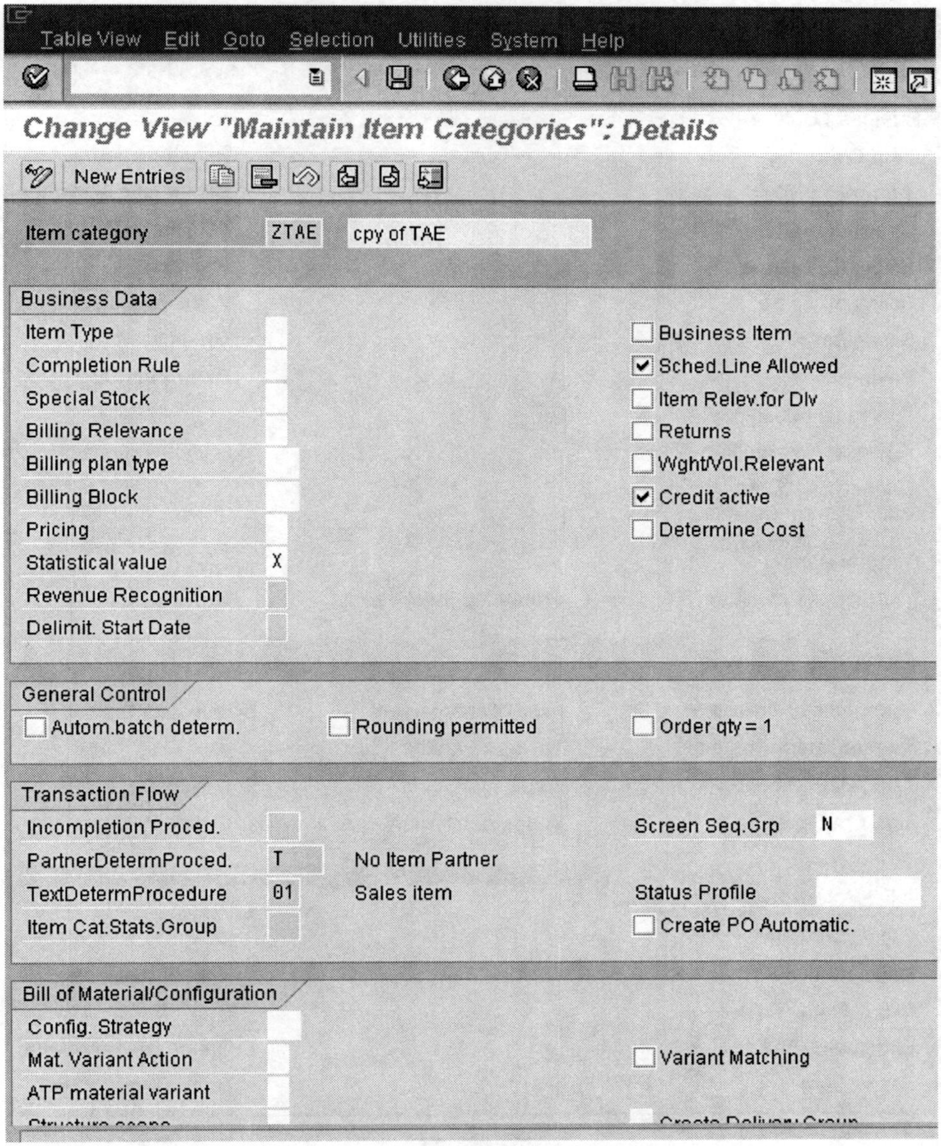

Fig: 6-30

Path: IMG- SD- SLS- SLS DOCS- SLS DOC ITEMS- Define Item Categories.

Note: OIC *ZTAE* is copied from SAP std TAE and the field 'Schedule Line Allowed' is marked. In this OIC; Billing, Pricing, Structure Break Down, etc are **not** applicable because this OIC is used as component.

[VOV7], Order Item Category ZTAP for parent item for KBOM testing.

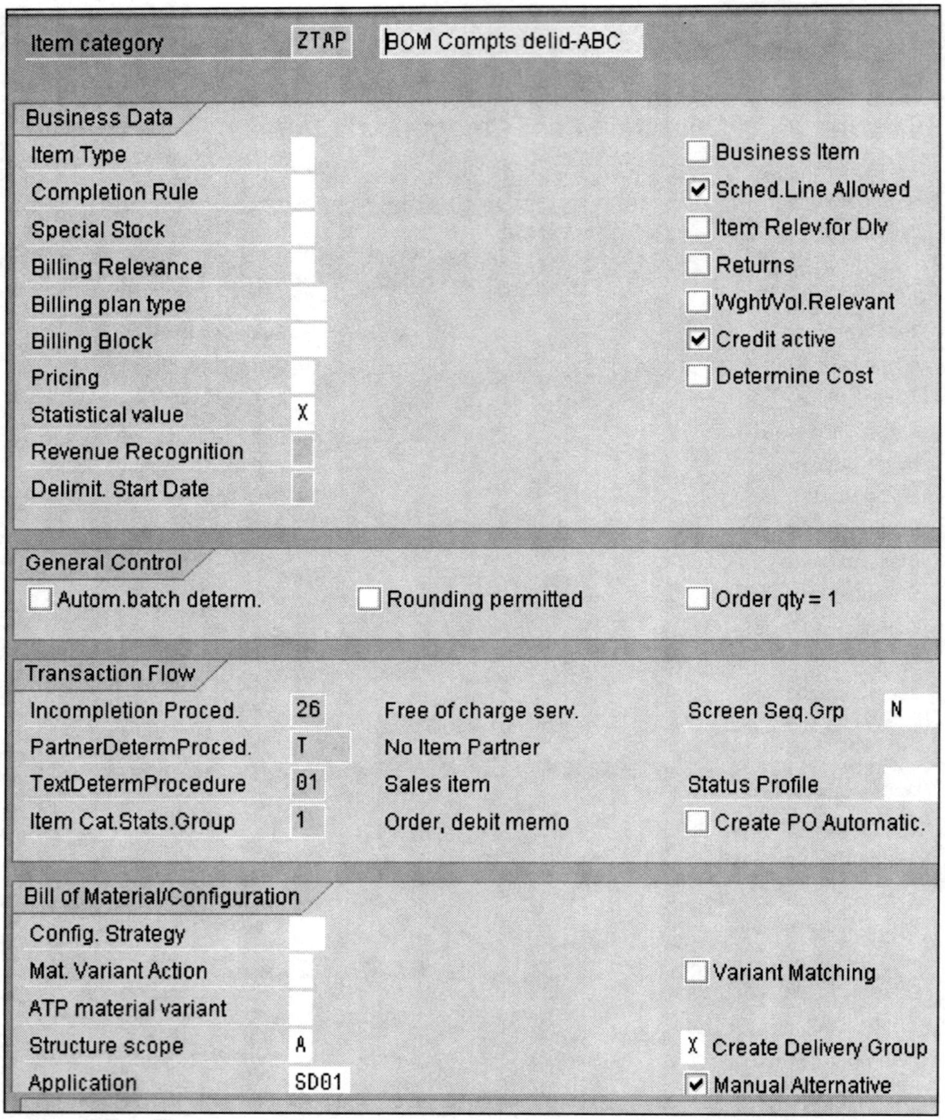

Fig: 6-31

Path: IMG- SD- SLS- SLS DOCS- SLS DOC ITEMS- Define Item Categories.

Note: The above given OIC is the copy of SAP standard OIC, *TAP* and modified. In this OIC: Billing and Pricing are not applicable, but Structure break down is applicable. Delivery(Schedule Line) is marked because otherwise we cannot enter quantity in SO. But delivery will not be applicable because the SLC or DIC will not have movement

type/ picking relevance.

[VOV7]. Order Item Category TAN for component for KBOM testing.

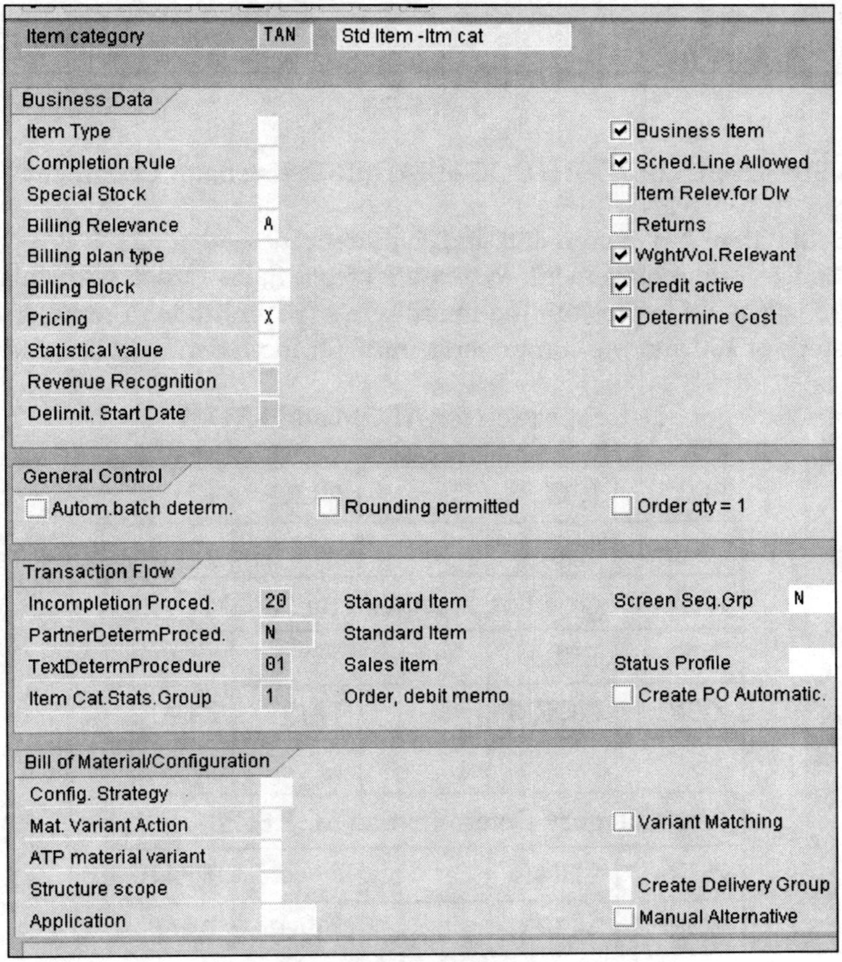

Fig: 6-32

Path: IMG- SD- SLS- SLS DOCS- SLS DOC ITEMS- Define Item Categories.

Note: The above given OIC is a SAP standard OIC. In this OIC: Billing, Pricing, Delivery(Schedule Line), etc are applicable. Structure Break Down is **not** applicable because it is used as a component.

[VOV8], SDT used for BOM process.

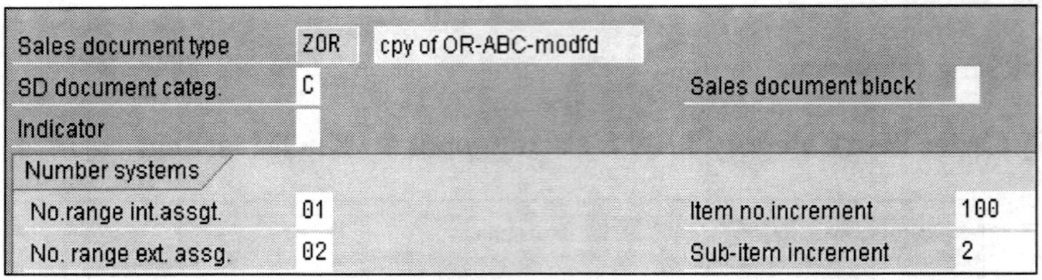

Fig: 6-33

Path: IMG-SD-SLS-SLS DOC-SLS DOC HEADER-Define Sales Document Types

Note the fields 'Item No. increment' and 'Sub item increment'. ZOR is a copy of OR and modified to our requirement. When we create Sales Order with this SDT and where there is a BOM explosion, the main item's (parent item's) number increment will be in steps of 100 and the components' number increment will be in steps of 2.

[VOV4], Item Category Determination for ABOM and KBOM

SDT	ICG	Usg	HLIC	IC
Item Category Determination for ABOM				
ZOR	ERLA			TAQ
ZOR	NORM		TAQ	ZTAE
Item Category Determination for KBOM				
ZOR	LUMF			ZTAP
ZOR	NORM		ZTAP	TAN

Fig: 6-34

Now let us test the BOM by creating sales orders.

Let us test ABOM first. For this, link item category group ERLA in the parent material COMPTR.

Now create a sales order by VA01.

[VA01],Creating an SO for material COMPTR with SDT,ZOR

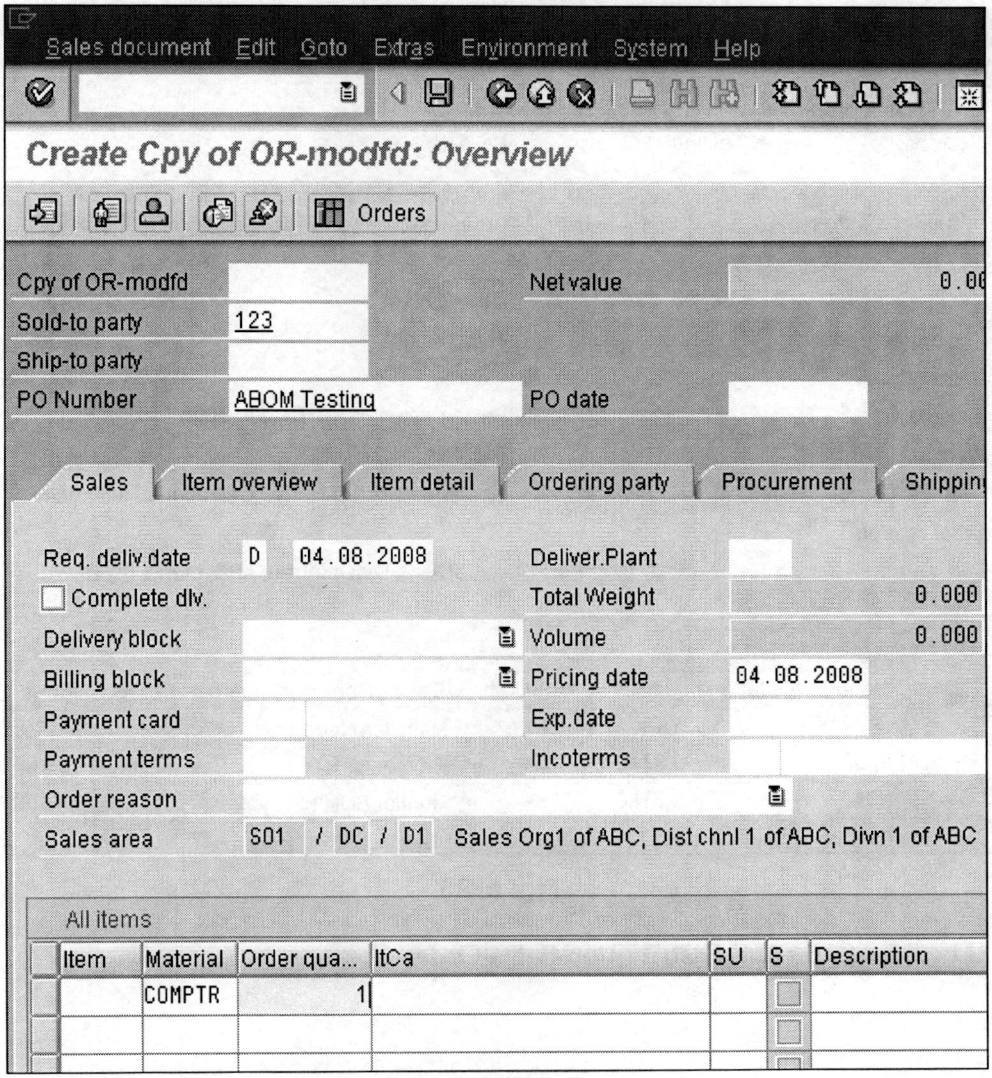

Fig: 6-35

Path: Logistics-Sales and Distribution-Sales-Order-Create.

Fill up the Parent material and it's order quantity and press Enter. The system explodes the BOM as shown in the next screen.

[VA01] Sales Order created to show BOM explosion for ABOM.

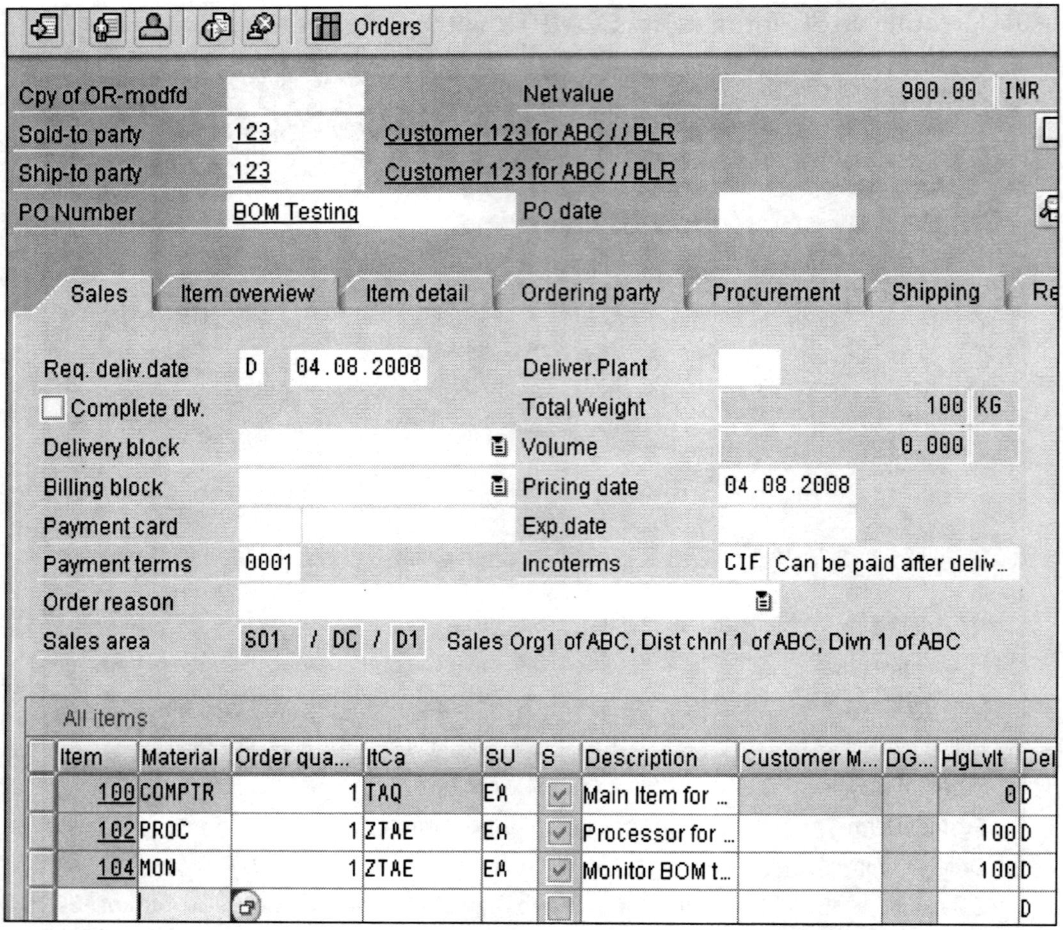

Fig: 6-36

Path: Logistics-Sales and Distribution-Sales-Order-Create.

Note:

The System has exploded the parent item to its components.

Note the net value, System allotted Item numbering(100,102 and 104), Item Category, Higher Level Item, etc. When you deliver the goods through [VL01N], picking will be active only for the parent item.

Now you can understand how the Higher level item category(HLIC) works.

Deliver the goods and see the stock balances for parents and components.

Now change the item category group of material COMPTR to LUMF and create another sales order.

[VA01] Sales Order created to show BOM explosion for KBOM

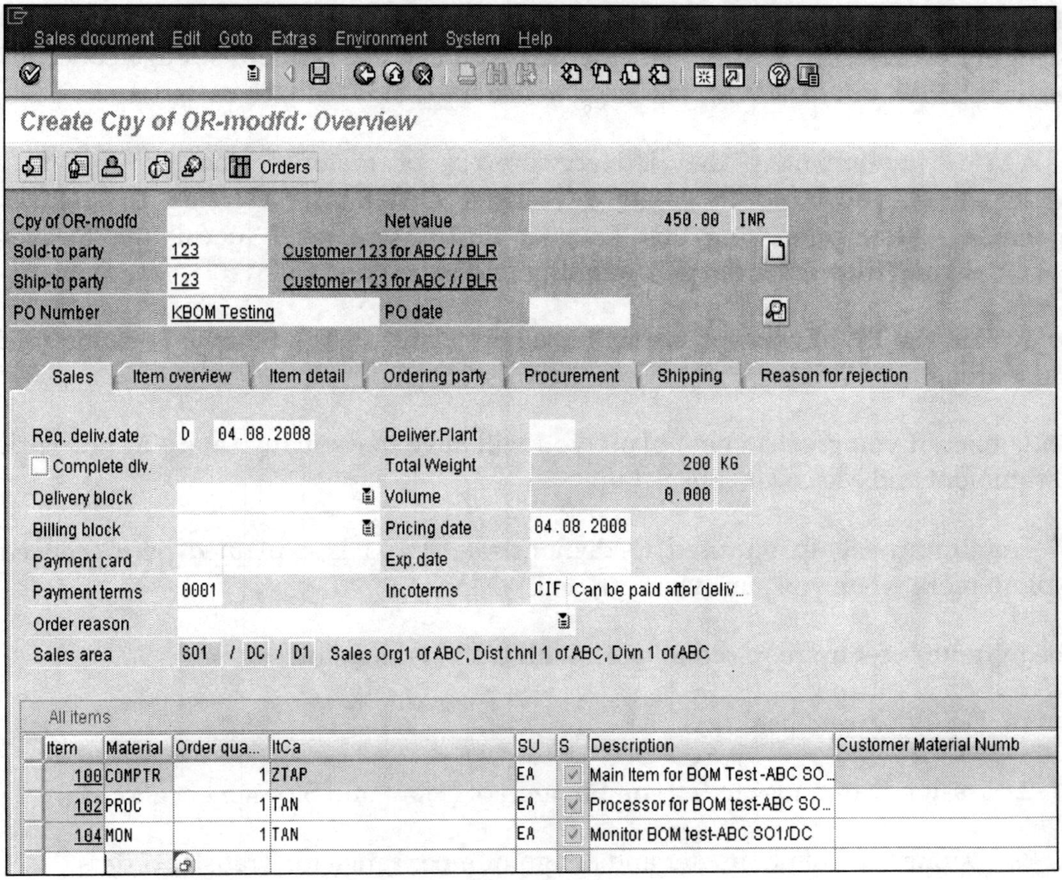

Fig: 6-37

Path: Logistics-Sales and Distribution-Sales-Order-Create

Note: The System has exploded the parent item to its components. Note the system allotted Item Category, net price, etc. When you deliver the goods through [VL01N], picking will be active only for component items PROC and MON. Further process of this Sales Order is as usual.

Note: The SLC Determination[VOV5] set up for parent and components are important in the delivery process of these items.

Lean Warehouse Management (LWM)

Lean WM is the simple form of warehouse management. If Full Warehouse Management(FWM) is implemented, the procedure of material management will be a lengthy process. If FWM is implemented, you can use random storage concept in the warehouse. But for LWM, you need to use fixed bins for each material.

If WM is implemented, the delivery process of material changes. If WM is implemented, you need to create a Transfer Order after creating the delivery document. After processing this Transfer Order, you need to call the Delivery Document and then enter the pick quantity and issue goods.

To explain the LWM concept, we will use new Plant(PLT5), Storage Location (SL5) and warehouse(WHL).

Remember, if you create a new plant, you will have to do many set up in Enterprise Assignment and Miscellaneous Set up.

The minimum set up required to demonstrate LWM is explained here. You can explore more when you start working on LWM.

The minimum set up required to work with LWM is as follows:

1. Define warehouse
2. Assign warehouse to the combination of (Plant and Storage Location).
3. Define control parameter and assign number range for Transfer orders.
4. Maintain number range intervals for transfer orders.
5. Define Storage Types.
6. Define Movement Types.
7. Control Plant/Storage Location/Warehouse number Assignment.(= Maintain 'Degree of activation' and 'Storage Type for picking')

Let us define a new warehouse WHL to test LWM.

Step1: Define Warehouse

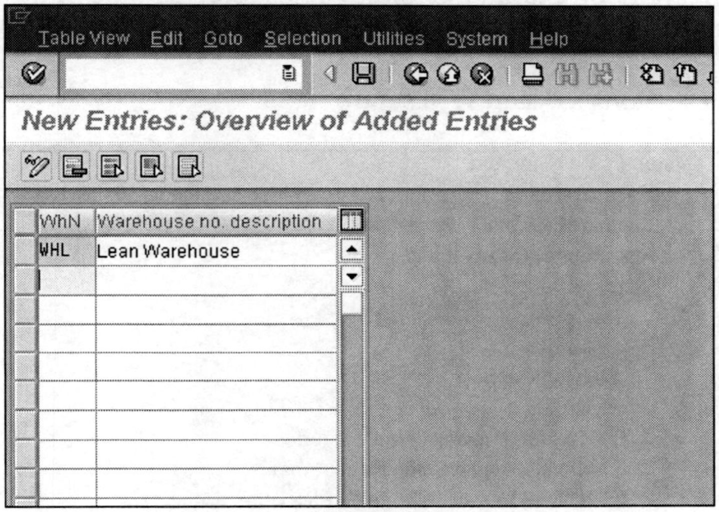

Fig: 6-38

Path: IMG-Enterprise Structure-Definition-Logistics Execution-Define, copy, delete, check warehouse number.

Let us assign this warehouse to plant PLT5 and storage location SL5.

Step2: Assign warehouse to the combination of (Plant and Location).

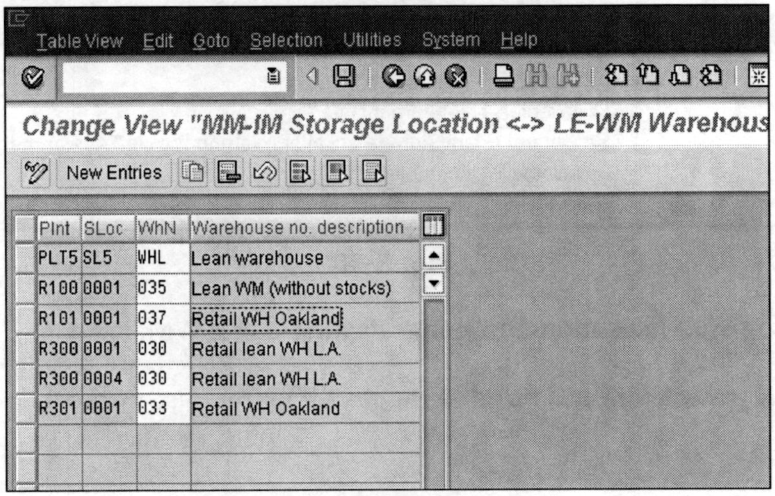

Fig: 6-39

Path: IMG-Enterprise Structure-Assignment- Logistics Execution- Assign warehouse number to plant/storage location.

Note: A combination of plant and storage location can be linked to only one warehouse.

Path for various sessions for lean WM set up

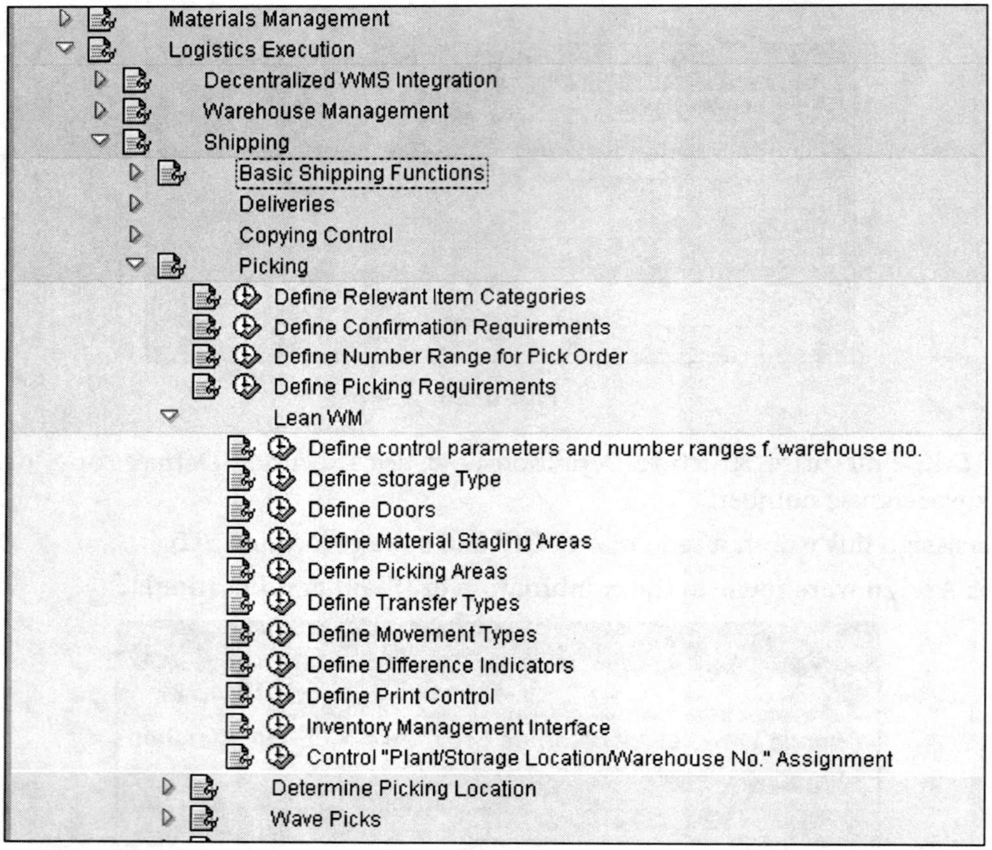

Fig: 6-40

Path: IMG- Logistics Execution- Shipping- Picking- Lean WM.

Define control parameters and number ranges for warehouse number.

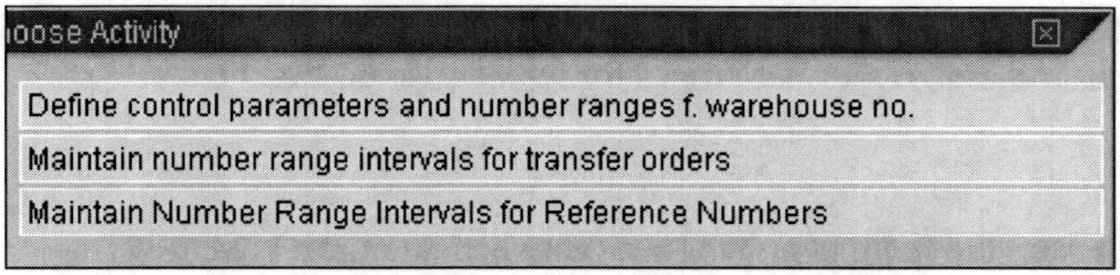

Fig: 6-41

Path: IMG- Logistics Execution- Shipping- Picking- Lean WM- Define control parameters and assign number ranges for warehouse number.

Step 3: Define control parameters and assign number ranges for warehouse number.

Choose the first option from Fig 6-41 to activate Lean WM and assign Number series for Transfer Order.

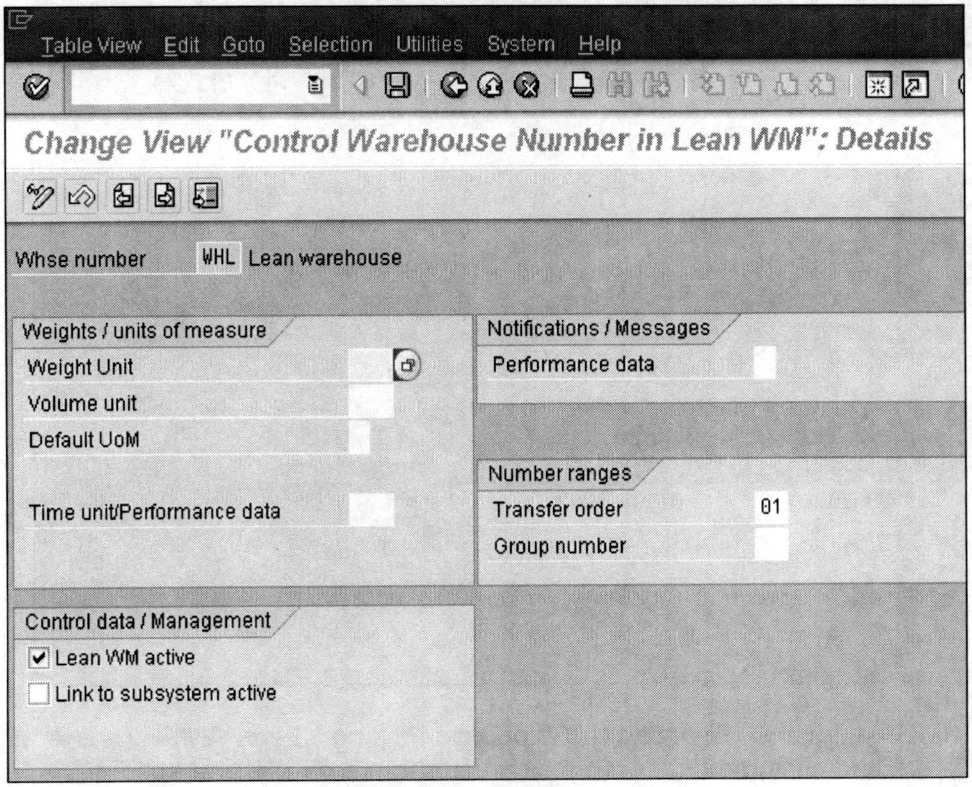

Fig: 6-42

Path: IMG- Logistics Execution- Shipping- Picking- Lean WM- Define control parameters and assign number ranges for warehouse no-first option.

Note:

1. Click on the field 'Lean WM active' to activate Lean WM.

2. The 'Transfer order' number (01) is very important. You are assigning the number range for transfer order here. What you put here must be defined in the session 'Maintain number range intervals for transfer orders'. Or you can assign this number range in the session [OMLW] .

Step 4: Maintain number range intervals for transfer orders

Choose the second option from fig 6-41 to define Number Range for Transfer Orders.

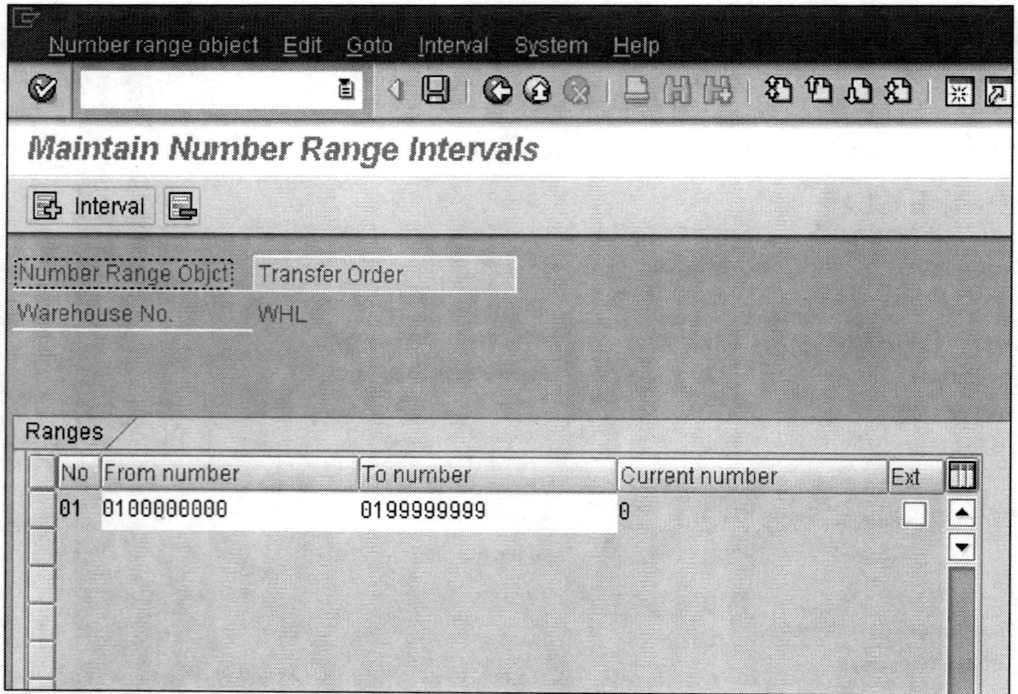

Fig: 6-43

Path: IMG- Logistics Execution- Shipping- Picking- Lean WM- Define control parameters and assign number ranges for warehouse no- second option

Note: This Number range can be assigned in the session [OMLW] also.

Step 5: Define Storage Types

There must be at least 3 Storage Types. The following three Storage Types are already defined by SAP in the system and hence, use them for your warehouse.

- For fixed bin storage (005)

- For Deliveries(916)

- For Differences (999)

Storage Type 005 for fixed bin.

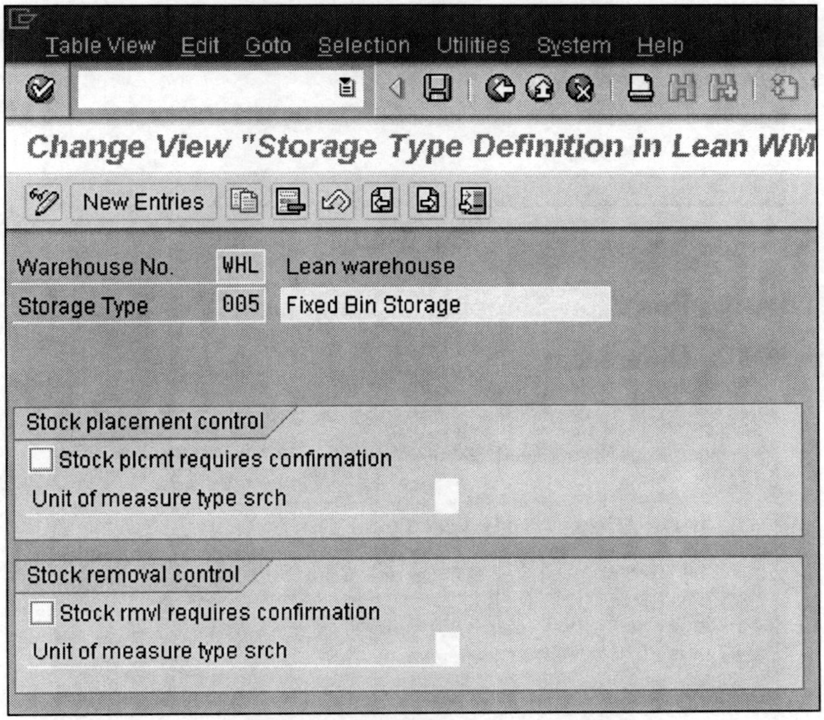

Fig: 6-44

Path: IMG- Logistics Execution- Shipping- Picking- Lean WM- Define Storage Type.

Storage Type 916 for Deliveries.

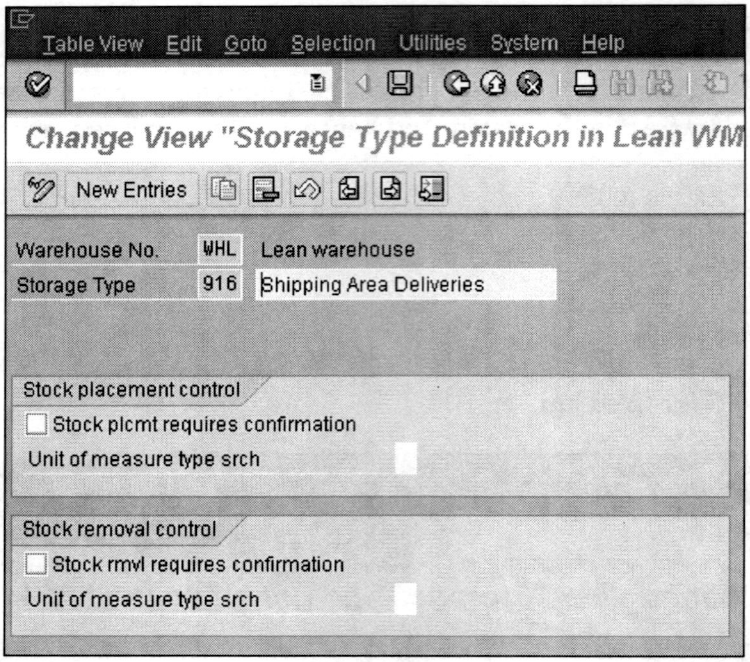

Fig: 6-45

Path: IMG- Logistics Execution- Shipping- Picking- Lean WM- Define Storage Type.

Storage Type 999 for Differences.

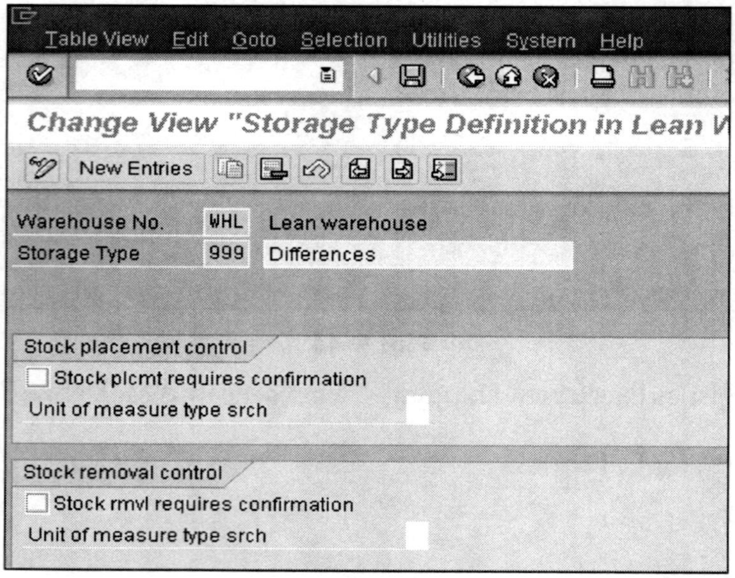

Fig:6-46

Path: IMG- Logistics Execution- Shipping- Picking- Lean WM- Define Storage Type

Fields:

Stock Placement control:

If ticked, when the materials are inbound (Put away) to the location, the Transfer Order is to be confirmed before processing in the delivery session.

Stock Removal requires confirmation:

If ticked, when the materials are removed from the location, the Transfer Order is to be confirmed before processing in the delivery session.

Hence, as we have not ticked these check boxes, we need to only create the transfer order and need not confirm the transfer order.

Step 6: Define Movement Types.

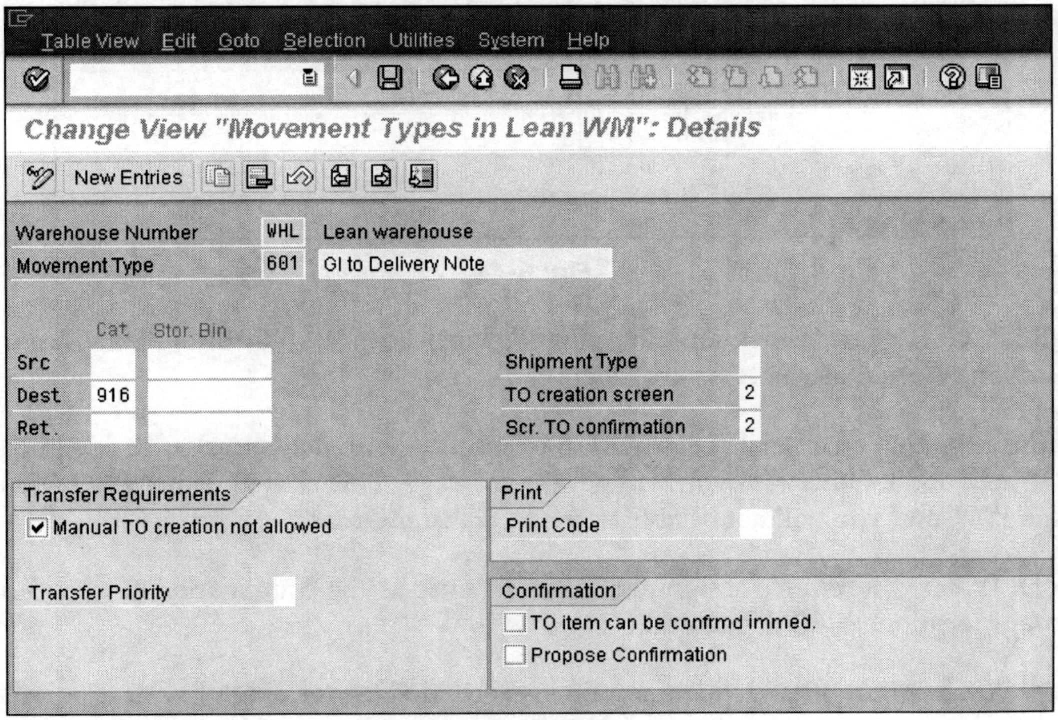

Fig: 6-47

Path: IMG- Logistics Execution- Shipping- Picking- Lean WM- Define Movement Types.

Here the Storage Type 916 is for deliveries.

Like this, you may have to define movement types for all the movement types you use in the sales transactions.

Step 7: Control "Plant/Storage Location/Warehouse No." Assignment.

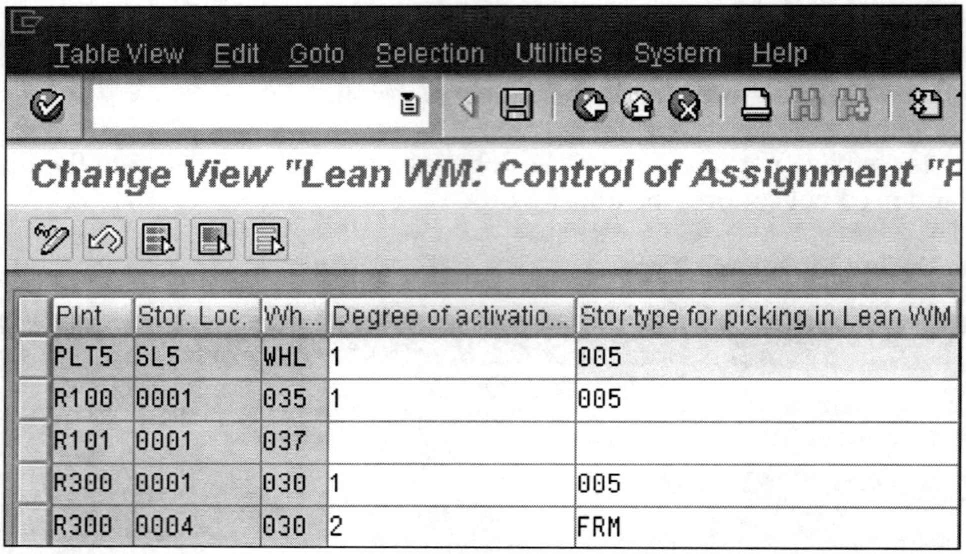

Fig: 6-48

Path: IMG- Logistics Execution- Shipping- Picking- Lean WM- Control Plant/Storage Location/Warehouse No. Assignment

In this session, you enter 1 (Lean WM in connection with deliveries) as the degree of WM activation. Otherwise you will get the message 'This activity is not available in Lean WM' and you will not be able to create Transfer Orders.

Note: When you remove assignment of warehouse to the combination of plant and storage location, this link gets cut.

Now you have completed the minimum steps needed to work with LWM.

Now, when you create a delivery document, the picking will not be active. Hence, you must save the delivery document and then create a transfer order as shown below. Then, call the delivery document, enter the pick quantity and proceed as usual.

Example to show Transfer Order [LT03]

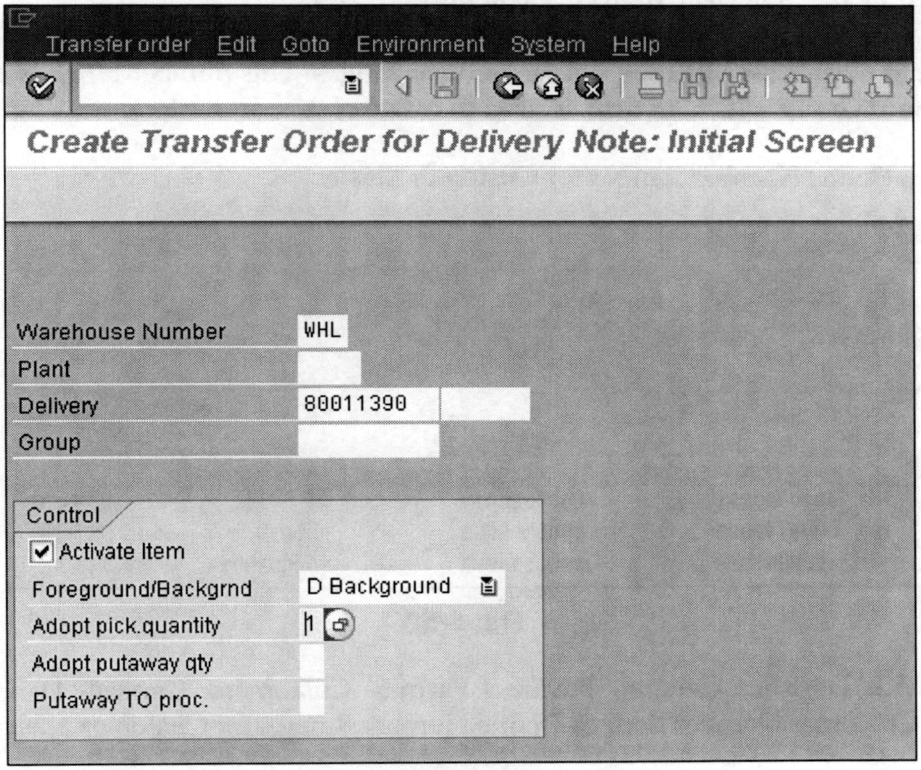

Fig: 6-49

Path: EA- Logistics- Sales and Distribution- Shipping and Transportation- Picking- Create Transfer Order-Single Document.

If Warehouse Management is implemented, you have to make transfer order to complete the sales cycle. This screen shows how to create a transfer order for a delivery document.

Number Ranges for various SD processes

The following are the number ranges used in our sales cycles.

1. Number Ranges for Customer Master [OVZC]

Customer master uses its own unique number ranges. This number range is entered in Account Group which, in turn, is used to create customer masters.

[OVZC], Define Number Ranges for Customer Master

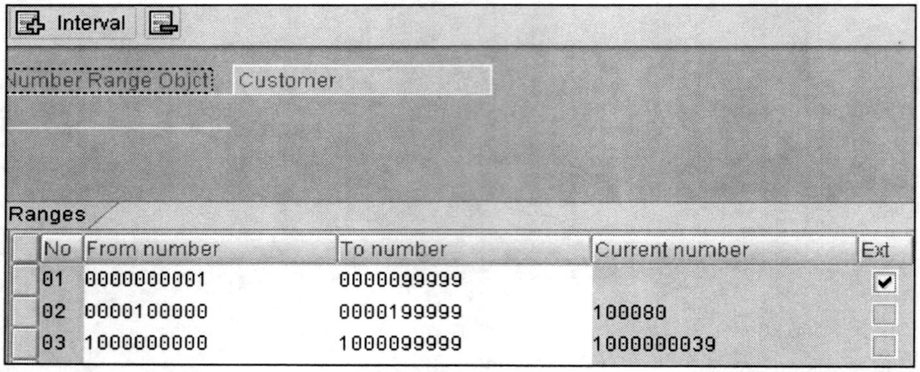

No	From number	To number	Current number	Ext
01	0000000001	0000099999		✔
02	0000100000	0000199999	100080	
03	1000000000	1000099999	1000000039	

Fig: 6-50

Path: IMG- Logistics General- Business Partner- Customers- Control- Define and Assign Customer Number Ranges-Define Number Ranges for Customer Master

The above session shows that the number range '01' is for external numbering and other number ranges '02' and '03' are for internal numberings.

2. Number Range for Materials [MMNR]

Like for customer masters, material master also uses its own number ranges.

[MMNR], Define Number Ranges for Materials

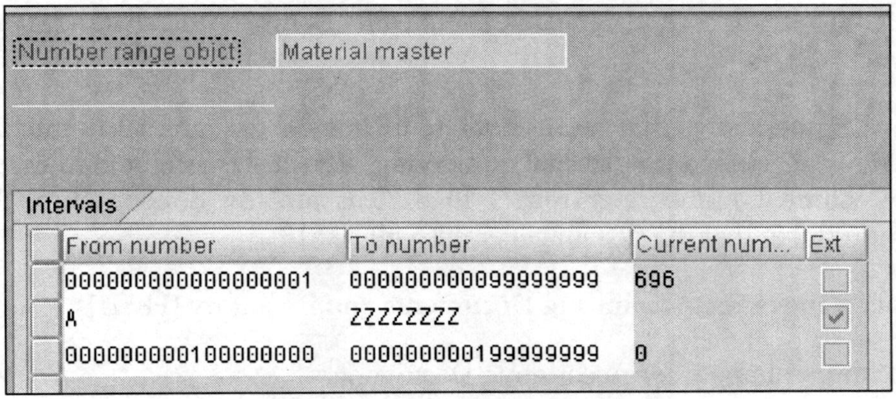

Fig: 6-51

Path: IMG-Logistics General-Material Master-Basic Settings-Material Types- Define Number Ranges for Each Material Type

For material master, there is no choice for selecting number range. It is set in the beginning commonly for a group of material types. As per the number range setting shown above, if you are using external numbers, you must add one alphabet compulsorily in the material code. In the case of internal numbering, the system has already allotted material numbers up to 696.

3. **Number Ranges For other Sales Documents [VN01]**

For other SD documents such as SDT, DDT, BDT, etc, number ranges are defined in this session.

[VN01], Number Ranges For other Sales Documents

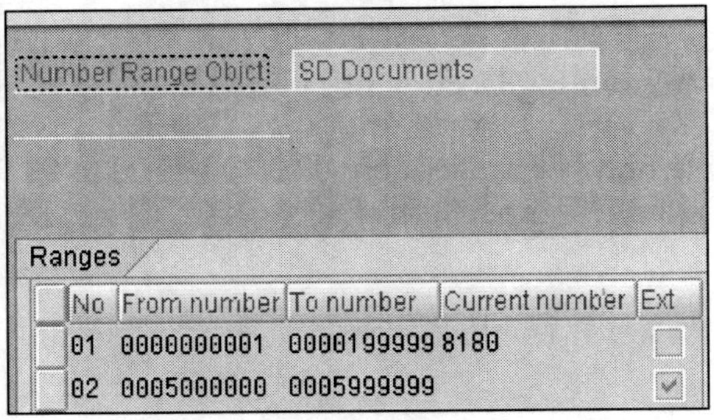

Fig: 6-52

Path: IMG-SD-SLS-SLS DOC-SLS DOC HEADER- Define Number Ranges For Sales Documents

The above figure shows that number range 01 is used for internal numbering and number range 02 is used for external numbering. Also it shows that in number range 01, the Document numbering from 1 to 8180 is already done. Hence, the next document number that the system generates will be 8181.

4. **Number Ranges For Accounting Documents and inventory [FBN1]**

[FBN1], Number Ranges for Accounting Documents

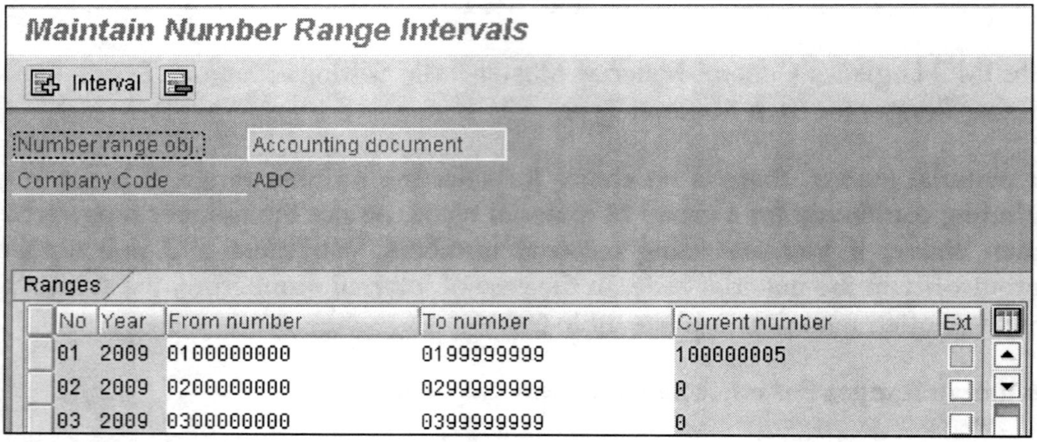

Fig: 6-53

Path: IMG- Financial Accounting- Financial Accounting Global Settings- Document- Document Number Ranges- Define Document Number Ranges

By default Number Series 49 is used for Stock Creation/ Update. Number Series 01 is generally used for Accounting Document Type *RV*.

Note that the available number range(here 00 00 00 00 00 to 99 99 99 99 99) must be distributed among various Number Series(here 01, 02, 03 etc) for the same year.

Abbreviations Used in this book

ABOM	Assembly Bill Of Material
ADT	Accounting Document Type (Document Type/ Accounting Type)
BDT	Billing Document Type (Billing Type)
CDD	Confirmed Delivery Date
DDT	Delivery Document Type (Delivery Type)
DIC	Delivery Item Category
FWM	Full Warehouse Management (Warehouse Management)
KBOM	Kit Bill Of Material
LWM	Lean Warehouse Management
OIC	Order Item Category (Item Category)
PCT	Price Condition Type (Condition Type)
PGI	Post Goods-Issue
RDD	Requested Delivery Date
SDT	Sales Document Type(Order Type)

Lightning Source UK Ltd.
Milton Keynes UK
UKOW03f2032080115

244224UK00005B/77/P